INCLUSION STRATEGIES & INTERVENTIONS

Toby J. Karten

Solution Tree | Press

a division of
Solution Tree

555 North Morton Street
Bloomington, IN 47404
800.733.6786 (toll free) / 812.336.7700
FAX: 812.336.7790

email: info@solution-tree.com
solution-tree.com

Visit **go.solution-tree.com/specialneeds** to download the reproducibles and access live links to the websites in this book.

Printed in the United States of America

14 13 12 11   2 3 4 5

Library of Congress Cataloging-in-Publication Data

Karten, Toby J.
  Inclusion strategies and interventions / Toby J. Karten.
      p. cm.
  Includes bibliographical references and index.
  ISBN 978-1-935543-23-7 (trade paper) -- ISBN 978-1-936765-13-3 (library edition)
 1. Inclusive education. I. Title.
  LC1200.K37 2011
  371.9'046--dc22
                            2010041642

Solution Tree
Jeffrey C. Jones, CEO & President

Solution Tree Press
President: Douglas M. Rife
Publisher: Robert D. Clouse
Vice President of Production: Gretchen Knapp
Managing Production Editor: Caroline Wise
Senior Production Editor: Lesley Bolton
Proofreader: Elisabeth Abrams
Text Designer: Raven Bongiani
Cover Designer: Jenn Taylor

The cover design was inspired by *Hidden Snails*, by Nikolas, age 9, San Antonio, Texas. Visit www.ldonline .org/kidsart to see more student art.

Acknowledgments

I would like to extend kudos to everyone who supports inclusive practices. This *includes* students and their families as well as professionals in schools and at Solution Tree. It *includes* my family, friends, and colleagues who continually offer encouragement and support. It also *includes* the new 21st century legislation that accepts and embraces inclusion.

Solution Tree Press would like to thank the following reviewers:

Cathy Deschenes
Learning Support Teacher
West High School
Iowa City, Iowa

Kristin Dreyer
Learning Disabilities English Teacher
Chantilly High School
Chantilly, Virginia

Peggy Katsilometes
Mathematics Teacher
Harmon Middle School
Aurora, Ohio

Debra Keith
Science Subject-Area Leader
Rodgers Middle School
Riverview, Florida

John Marc Murphy
Fourth-Grade Teacher
Leib Elementary School
Dover, Pennsylvania

Karrie Rage
Coordinator of Special Education Services
Fargo Public Schools
Fargo, North Dakota

Visit **go.solution-tree.com/specialneeds** to download the reproducibles and access live links to the websites in this book.

Table of Contents

ABOUT THE AUTHOR ix

INTRODUCTION 1

    Inclusion by Law 3

    About This Book 4

PART ONE

PROMOTING LEARNING IN THE INCLUSIVE CLASSROOM 7

CHAPTER ONE

UNDERSTANDING THE INCLUSIVE CLASSROOM 9

    Know What Your Students Know. 9

    Social, Emotional, and Academic Growth. 12

    Raising Awareness 13

    Behavioral Issues. 14

    Social Issues 15

    Communication Issues 17

    The Role of the Educator 18

    Moving Beyond Stereotypes. 18

CHAPTER TWO

ORGANIZING FOR INSTRUCTION 21

    Response to Intervention (RTI) 22

    Cooperative Learning 26

    Differentiated Instruction (DI) 27

    Understanding by Design (UbD) 28

    Universal Design for Learning (UDL) 30

    Multiple Intelligences, Sensory Modalities, and Technology. 32

    Organizing Structures and Instruction 35

CHAPTER THREE

ADDRESSING STUDENT NEEDS **43**

Fourteen Points for Success. 43

Strategic Learners 44

Attention and Motivation 46

Pacing and Complexity 47

Effective Co-Teaching Practices 49

Appropriate Interventions 50

Looking Past the Label 57

CHAPTER FOUR

USING ASSESSMENTS, ACCOMMODATIONS, AND DATA **63**

The Data 63

Accommodations and Modifications 64

Avoiding Learned Helplessness 68

Sample Curriculum Lessons. 70

Functional and Alternative Assessments 71

Functional Behavioral Assessments 75

The Merits of Mistakes 76

PART TWO

STRATEGIES FOR EFFECTIVE CURRICULUM PRACTICE **79**

CHAPTER FIVE

LITERACY AND COMMUNICATION **81**

Reading Differences 81

Reading Strategies 82

Writing Strategies. 86

Communication Strategies 90

Strategies for ELs. 93

CHAPTER SIX

MATHEMATICS **105**

Math Representations 105

Moving Math Beyond the Worksheet. 106

RTI Math Recommendations. 107

Math Strategies. 108

Strengthening Computational Fluency 109

CHAPTER SEVEN

SOCIAL STUDIES AND SCIENCE **117**

The Social Studies Curriculum 117

The Science Curriculum 118

Social Studies and Science Strategies 119

CHAPTER EIGHT

ART, MUSIC, AND MOVEMENT **129**

Artful Education 129

Music Matters 131

Moving Beyond the Pages 132

Life Skills 133

CHAPTER NINE

AN INTERDISCIPLINARY APPROACH **135**

Lesson Strategies 135

Thematic Planning 139

CHAPTER TEN

TRANSITIONAL PLANS **141**

Setting Goals 141

Strategies 142

PART THREE
MAINTAINING THE INCLUSIVE CLASSROOM 147

CHAPTER ELEVEN

PROFESSIONAL COLLABORATION **149**

Inclusion Players 149

Communication 151

Professional Development 153

Interventions 154

CHAPTER TWELVE

HONORING INCLUSION **159**

Disability Awareness 159

Helping All Learners to Succeed 162

Inclusion as an Evolutionary Process 163

APPENDIX A

ABBREVIATIONS **165**

APPENDIX B

LEGAL ASPECTS OF INCLUSION 167

REFERENCES AND RESOURCES 171

INDEX 191

About the Author

 **TOBY J. KARTEN** is an experienced educator who has worked in the field of special education since 1976. An accomplished author and researcher, she has presented successful staff development to local, national, and international audiences. Toby is a lecturer at Drew University and an adjunct professor and graduate instructor at the Regional Training Center, which is affiliated with Gratz College, the College of New Jersey, and Washington College. She has been a resource teacher, staff developer, adult educator, and inclusion consultant in New York and New Jersey schools and in many districts nationally and globally for students and educators in grades K–12 and beyond. She is currently working with Time To Know as the lead instructional math coach for New York City schools.

In addition to her roles as mentor and resource teacher, Toby designed a graduate course titled Skills and Strategies for Inclusion and disABILITY Awareness and has trained other instructors in three states to teach her course. She has been recognized by both the Council for Exceptional Children and the New Jersey Department of Education as an exemplary educator, receiving two Teacher of the Year awards.

Toby has authored several books and resources about inclusion practices, which are currently used for instruction on many college and university campuses and in schools throughout the world.

She earned an undergraduate degree in special education from Brooklyn College, a master of science in special education from the College of Staten Island, and a supervisory degree from Georgian Court University.

Introduction

The general concept of inclusion is the meshing of general education and special education to benefit all learners. This includes valuing cultural, academic, social, behavioral, and emotional differences. In inclusive classrooms, students with special educational needs are treated as integral members of the general education environment and are provided with collaborative support systems that honor peer relationships and provide access to meaningful curricula (Causton-Theoharis, 2009).

While the concept of inclusion seems simple enough, researchers, practitioners, and legislators express differing thoughts about inclusion's implementation. Societal attitudes, legislation, educational philosophies, administrative directives, family involvement, and teacher expectations are all factors that influence the implementation and effectiveness of inclusive school programs. For example, common core assessments have been designed to provide the appropriate accommodations from a test's inception rather than adding them on later as an afterthought. This may replace the need for alternate assessments based on modified achievements (Samuels, 2010). Some teachers, administrators, students, and families embrace these new test designs, while others do not approve of the changes. Even though common legislation exists, inclusion must be individually defined and implemented through a variety of applications.

No one method is appropriate for all inclusive classrooms. Educators must explore a variety of strategies to determine which create the desired connections between the students and the curriculum, taking into account students' academic, social, emotional, and behavioral levels; interests; and diverse abilities.

Inclusion interventions are meant to honor the belief that all students are capable of meeting high expectations and to offer the academic, social, emotional, and behavioral benefits that allow students to achieve their highest potential. Inclusion interventions connect the instruction to each and every student's unique needs.

Inclusive classrooms need to be equitable and heterogeneous and offer placement, instruction, and support for students with exceptionalities (Winzer & Mazurek, 2009). Providing students with opportunities to achieve regardless of current circumstances, prior attainments, or predetermined expectations is part of the inclusion process (Ollerton, 2009). In other words, teachers should hold high expectations for their students, regardless of students' past achievements. Intentional design with deliberate planning and continual communication is crucial (Dukes & Lamar-Dukes, 2009).

The goal of inclusion is more than just preparing students to pass standardized tests and increasing academic levels. Students with developmental needs may have behavioral, social, emotional, or communication goals included in that general education setting. Research asserts that teaching students how to behave and interact with each other fits naturally within integrated school environments (Marchant & Womack, 2010). For example, students with autism showed improvements in the areas of behavior management, communication, and social skills when inclusion interventions such as applied behavior analysis and inventories were infused in the curriculum (Waddington & Reed, 2009; McGarrell, Healy, Leader, O'Connor, & Kenny, 2009). Such methods help students acquire and maintain skills in discrete steps through much practice and positive reinforcement with appropriate rewards, such as smiles, increased verbal praise, and tokens.

Full inclusion, which refers to placing students of all abilities in the general education classroom regardless of the type or severity of the disability, has many challenges (Ferguson, 2008; Karten, 2010a). Proponents of full inclusion want the general education classroom to be the only placement, yet without the appropriate accommodations, students may very well end up being excluded under the guise of inclusion. The general education classroom needs to be restructured in a way that allows students' needs to be appropriately met. Many students with special needs who succeed in the general education classroom receive appropriate scaffolding that allows for the provision of necessary academic, physical, emotional, social, and behavioral accommodations and modifications. If the programs are not modified, the general education classroom is actually excluding students with special needs even though they are physically included.

Although inclusion is not always an easy process to implement, collaboration and structured plans will yield successful results for students (Hollingsworth, Boone, & Crais, 2009). Overall, inclusion has been a unifying concept for special and general education (Gavish, 2009). For example, when special education practices enter the classroom, general education teachers are able to see the benefits of differentiated instruction. When general and special education teachers collaborate, all learners are viewed as exceptional students who are worthy of achieving solid educational foundations within the inclusive environment.

Inclusion Strategies and Interventions focuses on helping educators maximize learning in today's inclusive classrooms, where learning, physical, communicative, emotional, social, behavioral, sensory, perceptual, or cultural differences exist. Interventions are meaningless unless they are connected to the individual profiles of unique students. Diversity is a way of life in inclusive classrooms that honor individual student levels and abilities. Education is never exclusively about the subjects taught; it is also about who is seated in the room. The classroom audience defines the lesson delivery, the depth of the concepts, the intervening strategies, the pace of the lessons, the types of collaborative structures, the lesson plans, and the curricular decisions made. Savvy inclusive educators always remember that inclusive classrooms consist of individual learners.

Inclusion by Law

The Individuals with Disabilities Education Act (IDEA) is very influential in current inclusion programs. IDEA stems from the Education of All Handicapped Children Act (PL 94–142) of 1975 and was written to allow students with disabilities access to the general education curriculum in what is determined to be their least restrictive environments (LREs). Individualized education programs (IEPs) are developed for each student. In Canada, individualized program plans (IPPs), which are similar to IEPs, are designed by program planning teams to place students in their appropriate educational settings. Each province adopts its own regulations with roles and expectations defined.

In the United States, the general education classroom, or the *regular classroom*, is the first option of placement unless the nature or severity of the disability is such that even with the necessary supports and aids in place, the student would not achieve a satisfactory education in such an environment. Not all children belong in the general education classroom. Sometimes a student's academic, behavioral, emotional, or social needs call for special classes and a separate school even though these are viewed as more restrictive environments. Canadian schools have challenges as well with the restructuring of general education to establish fair, equitable, and sensible placements for all students (Porter, 2008).

Inclusion sometimes involves a combination of services and environments, such as a student receiving replacement instruction for mathematics in a separate smaller resource room, while the rest of his or her instruction is achieved within the larger inclusive classroom. Sometimes students are placed in the general education classroom with a co-teacher or instructional assistant. Each placement is unique to each student.

Legislation drives many decisions regarding inclusion. For example, the No Child Left Behind (NCLB) Act of 2001 (the reauthorization of the Elementary and Secondary Education Act [ESEA] of 1965) advocates high outcomes for all children to narrow achievement gaps. NCLB's contention is that all students are entitled to quality education that is delivered by prepared educators. This includes a system of accountability that demands increasingly successful learning opportunities for students with disabilities within general education settings. The tremendous emphasis upon accountability has caused many school systems to revamp their inclusion programs. Schools continually plan and monitor goals and objectives and communicate these with all involved parties throughout the school year.

Laws such as IDEA, Section 504 of the Rehabilitation Act of 1973, and the Americans with Disabilities Act (ADA) extend accommodations and modifications to students with disabilities in school environments and other public and private settings. Educational staff collaborate with the student's family to determine the appropriate placements and related services, including accommodations for both instruction and assessments.

IEPs unique to each student are developed to outline the type of placements, supports, accommodations, modifications, and related services the student will require to reach his or her fullest potential. IEPs are not magical documents that automatically ensure that students' achievements will be gained by the presence of formal signatures that agree to adhere to the goals presented. Some IEPs, intervention plans, or Section 504 (Rehabilitation Act of 1973) plans, which also provide student classroom accommodations, are not meaningfully written, individualized, or comprehensive enough if they do not include pertinent assessment information, baseline data, short-term objectives, or appropriate accommodations (Capizzi, 2008). In addition, many groups oppose the fact that states are not required to place short-term objectives in all IEPs, claiming that the monitoring of progress is somewhat limited with less accountability of educators' steps taken toward meeting students' individual needs (Cortiella, 2005; Wright & Wright, 2006; National Committee of Parents and Advocates Organized to Protect IDEA, 2006). However, IEPs are worthwhile educational road maps if they are continually reviewed and amended based upon students' progress and ongoing needs.

As an offshoot of IDEA, response to intervention (RTI) looks at student learning and screening data, determines appropriate interventions, and monitors students' progress with interventions before considering whether students are eligible to be evaluated for a learning disability. With RTI, we do not wait for students to fail but instead find ways to deliver the curriculum to achieve successful outcomes. RTI is a viable way for struggling students to learn on their individual levels within inclusive classrooms before they are given labels involving special education.

More details about specific legislation are presented in appendix B.

About This Book

This text is divided into three parts. Part 1 centers on promoting learning in inclusive classrooms. The first chapter introduces the students in inclusive classrooms and focuses on the unique abilities that they possess, providing the foundation for the rest of the book. Once this baseline knowledge is established, chapter 2 then describes ways to organize the inclusive classroom utilizing principles such as RTI, differentiated instruction, understanding by design, universal design for learning, multiple intelligences, multisensory approaches, peer mentoring, and cooperative learning. Appropriate related services such as assistive technology are also discussed. Chapter 3 moves into the actual creation of an inclusive classroom and outlines interventions for particular categories of learners. Effective co-teaching practices are also described. Chapter 4 highlights realistic accommodations and how they are directly linked to students' assessment data to establish meaningful accountability.

Part 2 offers strategies for effective curriculum practice, stressing the importance of creating strategic learners who are equipped with study skills through educationally solid collaborative lesson deliveries. Chapter 5 concentrates on literacy and communication, and presents multisensory and structured reading programs, along with explicit writing instruction. Strategies for English learners are also included. Chapter 6 delves into mathematics instruction and provides RTI math recommendations. The disciplines of social studies and science are explored in chapter 7, while chapter 8 dives into the important but often overlooked domains of art, music, movement, and life skills. Chapter 9 demonstrates the merits of an interdisciplinary approach, which links the instruction across the curriculum and proves that subjects do not have to exist in isolation. To close part 2, chapter 10 discusses transitional plans for successful postsecondary outcomes.

Part 3 outlines how to nourish and continually maintain the inclusive classroom, focusing on what needs to be done to consistently achieve the desired outcomes for students, teachers, and families. Chapter 11 discusses professional collaboration and the inclusive players who create that collaborative environment, including co-teachers, related staff, administrators, professional learning communities, families, and the students themselves. Chapter 12 ties it all together and serves as a conclusion to the book with reminders about how evidence-based practices can effectively meet and honor students' needs within inclusive classrooms. This final chapter also includes an investigation of where we are now, along with curriculum implications and a review of the inclusive practices.

The appendices offer handy resource material, including a list of abbreviations, a look at the legal aspects of inclusion, and a reference list. Visit **go.solution-tree.com/specialneeds** to download the reproducibles and access live links to the websites in this book.

There are several ways educators can deliver the standards minus the standardization. Differentiated instruction, universal design for learning, understanding by design, team planning, cooperative learning, peer mentoring, and collaborative communications are all viable ways in which inclusion is applied to today's classrooms. It is important that teachers are not overwhelmed by the complexities inclusion presents but instead are prepared with an awareness about their students that is combined with an array of inclusive strategies. This book highlights daily school interventions that help teachers to tap into students' academic and emotional abilities, potentials, levels, and interests. *Inclusion Strategies and Interventions* encourages educators and learners to effectively work together as a team to achieve inclusive schools within accepting and inclusive worlds.

PROMOTING LEARNING IN THE
INCLUSIVE CLASSROOM

ONE
Understanding the Inclusive Classroom

"I hated the shorter line when we went to lunch and specials. My class only had ten kids in it with two teachers. The other classes had so many more kids. I just knew that everyone was looking at me and thinking, Boy, is he stupid or what! Now, because I did OK in that other class, I am back in the bigger classroom with my friends for most of the day. That's where I have social studies and science and go to gym, art, and music with the kids who ride the bus with me and live on my block. I still do my reading and math in a separate room with a different teacher and other kinds of books. Sometimes the smaller room is OK. When I'm with the resource group, I don't care as much about messing up, and the teacher helps me learn the things I need to know. When I was younger, I hated school and sometimes myself. Now, I have more friends, and school isn't so bad."

It is tough for some kids to fit in when others view them as being different. This affects their self-esteem, which in turn influences academic performances and social interactions. Special education classes that set kids apart and flag them as "different" still exist today, but they are rapidly being replaced by classes that employ teaching strategies that accept and embrace all students (without the stigmatization). Today, differences are becoming the norm in heterogeneous inclusive classrooms.

Know What Your Students Know

There are thirteen classifications of disability under IDEA (2004) for students aged three to twenty-one:

1. Autism
2. Traumatic brain injury (TBI)
3. Deaf-blindness
4. Visual impairment including blindness
5. Deafness
6. Speech/language impairment
7. Hearing impairment

8. Mental retardation (still a legal term, although *intellectual disability* is often used instead)

9. Emotional disturbance (ED)

10. Orthopedic impairment

11. Multiple disabilities (MD)

12. Specific learning disability (SLD)

13. Other health impairment (OHI)

The term *developmental delay* may be used as another category by local education agencies (LEAs) for children aged three through nine who need early intervening services because of cognitive, physical, communication, social, emotional, or adaptive delays.

Inclusive classrooms often consist of learners from diverse cultures who speak many different languages. Different levels of understanding and expression exist within this group, labeled English learners (ELs) (Pransky, 2009). While statistics consistently point out the overrepresentation of students with specific learning disabilities, intellectual differences, and emotional disturbances who are also culturally and linguistically diverse or ELs (Artiles, Trent, & Palmer, 2004; Macswan & Rolstad, 2006; Klingner & Harry, 2006; Hart, 2009), approximately one million students classified as ELs also have learning and emotional difficulties and challenges that may place them into the special education spectrum (Hart, 2009; Baca & Cervantes, 2004; Artiles, Rueda, Salazar, & Higareda, 2005).

A student's classification helps an educator to establish basic knowledge of his or her needs, but this knowledge is not enough to help the student achieve his or her highest potential. Each student with a disability has a unique personality with individual likes and dislikes. As differentiated instruction expert Carol Tomlinson (2010) points out, we need to study the students we teach.

Within any given inclusive classroom today, students' levels of competency, rates of learning, and degrees of motivation to acquire concepts and skills will vary. *Knowing what your students know is essential.* It is also important to understand how the students view themselves and others during learning experiences. For example, students with autism or Asperger's often have excellent prior knowledge and specific interests that need to be tapped. A student with Down syndrome may not verbally communicate his or her likes or dislikes but certainly has individual preferences that need to be acknowledged. Physical, sensory, emotional, behavioral, social, or learning differences do not always translate into disabilities if educators recognize and utilize the students' stronger modalities and intelligences.

Learning is halted when abstract concepts are not connected to students' prior knowledge. Without motivation or the desire to listen to the lessons, the students' learning gains are minimal, nonproductive, and temporary. Teachers who confidently know their students, the subject matter, and the best delivery approaches realize the value of applying metacognitive strategies, which encourage students to think about their thinking. It is no longer OK to just mark an answer as correct or incorrect; students need to understand why an answer is right or wrong. Metacognitive strategies may involve self-checking exercises, self-talk, self-regulation, and more.

Students should know themselves better as well. Students who assume responsibility for their learning gain strides with realistic self-perceptions. Research denotes that self-reflective learning yields positive effects for students' academic and social development (Joseph, 2010).

In addition, students benefit from the self-reflection of administrators, related school staff, and families. The following questions should be addressed by the respective inclusive stakeholders.

Student:

- Do I ask questions during the lesson, or do I just pretend that I am getting it with lots of smiling and meaningless head nodding?

- Do I care about learning or just about the grade?

- Who can I go to for additional help?

Teacher:

- What do I know about my students' strengths?

- Is my lesson effectively reaching all of my students, or are some of them lost due to the pace or complexity?

- What lesson elements can I change, repeat, or abandon?

- How can I strengthen my skills with evidence-based practices?

- Do I share and plan strategies with co-teachers, paraprofessionals, related staff, and families?

- Who can I collaborate with for more ideas?

Administrator:

- Am I supporting my teachers with appropriate student data, resources, and planning time without overwhelming them with the latest best practices?

- Do I collaborate with my staff in an atmosphere that values a team mentality?

Family:

- Do I support the school and teachers in their inclusion efforts?

- Is there an open line of communication between the school and me?

- Who can offer additional resources or support?

Social, Emotional, and Academic Growth

Inclusion is more than a philosophy. It is a setting in which students connect to both the curriculum and their peers, allowing for academic *and* social growth. Cognitive psychologist Lev Vygotsky was a firm believer in healthy relationships between individuals and saw cognitive development as closely related to social engagements (Kearsley, 2009). Researchers such as Howard Gardner and Daniel Goleman also affirm the importance of students' interpersonal and intrapersonal skills and connect emotional intelligence to successes (Hoerr, 2009). Emotional, social, and behavioral issues affect classroom lessons for students of all abilities and must be emphasized as much as academic gains. In fact, how students feel about themselves cannot be separated from how they learn. Messages from peers, families, and educators influence students' self-image and performance. For example, when teachers consistently praise students, those learners are encouraged to achieve more. When students receive encouragement from their families or caregivers, this boosts their self-esteem, translating to greater self-worth.

Belonging is a difficult issue for students with special needs who try to fit in with the general education population, and their level of academic attainment is often contingent upon appropriate emotional scaffolding. Even though students with disabilities are physically included in general education settings and work side by side with other students, they are not always socially accepted. They discover early that they are different from their peers, and this creates difficulties outside of their respective disabilities. Students with emotional differences often experience rejection from peers, loneliness, and social isolation due to poor interpersonal skills (Mathur, Quinn, Forness, & Rutherford, 1998). Students with intellectual disabilities are more accepted in nonacademic classes than academic classes, but social inclusion outside of school is not common (Siperstein, Parer, Bardon, & Widaman, 2007). Other children often wish to distance themselves from those with behavioral differences. Even teachers, at times, find it difficult to separate the behavior from the child (Karten, 2010a). Consequently, this affects the degree of personal contact and social inclusion the student with special needs experiences both within and outside school.

So, for example, even though a student with a nonverbal learning disability who has difficulties with executive functioning or organization may very well belong in the general education setting, without the proper social and emotional scaffolding, he is still excluded, which further diminishes his feelings of self-worth and capacity for emotional regulation. The sense of being excluded also influences his choices and actions, further impacting academics when participating in cooperative work, classroom discussion, and assessments. Students with special needs want to be on par with their classmates, academically and socially, but might not ask for extra help or clarifications for fear of being ridiculed or viewed as too needy. When students are young, they are less hesitant to ask for extra help, since they are not as aware of the social consequences or stigmatization of being different. As students with special needs advance in the grades, however, they become increasingly more cognizant of their needs and are often hyperconscious of how they are viewed by others. Students are then less likely to ask for additional help, ultimately harming their academic efforts. It is important that educators understand how the students feel about the inclusive environment (Miller, 2008).

Since childhood relationships with peers influence adult social adjustments, inclusive classrooms must be accepting and support and promote social competence (Meadan & Monda-Amaya, 2008). Yes, curriculum standards must be delivered, but social, emotional, and behavioral skills also need to be given respect—and direct skill instruction—to increase students' achievements. This requires an inclusive classroom atmosphere that models positive interactions. Teachers who offer positive learning climates embrace students' minds and souls. They not only teach academics, but also observe, hear, and honor their students' emotional, social, and behavioral needs within a nonjudgmental yet constructivist learning environment that allows the students to shape their own experiences. Remember, inclusion means that students are learning *together* in *supportive* environments while supporting themselves as well.

Raising Awareness

A powerful tool for raising awareness about disabilities is bibliotherapy. It is often more effective for students with disabilities and their peers to read about fictional characters and then translate those messages to everyday classroom scenarios than to digest information presented in a lecture about disabilities. Students identify with the protagonists and absorb the subliminal messages through stories that often have common themes and are not exclusively about disabilities.

Bibliotherapy has been used successfully to build both academic and social skills of students with social and emotional difficulties (Regan & Page, 2008). Through this medium, educators can send out the message that kids with disabilities have the same issues as their peers. At the same time, reading books such as these increases students' awareness of diversity and differences and minimizes preconceived stereotypes. Such books also address the insensitive actions of peers. Students constructively draw healthy parallel emotional conclusions with fictional characters' experiences. Knowing that they are not alone helps students with disabilities work through some of the issues they face in a nonthreatening, less confrontational manner.

Table 1.1 (page 14) offers a few books to explore about abilities and differences according to grade level and disability. Select literature that portrays students with disabilities in a positive way with pluralistic themes rather than literature that focuses solely on the disability or portrays people in a negative light.

Table 1.1: Bibliotherapy to Increase Disability Awareness

	K–2	3–5	6–8	9–12 and beyond
Learning Disabilities	The Don't-Give-Up Kid by Jeanne Gehret Leo the Late Bloomer by Robert Kraus	Thank You, Mr. Falker by Patricia Polacco I Got a "D" in Salami by Henry Winkler and Lin Oliver	My Thirteenth Winter by Samantha Abeel Many Ways to Learn: Young People's Guide to Learning Disabilities by Judith M. Stern	Learning Outside the Lines by Jonathan Mooney and David Cole
Physical Disabilities	Rolling Along With Goldilocks and the Three Bears by Cindy Meyers	All Kinds of Friends, Even Green! by Ellen B. Senisi	Freak the Mighty by Rodman Philbrick	The Dive From Clausen's Pier by Ann Packer
Sensory Disabilities	Silent Lotus by Jeanne M. Lee	Follow My Leader by James Garfield	Singing Hands by Delia Ray	Of Sound Mind by Jean Ferris
Autism	Ian's Walk by Laurie Lears	My Friend With Autism by Beverly Bishop	Al Capone Does My Shirts by Gennifer Choldenko	The Way I See It by Temple Grandin
Asperger's	All Cats Have Asperger Syndrome by Kathy Hoopmann	Blue Bottle Mystery by Kathy Hoopmann Buster and the Amazing Daisy by Nancy Ogaz	Look Me in the Eye by John Elder Robison	The Curious Incident of the Dog in the Night-time by Mark Haddon House Rules by Jodi Picoult
Down Syndrome and Intellectual Disabilities	Be Good to Eddie Lee by Virginia Fleming	The Summer of the Swans by Betsy Byars	The Man Who Loved Clowns by June Rae Wood	The Memory Keeper's Daughter by Kim Edwards
Social, Emotional, or Behavioral Disabilities	How to Behave and Why by Munro Leaf	Matt the Moody Hermit Crab by Caroline C. McGee	Help! I'm in Middle School . . . How Will I Survive? by Merry L. Gumm	Running With Scissors by Augusten Burroughs

Behavioral Issues

Developmental, learning, physical, and emotional differences often impact students' attention and progress with academic and social behaviors. For example, students with traumatic brain injury may exhibit frustrations with memory issues during instruction and assessments. Sometimes medications are prescribed to modify unwanted behaviors, but even so, students need self-control strategies as well as those medications. Being aware of how psychological factors affect behavior is part of the preparation that makes some inclusive classrooms better than others.

Students with emotional and behavioral differences often require extra attention from educators and the administration, impacting the learning of other students and the schedules of school personnel. If that is the case, then appropriate behavioral plans must be proactively implemented to monitor positive strides and decrease the negative unwarranted behavior.

Behavioral student contracts help students exhibit more self-control and become more emotionally regulated. It is sometimes difficult to realize that self-control or paying attention is an evolutionary process, but if improvements are monitored and charted, then behavioral and social skills become more tangible concepts for educators, students, and families. Sometimes educators will need to break down the components of social behaviors into their subskills and offer increased verbal reinforcement, modeling, discussion, and practice across settings to ensure student generalizations.

Simulations and modeling appropriate interactions through hypothetical scenarios reinforce appropriate behavioral actions. Students also need to practice seeing things through other people's perspectives and viewpoints that differ from their own. Students need not agree with the viewpoints, but they must learn to tolerate and even accept such views. Understanding other perspectives is a crucial life skill.

There is a difference between the remediation necessary for acquiring skills and the remediation necessary for performing skills. Within inclusive classrooms, strategies differ depending upon whether students are acquiring or performing the skills, as is shown in table 1.2. The overall desired outcome is for students to be able to apply these skills in settings beyond the inclusive classroom walls.

Table 1.2: Types of Behavioral Interventions

Remediation for Acquiring Skills	Remediation for Performing Skills
Modeling	Prompting
Coaching	Shaping
Direct instruction	Direct reinforcement

Source: Gresham, Cook, Crews, & Kern, 2004.

Social Issues

Educators cannot assume that students who enter the school doors possess appropriate social skills (Johns, Crowley, & Guetzloe, 2005). Sometimes students with special needs are not aware of the impact their behavior has on their peers or how their comments, body language, lack of experience, or inappropriate choices may isolate them and offend others. Just as academics require direct skill instruction, socialization often requires direct skill instruction for many students with disabilities. Accountability, accommodations, and data are not exclusive to academics.

Students with Asperger's syndrome, autism, or emotional differences often have difficulties with social situations, difficulties that spill over to academics. These difficulties are found in a variety of interactions: playing at recess, working in cooperative groups, giving eye contact to others, engaging in appropriate conversation, waiting turns, transitioning, asking for help, exhibiting nonverbal cues, and more. Social interactions are a part of daily life and therefore important both in and outside of school. Reciprocating socially, living independently, and handling stressful situations are significant skills, even though they do not appear on standardized tests with neatly bubbled responses.

Teachers need to be aware of how students process social cues and just what skills are necessary to improve social competencies (Meadan & Monda-Amaya, 2008). Social skills involve showing empathy for others, being responsible, making appropriate decisions, exhibiting ethical behavior, and being able to handle a variety of situations and relationships (Zins, Weissbert, Wang, & Walberg, 2004).

One example of social skills instruction is the use of social stories with students with autism to increase their game-playing skills (Qirmbach, Lincoln, Feinberg-Gizzo, Ingersoll, & Andrews, 2009). Social stories by Carol Gray (www.thegraycenter.org) help students with ASD (autism spectrum disorder) understand more about the perspectives of others. Jed Baker offers excellent social pictures that visually outline appropriate behaviors in his *Social Skills Picture Book*. Another publication of Baker's, *No More Meltdowns*, helps students to better manage their emotions through acceptable plans and strategies. Students can view pictures and then act accordingly to visual prompts and models for schedules, directions, transitions, and unfamiliar learning content.

It is important that social skills are taught and assessed within caring, structured learning environments. Teachers should not draw undue attention to students in front of peers. Private conferences and signals increase students' awareness and avoid embarrassments and self-consciousness. A student with behavioral and emotional differences needs increased self-reflection and feedback to improve his or her behavior. Students with disabilities such as obsessive-compulsive disorder, oppositional defiant disorder, attention-deficit/hyperactivity disorder, bipolar disorder, and depression do not deliberately exhibit the wrong behavior. They require outside regulation, guided practice, modeling, and then more self-regulation to understand and improve their social skills.

When students have social deficits, it is crucial that educators accept and effectively apply the knowledge offered by evidence-based practices to help students gain increased social and behavioral acumens, specifically targeting social areas of need with appropriate interventions (Barton-Arwood, Murrow, Lane, & Jolivette, 2005; Lane, Gresham, & O'Shaughnessy, 2002; Lane & Wehby, 2002). This includes establishing specialized programs within school settings and general education environments that promote success with consistent attention and positive reinforcement of appropriate behavior.

Appropriate social behavior needs to be reinforced to improve social deficits. Students often know how to perform correctly but need additional attention that recognizes them when they behave properly to increase the frequency of that appropriate behavior (Gresham, Cook, Crews, & Kern, 2004). Reinforcements can range from simple verbal praise to token economies or self-selected items at the school store. Effective rewards are student specific, based upon interests and developmental levels.

The Council for Exceptional Children and the Interstate New Teacher Assessment and Support Consortium (INTASC, 2001) both advocate not only the intellectual but also the intertwined social and personal development of each learner. Recognizing and praising appropriate behaviors, teaching anger management, instituting conflict resolution, and capitalizing on the teachable moments are crucial ingredients that make classrooms emotionally healthy (Johns, Crowley, & Guetzloe, 2005). In addition, schools should provide guidance counselors and structured rules to circumvent undesirable behaviors. A schoolwide policy of zero tolerance for bullying, whether it is displayed in a classroom, on a school bus, or in the lunchroom, must be consistently reinforced.

Social competencies spill over into all school and personal endeavors and therefore warrant special instruction. Social skills instruction broadens opportunities to learn but if not appropriately addressed can lead to social isolation (Deshler, Ellis, & Lenz, 1996).

Communication Issues

There are many aspects of communication and thus many possible areas of difficulty. *Receptive language* refers to understanding or interpreting what others say. *Expressive language* allows people to communicate their understanding through a multitude of ways, such as oral and written language, body gestures, and interactions. *Pragmatic language* uses speech for socialization. This includes holding conversations, organizing speech, waiting to speak when someone else is talking, and staying on topic. Communications affect interactions with peers and teachers as well as academic advancements.

Students with learning, sensory, perceptual, communication, developmental, emotional, and behavioral differences process information and communicate differently. Often students with disabilities have difficulties expressing their thoughts in conventional ways such as speaking and writing. For example, approximately one-third to one-half of students who fall under the ASD umbrella do not use functional speech as their means of communication (Light, Roberts, DiMarco, & Greiner, 1998; National Research Council, 2001). Some communicate in nonverbal ways with concrete objects, pictures, gestures, and body language. For these students, decoding, encoding, and comprehension issues affect reading, writing, speaking, and listening skills, which in turn influence understanding.

Students with communication issues might need additional support from speech-language pathologists who can preteach unfamiliar content-related vocabulary and appropriate ways to converse with peers. Students with hearing, visual, or physical difficulties require individual IEP-driven classroom accommodations (Kirch, Bargerhuff, Turner, & Wheatly, 2005) that highlight their competencies, not their sensory or communicative differences.

Inclusive environments offer students opportunities for communication growth with both receptive and expressive language since the natural setting of the general education classroom has many peer role models and offers more exposure to social opportunities and pragmatic conversation. For example, one study affirms the positive influence that ongoing inclusive environments have upon the communication weaknesses of learners with Down syndrome as compared to separate special education classrooms (Buckley, Bird, & Sacks, 2006). Students who are hearing impaired or deaf can also gain communication skills in inclusive classrooms if the right supports and accommodations are in place. This may include circular seating if a student who is deaf lip-reads, lessons on sign language, or sound-field enhancement or assistive listening systems.

Communication is a lifelong skill that people use to express feelings and interact with their environment, and inclusive classrooms offer students opportunities to advance their communication skills when prepared teachers and accepting peers are present.

The Role of the Educator

At the core of all successful inclusive environments is the connection between the educator and student. The effective educator uses a student's passions, interests, and goals to further maximize learning engagements. He or she teaches the student about consequences and lets him or her have a stake in setting up the rules for behavior, communicating that the student is an integral part of the social and behavioral processes. That educator's hello with a supportive smile before jumping into the lesson communicates genuine concern. When addressing inappropriate behaviors, the educator communicates to the student that it is the behavior that is disliked, not the student. Most important, the educator builds a trusting relationship with the student.

Sensitive, well-trained educators who communicate a philosophy that differences are expected, accepted, and exceptional set up nurturing inclusive environments. When teachers take the time to humanize educational experiences, they are able to motivate students to buy in to the lessons.

Moving Beyond Stereotypes

The educational waters become murky when teachers' perceptions of students' abilities interfere with their beliefs that all students are capable of meeting high expectations. Students within inclusive classrooms have varying prior knowledge, receptive and expressive language levels, and perceptual, sensory, physical, academic, social, behavioral, and emotional skills. The educator's knowledge of his or her students' characteristics needs to always advance his or her perceptions of the students, not thwart his or her confidence in their abilities.

In the following exercise, match the student comment to the learner. Responses can be either free choice or taken from the word box provided.

Student Comment:

1. Let me listen to the books on tape! _____
2. No way will I do that! _____
3. I have to redo it, again! _____
4. I can't talk in front of the class! _____
5. Why do I have to write an essay? _____

6. I like to move when I learn. _____

7. I'll shout out my answer if I want to! _____

8. How will I ever get organized? _____

9. Math is *so* not cool! _____

10. *They* are not like *me*! _____

11. I want to do it my way! _____

12. Gym is too tough! _____

13. The brook I read was a good one! _____

14. I better hold the paper closer. _____

15. These tics are so embarrassing. By the way, I don't swear. _____

16. The world is awful. I wish I could sleep more. _____

17. Please look at me when you speak. _____

18. It's embarrassing to be in the nurse's office so much. _____

Learner's Difference:

a. cerebral palsy	b. dyslexia	c. Tourette's	d. autism	e. diabetes	f. dysgraphia
g. ADHD	h. visual impairment	i. articulation disorder	j. learning disability	k. dyscalculia	l. OCD
m. oppositional defiant disorder	n. selective mutism	o. depression	p. CAPD	q. deafness	r. Asperger's
s. other health impairment	t. spina bifida	u. hearing impairment	v. TBI	w. emotional difference	x. multiple disabilities

Are you looking for an answer key, or were the preceding student statements easy to identify based upon your prior knowledge? Prior knowledge is helpful, but sometimes that same prior knowledge skews views about students' potentials, lowers expectations, and encourages statements such as:

- He has ADHD; I'll never get him to sit quietly to learn.

- Oh no, there's a change in schedule; that Asperger's kid* will just flip.

- I better not teach this; the LD boy* will never understand.

- Kids with ED just disrupt the class.

*Note: Always use people-first language, for example, "a child with Asperger's" or "a boy with a learning disability."

The point of this exercise is to emphasize that we teach students, not labels. Students do not fit into stereotypical patterns or neatly compartmentalized boxes. Yet every day teachers differentiate their lessons to meet the needs of children labeled *a* through *x*. Students with certain disabilities may have similar characteristics, but each child is most certainly an individual with his or her own way of seeing the world and his or her own likes and dislikes.

Question to Investigate

What are some essential ingredients for emotional well-being that teachers need to infuse in their daily lessons?

The establishment of clear expectations is essential for academics, as are behavioral and social opportunities to allow all students to learn and grow in emotionally healthy classrooms. Students who are depressed or seem apathetic need encouragement to tune in to the lessons. Some activities to accomplish this are more teacher-student conferences; open discussions; writing, art, and drama projects; reading choices; and personal logs. Realistic praise increases students' time on task and the desire to keep trying, even when the topic seems a bit tough.

Caring and attentive educators make positive differences in students' lives. Pay attention to a student who is depressed or has shut down. Notice changes in clothing, self-care, and moods. Enlist the assistance of caregivers at home, school psychologists, guidance counselors, and other school and community resources. Involve the student in his or her interests to promote healthy outlets for experiencing good feelings, whether it is through more physical activities in gym or subjects and clubs such as art, chess, creative writing, computers, chorus, band, or cheerleading. School is about stimulating minds, but we cannot ignore the child's demeanor and emotional health. It is sometimes the quietest students who scream the loudest.

TWO
Organizing for Instruction

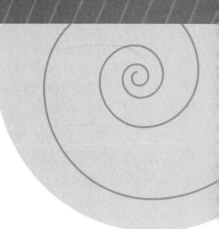

"Fine, I'll help that kid with the social studies project, but she better not get a better grade than me."

"I like the kid who acts out; we learn less algebra when he's around."

"If I hear one more thing about the test, I'll explode. I hate school!"

"Finally, someone gets me and knows that I need help."

Every student is different. What matters to one is inconsequential to another. Some students welcome differences, while others cannot accept the fact that *fair* does not translate to equal. The pace, complexities, and assessment demands overwhelm some students, while other students appreciate the learning and help offered.

Considering the learners' diverse needs in delivering the curriculum is an important aspect of any inclusive classroom. Students who have difficulties must not be ignored; instead, they should be supplied with the appropriate interventions and supports (Ervin, 2008). The days of teaching students with choral reciting of facts have long passed. Successful inclusive educators employ evidence-based practices that proactively prepare for student differences and apply interventions that connect to the levels and abilities of their heterogeneous students. Instructional and assessment practices that advocate current inclusive teaching principles fall under domains such as response to intervention, cooperative learning, differentiated instruction, universal design for learning, understanding by design, multiple intelligences, and sensory modalities.

Educators need to be abreast of the latest research on effective teaching strategies. For instance, research indicates that differentiated instruction and RTI hold excellent promise in reducing the overrepresentation of students with cultural, linguistic, and learning differences by offering proper instruction that uses preventative measures to address reading differences (Walker-Dalhouse et al., 2009). Success lies not in what you are teaching, but in your selection and application of appropriate instructional interventions and programs. This chapter outlines a selection of effective programs as part of the organization structure of inclusive classrooms.

Response to Intervention (RTI)

Special education has entered general education classrooms with responsive early intervening services under the reauthorized Individuals with Disabilities Education Act (2004). These interventions are intended to reach a broad range of students with learning, sensory, perceptual, developmental, communication, and cultural differences (Vaughn & Ortiz, n.d.; Fletcher, Lyon, Fuchs, & Barnes, 2007; Stuart & Rinaldi, 2009). RTI ensures that students with language barriers and/or different learning abilities are offered appropriate interventions based upon their levels and needs.

In RTI, evidence-based instructional practices are used, student progress is monitored, and educators meaningfully use the data to decide upon instructional interventions. Educators determine where the students are now, where they want them to be, and the routes the students and teachers will travel to reach their destination. RTI includes an instructional itinerary of the following legs of the journey:

- Beginning phase—review of data and assessment of who needs help

- Middle phase—determination and implementation of appropriate services

- Review phase—reflections on whether the interventions work

Interventions are offered in tiers to help narrow students' gaps in learning or to provide advanced learning to meet the needs of students with higher abilities. These tiers are usually:

- Tier 1—whole-class core instruction

- Tier 2—smaller groups with strategic interventions

- Tier 3—more intensive targeted or individualized instruction

In some classrooms, at Tier 1, approximately three-fourths or more of the class receives and responds to the whole-class instruction. At Tier 2, smaller targeted groups receive explicit skill instruction, while Tier 3 calls for more intensive interventions for individual students. All of the tiers require students' progress to be monitored. As explained in the following section, teams meet to plan whether to continue, tweak, abandon, or expand interventions as they review the frequency, duration, and location of the RTI programs, baseline data, and the overall effectiveness of interventions.

Table 2.1 provides examples of how to plan across the tiers for primary, middle school, and high school students. (Products are listed as examples only, not as recommendations.)

Table 2.1: RTI Curriculum Examples

Literacy	
Grades K–5	It is important that students accurately and automatically read text. This fluency then aids with comprehension across content areas. Reading accuracy is determined by the number of words read correctly per minute (WPM). Assessments are given at least three times during the year at the beginning, at midyear, and at the end of the school year. Intensive interventions are monitored more frequently. Types of errors—deletions, omissions, substitutions, reversals, repetition, and self-corrections—are recorded. Reading specialists visit the classroom to offer guided instruction to students at different tiers.

Baseline Data	Independent level: reading accuracy 98 percent or higher		
	Instructional level: 95–97 percent		
	Frustration level: below 90 percent		
	Tier 1 Notes	**Tier 2 Notes**	**Tier 3 Notes**
Objectives, Procedures, & Materials	Explicit instruction with syllable types including modeling and structured daily skill practice is given to the whole class. Visual (pictures and color-coded flashcards), auditory (clapping and speaking), and kinesthetic-tactile elements (writing in salt, finger blending, tapping) are used. Materials: Wilson Fundations® for grades K–3 and Wilson Reading System® for grades 4–5 (www.wilsonlanguage.com)	Eight students require additional practice to classify and pronounce the two- and three-syllable word lists. Guided instruction is given to read nonsense words from the Wilson program. Some students in the class surpass others and are offered cloze practice enrichment while small-group intervention is given to these eight students.	After five weeks, four of the eight students require more intensive interventions with additional instruction for open and closed syllables. Structured twenty-minute daily sessions with a review of all consonant and vowel sounds in conjunction with syllable practice are implemented and monitored. Trained teachers and reading specialists circulate and assist students.
Assessment	Fluency monitoring with administration of pre-, inter-, and postassessments of word lists, sentences, and timed orally read passages.		
Mathematics			
Grades 6–8	Students who have a strong command of mathematics across the operations with whole numbers, decimals, and fractions relate this learning to functional daily applications and higher-level mathematics. Professional learning committees collaboratively review and jigsaw sources from the National Council of Teachers of Mathematics (www.nctm.org/eresources/school_level.asp?lv=2) to determine appropriate yet challenging grade/course activities. Interdisciplinary lessons with grade-level teachers are continually planned throughout the year.		
Baseline Data	Students' math levels are assessed with percent-correct scores on daily curriculum unit math drills, weekly quizzes, unit tests, and collaborative small-group problem solving. Students' progress is graphed and kept in portfolios.		
	Tier 1 Notes	**Tier 2 Notes**	**Tier 3 Notes**
Objectives, Procedures, & Materials	Whole-class instruction is used to increase students' computational and problem-solving skills with application to real-life situations. Concepts addressed include number sense, algebra, geometry, measurements, data analysis, and probability. Problem-solving strategy charts are distributed to all students. Materials: *Connected Mathematics 2* (www.phschool.com/cmp2)	A few of the students require a review of basic computations of subtraction with regrouping, two-digit-by-two-digit multiplication, and division by two-digit divisors. These students receive skill instruction three times a week for thirty to forty minutes from math teachers. The rest of the class cooperatively completes assignments in math stations for advancements with teacher guidance and instruction.	Based upon initial mathematical assessments, the students who have moved to Tier 3 require intensive math instruction with math vocabulary, computation skills, and problem-solving steps. Discrete task analysis is conducted to determine and strengthen weaker areas. Basic-skills math teachers provide daily modeling with guided practice for thirty-minute intervals.
Assessment	Math portfolios with formal and informal assessments are graphed and reviewed with students to increase self-regulation.		

continued ➲

Literacy			
Grades 9–12	Literacy is on a downward spiral for adolescents. They would rather text their friends a message than write a formal letter. More encouragement is needed to invite students to read books from various genres and periodicals and to develop better research skills. Teachers administer reading tests to ascertain fluency, vocabulary, and comprehension levels of the students at the beginning of the year and again at quarterly marking periods. Students receive direct instruction from both general and special education staff and other related personnel using a variety of genres. Instruction is given to the whole class, to small groups, and in collaborative ongoing classroom vocabulary centers.		
Baseline Data	Online quiz and short reading passage with a cloze exercise are given to all of the students to ascertain a baseline vocabulary level (worksheet is generated from www.teach-nology.com /worksheets/language_arts).		
	Tier 1 Notes	Tier 2 Notes	Tier 3 Notes
Objectives, Procedures, & Materials	To raise students' vocabulary levels, the class reviews Greek and Latin word derivations in lists, short passages in various genres, and informational texts. Whole-class instruction is given in the computer lab with monitoring of online exercises and teacher-generated activities from these sites: • www.studyisland.com • www.awrsd.org/oak/Library /greek_and_latin_root _words.htm • http://grammar.ccc .commnet.edu/grammar /quizzes/vocab/match2.htm	Some students have difficulties breaking up words into affixes or identifying the stem words. Three times a week, those students receive small-group thirty-minute instruction with content-related words. Pre- and posttests are given every week. Students color-code the words, highlight them on photocopied passages, and use them in contextual sentences. Work samples are graded with student conferencing. Study Island sessions are repeated.	Two students are reading significantly below grade level. Individualized class and modified homework assignments are assigned and monitored by the general education and support teachers. The special education and general education teachers alternately listen and guide students as they orally read selected grade-level passages and excerpts (from www. timeforkids.com/TFK). Students receive direct skill instruction, focusing on one word family at a time five days a week for forty minutes from the school reading specialist.
Assessment	Online quiz and short reading passage with cloze exercise are readministered, and the results are compared to the baseline data.		

Team Planning

Because of their collaborative approach, RTI models hold great promise in the identification and implementation of interventions for students with differences when interventions are organized, implemented, and reviewed correctly (Murawski & Hughes, 2009). School teams may be comprised of principals, supervisors, other administrators, grade-level general and special education teachers, reading and math basic-skills teachers, resource teachers, behavioral specialists, and other support staff. (Information is also reported to parents and families.) Teams meet to review students' progress and make appropriate recommendations. Staff who observe the students share their insights with other related staff, and the team collaborates with active discussions and consultations.

For the RTI process to be successful, it must be structured in a way that does not burden or overwhelm the classroom teachers, but instead provides them with continuing support in terms of physical resources and knowledge. RTI requires the right materials and equipment for instruction and data collection, along with the appropriate environment, and of course collaboration and insights from supportive people. This may involve the provision of separate testing areas, extra folders, ongoing professional development, technological monitoring systems for data collection, and time and support from all team members.

Examination of the data yields specific instructional plans and ways to address learners' needs based upon viable information rather than arbitrarily written lesson plans that only take into account the curriculum, not diverse students' levels. Data identify students' strengths and weaknesses and are the driving force that helps teachers to determine the required interventions. Through ongoing classroom assessments, such as quarterly reading tests, graded homework assignments, class projects, participation, written work samples, and unit tests and quizzes, students' progress is continually monitored. Grade-level teams then collaboratively formulate ways to deliver the curriculum.

Progress Monitoring

An intervention's effectiveness is determined when students' progress is monitored at set times during the school year (Johnson, Mellard, Fuchs, & McKnight, 2006). For students in Tier 1, that monitoring can be initiated at the beginning of the year and then repeated midyear and at the close of the school year. For students in Tier 2 or Tier 3, assessments are usually more frequent—daily or weekly—and include a review of the data after a month or perhaps five to eight weeks of intensive instruction. Assessments reveal whether the students are benefiting from direct instruction and appropriately responding to the interventions.

Progress needs to be monitored and valued for the students with the highest skills as well as the struggling students who need the most help (Hughes & Rollins, 2009). Students who fall into the top 25 percent of the class deserve an equal opportunity to improve their skills, and when RTI is properly implemented, achievement is valued for *all* students.

Curriculum-based measurement (CBM) can be used to review the progress of the class as a whole, small groups, or individual students. CBM can include teacher-created quizzes and tests, observations, and other formal or less formal assessments. To gauge improvements, the measurements used for pre- and posttests must be of equal difficulty. Graphing the progress of students receiving interventions yields a quick picture of how well the interventions are working. Inspired educators then use this data collection and progress monitoring to judge the effectiveness of daily lessons and interventions in inclusive environments.

Students' responsiveness to interventions can be documented in the RTI Intervention Plan and RTI Progress Monitoring forms (pages 38 and 40, respectively).

RTI is in its infancy, but it holds tremendous promise as the systems of intervention enter all grades. Overall, RTI acknowledges that uniformed instruction has no appeal in today's classrooms and that students benefit from intensive interventions, team planning, CBM, data analysis, and progress monitoring. RTI is a problem-solving process that monitors students' progress with interventions through team planning sessions and necessary scaffolding. Assessments are viewed as valuable information and guide instructional decisions. Gains from RTI programs and interventions have been noted; in RTI, struggling students are no longer ignored, but instead offered differentiated instruction (Barton & Stepanek, 2009).

Cooperative Learning

Students should always be the primary focus of educators' instructional and classroom management decisions. In cooperative inclusive classrooms, progress is achieved not only through educators' actions or the instructional materials chosen, but also through the help and interaction of peers. Teachers act as facilitators rather than strict disseminators of the learning, and students learn how to learn together.

Because they are drawn to the members of their own age group, students often prefer listening to their peers over listening to their teachers. Cooperative inclusive classrooms are organized in such a way that encourages learners to share ideas in a collaborative, trusting atmosphere. A healthy classroom climate values the abilities of all of the students present, and cooperative classrooms value the students as integral people who enhance the curriculum. Through cooperative learning, students work together to achieve positive academic goals.

Cooperative learning is not just clusters of students learning together; individual accountability and positive interdependence are achieved. Specific roles, such as researcher, reader, writer, artist, musician, focuser, speaker, or checker, are assigned for student interactions. No single person or group monopolizes the learning since the process is about collaborating for results rather than competing for rewards. Ideas and learning are transferred as smaller groups formulate ideas and outline steps to solve problems and then join larger groups to digest, expand, and apply their thoughts. Groups can create collages, approach problem-based learning questions, conduct scientific experiments, organize debates with telling points, write essays, read novels, solve discrete math problems, form study groups, and join together for instructional purposes in an infinite number of configurations.

When appropriate and if willing, peers can also help or tutor each other in their areas of strength, from math concepts to curriculum vocabulary applications. If properly implemented and monitored, peer-mentoring programs add social-cognitive growth for both the mentors and mentees as students work together to achieve desired goals in a noncompetitive atmosphere. Of course, students should be instructed on how to help each other without simply providing the answers.

In cooperative learning environments, even jobs within the classroom are shared. Teachers divide the classroom responsibilities and allow students to take ownership of particular roles, such as pencil sharpeners, schedule writers, homework monitors, and paper passers. The assigned jobs are rotated, and students learn that their efforts have positive effects on the classroom dynamics.

Collaboration is a marketable 21st century skill that involves learning, application, and mastery within healthy social contexts. Vygotsky (1962) poignantly stated that what students do together today, they could do alone tomorrow.

Differentiated Instruction (DI)

DI acknowledges that learners in inclusive classrooms possess varying abilities, interests, and prior knowledge. Even though it may seem like a buzzword in special education, differentiated instruction is not a new concept. One-room schoolhouses utilized this method of teaching out of necessity. In DI, all aspects of instruction are differentiated: content (what is taught), process (how students learn the content), and product (how students show learning). Educators assess students' levels, offer learning choices, and scaffold as appropriate. Students who are engaged with the lesson goals and objectives become stakeholders in their learning. Schools that implement differentiated instruction receive higher standardized assessment scores than schools that practice the one-size-fits-all instructional philosophy (King-Sears, 2008).

To accomplish differentiation, flexible learning options must match the curriculum to the students' needs and levels, utilizing materials, supports, and proactive planning. In a DI class, some students may write research reports, and other students may write paragraphs or sentences. Some students need assistance to break up more difficult words into syllables to improve their fluency and understanding before they even begin to write. Content-related vocabulary may need to be pretaught, retaught, pantomimed, and/or illustrated through any combination of visual, auditory, or kinesthetic-tactile modalities.

Differentiation involves administering pre-, inter-, and postassessments that are reviewed to ascertain students' progress and determine whether to tweak, refine, or rethink instructional practices (King-Sears, 2008). With each assessment, teachers ask these two questions based upon the students' starting levels and outcomes:

1. What should I teach?
2. Was the instruction effective?

If the instruction was not effective for certain students, then alternate instructional interventions are warranted. Instructional plans, deliveries, and assessment choices need to appeal to the diverse abilities of the students in the class. True differentiation allows educators to simultaneously challenge and support their students.

Topic-related centers or stations allow for differentiation options in a classroom (King-Sears, 2005, 2007; Tomlinson & McTighe, 2006). At these stations, groups of students work cooperatively to complete assigned tasks during different periods of the day or week for instructional, enrichment, or review purposes. At the same time, individual teachers, co-teachers, or instructional assistants circulate about the classroom. Help is offered to students on a one-on-one basis or within small groups to either advance or remediate skills. Stations can expand across the curriculum to include many disciplines. The following station titles may spark your imagination: Meet the Author, Poet's Corner, Money Madness, Math in Sports, Time Travelers, Healthy Habits, Reaching for the Stars, Pleasing Palettes, and Study Buddies. Corresponding student instructions, tasks, resources, and worksheets will vary depending upon the complexity of the topic and prior knowledge.

Understanding by Design (UbD)

In the UbD method of instruction, educators outline learning outcomes with student growth, curriculum objectives, and state or provincial standards in mind *before* they plan instructional strategies (Wiggins & McTighe, 2006; Tomlinson & McTighe, 2006). Students participate in planned activities that guide them toward the achievement of those outlined goals, and assessments focus on what was taught, not minute details. The following steps sum up UbD instruction:

1. Identify what students are going to learn.

2. Determine the type of assessment to be used.

3. Design a learning activity that allows each student to achieve that objective based upon his or her highest potential.

UbD is more about maximizing understanding than promoting memorization. Yes, teachers use textbooks, worksheets, and technology to plan activities, but they first determine the purpose of those activities and materials. Thinking about the assessments before the lessons helps to avoid a focus on trivial or superfluous facts that sometimes just assess who the best memorizers are rather than which students are truly gaining understanding. The assessment then drives the types of instruction that are required to achieve planned learning objectives.

Educators in inclusive classrooms connect the outlined outcomes of UbD to students with appropriate scaffolding, presentations, and relevant information. This involves accommodations such as teaching students to paraphrase information, using more graphic organizers, offering continual feedback, sharing more visual supports, or combining appropriate adaptations that allow students of all abilities to better understand the central concepts and all important questions.

A benefit of UbD is that students develop more self-awareness as they are encouraged to assess their levels and ways to achieve higher successes. This process of self-regulation can take place at any grade level—and continue throughout learners' lifetimes.

Figures 2.1 and 2.2 (pages 29–30) illustrate UbD in the subjects of mathematics and literacy. Notice how UbD is connected to DI; both offer students multiple pathways to attain concepts and achieve preplanned outcomes.

UbD essentially plans for, interprets, and values students' achievements. Thinking about the desired results first requires understanding not only the design, but also the students who ultimately construct and master the design.

Thinking of your curriculum, create your own UbD plans using the following prompts:

- Topic

- Concept to be taught

- Essential question

 ● Desired learning outcome

 ● Types of learning activities and materials

Topic: Mathematics

Concept to be taught: Multiplication

Essential question: What does multiplication look like?

Desired learning outcome: Students will relate multiplication to visual representations and concrete models in everyday situations.

Types of learning activities and materials: Students are taught to apply repeated addition to the idea of multiplication ($3 + 3 + 3 + 3 = 3 \times 4$). They will solve and create one- and two-step word problems involving multiplication and/or addition and subtraction. They will also determine how multiplication concepts and facts are related to division. They can create math skits to act out a multiplication problem. Manipulatives such as buttons, paper clips, pencils, and pairs of shoes will be used. The next tables offer more learning activities.

Students fill in tables to skip-count and form patterns.

1	2		4	5			8		10
2	4	6		10		14	16		20
3	6	9		15	18		24		30
4			16		24		32	36	
5	10		20			35		45	
6	12			30		42			60
7		21		35			56		
8		24			48			72	
9			36			63			90
10		30		50			80		

Students create arrays on graph paper, like this one, which vertically displays 5 groups of 2 (2×5) or horizontally shows 2 groups of 5 (5×2) with 10 as the product.

☺	☺	☺	☺	☺
☺	☺	☺	☺	☺

Figure 2.1: Example of UbD in math.

Topic: Literacy

Concept to be taught: Story elements

Essential question: What is the structure or common elements of all stories?

Desired learning outcome: Students will cooperatively identify the characters, setting, plot, climax, and resolution in historical fiction with oral and written reports.

Types of learning activities and materials: Literature circles consist of groups of students with each group reading and reporting on different novels in the genre of historical fiction. Members will assume the following cooperative roles and share their presentations with each other and then the rest of the class:

- **Setting seeker**—this person identifies the various times and places in the novel and conducts research online or through texts to discover more information about the location and time period. Materials used can include student-created maps and timelines, atlases, gazetteers, or online sources.

- **Character artist**—this student outlines the physical and personality traits of the protagonist, antagonist, and other major and minor characters in paragraph form, with bubble dialogue, or using a Venn diagram that compares two or more characters.

- **Plot person**—this student shares the most important events of the story in sequential order up to the story's high/turning point. He or she can communicate the plot by writing a poem, singing a rap song or ballad, or pantomiming story events.

- **Mountaineer**—using programs that create graphic organizers, such as the program found at www.kidspiration.com, this student illustrates the events that immediately preceded and followed the story's climax. Pictures may be hand drawn or involve computer graphics.

- **Finisher**—using a gift box, index cards, and ribbon, this person sums up the novel by wrapping up and reviewing each of the story elements.

Choices for historical fiction novels include: *My Brother Sam Is Dead* by James Lincoln Collier, *Daniel's Story* by Carol Matas, *The Egypt Game* by Zilpha Keatley Snyder, *The Cay* by Theodore Taylor, *Early Sunday Morning: The Pearl Harbor Diary of Amber Billows* by Barry Denenberg, *Once Upon a Quinceanera: Coming of Age in the USA* by Julia Alvarez, and *Baseball in April and Other Stories* by Gary Soto. Afterwards, to tie the experience together, the students collectively create a mural with elements from all stories.

Figure 2.2: Example of UbD in literacy.

Universal Design for Learning (UDL)

Educators who incorporate UDL in their lessons vary their objectives, methods of instruction, and types of assessments to honor the students present. A UDL classroom welcomes all students with learning, behavioral, communication, sensory, physical, and developmental differences and differentiates for all of its students without singling anyone out as being needier.

Universal design was originally a term that described architectural access for all people, not just those with disabilities. It called for environments to be barrier-free, allowing individuals easy access, without waiting for specific needs to arise. For example, the doorway of a restaurant, restroom, hotel room, or classroom needs to be wide enough to allow someone in a wheelchair to easily maneuver himself or herself inside. In addition to helping someone in a wheelchair, the curb cuts on city sidewalks provide access to a person rollerblading or a mother pushing a toddler in a stroller. Elevators and hotel rooms have Braille numbers in place. Closed captioning allows an individual who is deaf to follow a television program; it also helps people with dyslexia and English learners.

In the classroom, UDL offers access to the content through varying opportunities for presentation and with multiple choices for practice and learning (Palincsar, Magnusson, Collins, & Cutter, 2001). UDL lessons recognize students' diverse motivations, emotions, and abilities and include varied content and delivery processes. Educators offer students choices and control to empower them as learners. Research shows that teachers who had specific trainings in their graduate studies on UDL approaches made their lessons more accessible for heterogeneous groups of learners, while those who had no UDL training or instruction were less likely to differentiate their lessons or implement necessary modifications (Spooner, Baker, Harris, Ahlgrim-Delzell, & Browder, 2007).

When a teacher allows students to listen to online talking sites to gain information, then a student with a reading issue is not held back from understanding concepts, nor will a student with blindness be kept apart from the rest of the class. Guided notes help students with dysgraphia while also aiding those students who have ADHD or memory, concentration, or auditory difficulties. In UDL classrooms, many different materials are on hand because the educators are proactively prepared to reach a wide range of students.

The following are examples of UDL assignments:

- *Respond to two of the following five essay choices.* Students are allowed to use writing frames and/or refer to the Transitional Word Lists or Sensory Word Lists (pages 99–100 and 101–102, respectively).

- *Create a song about one of the primary documents.* Students are given the option to listen to the document with a text-to-speech feature. There is also a simplified version of each primary document with vocabulary paraphrased.

- *Design a graphic novel or skit on the book we just read.* Students are allowed to free draw or use software such as Comic Life (http://comiclife.com).

- *Set up a controlled science experiment.* Students are provided with step-by-step directions on PowerPoint slides and podcasts.

- *Write a math word problem starring your favorite celebrity.* Students are allowed to work independently or cooperatively with peer mentors. Teachers model a sample problem with the whole class.

- *Create a PowerPoint presentation from this list of explorers or solve this WebQuest.* A rubric outlining the requirements—for example, the number of slides—is created at www.rubrics4teachers.com and distributed to the students before the assignment.

When teachers take into account the diversity of their students, they build flexibility and differentiation into their lessons. A teacher in an inclusive classroom who follows the principles of UDL will vary his or her presentation style to include formats from straight lecture to detailed descriptions, cooperative learning, open discussions, debates, and hands-on stations and centers. UDL's goal is to increase student participation and engagement. Therefore, visuals and graphic organizers, multimedia presentations, interpersonal or intra-personal activities, and a variety of other mediums to absorb the learning are included in instructions, representations, and assessments. UDL opens many inclusive doors to a truly universal education!

Multiple Intelligences, Sensory Modalities, and Technology

Curriculum demands are heavy as the breadth of knowledge students are expected to have constantly increases. Students have specific preferred learning styles, and educators have preferred styles of teaching. Dilemmas arise when teachers' presentation styles differ from students' preferred styles of learning and students' preferred intelligences and modalities are not acknowledged during lessons or assessments. However, when educators allow students to tap to songs to learn multiplication facts or create a dramatic play, PowerPoint, or iMovie with characters demonstrating the forces of gravitation, magnetism, and friction, then different intelligences and preferred modalities are honored and curriculum demands are met. Mathematics comes alive when educators provide concrete examples—for example, by sectioning an apple to teach about fractions or counting objects in groups of three or four to learn multiples. Acting out a play in social studies or conducting science experiments adds crucial visual, auditory, kinesthetic/tactile (VAKT) elements that honor students' modalities and multiple intelligences. Students of all ages and ability levels need to understand the learning on a concrete or representational level before the abstract learning stands alone. Multiple intelligences, sensory modalities, and technology options are effective in accomplishing this and are applicable to all disciplines and certainly all students.

Multiple Intelligences

The theory of multiple intelligences, as initially outlined by Howard Gardner in Project Zero at Harvard University, challenges traditional fixed views of intelligence. Gardner named nine different intelligences. Prior to the application of multiple intelligences within school settings, students were often defined by what IQ tests and more formal standardized testing revealed. The theory of multiple intelligences values the whole child, not just his or her reading and writing abilities, which only reveal the verbal-linguistic and logical-mathematical intelligences. Recognizing and utilizing multiple intelligences allows educators in inclusive classrooms to both present and assess information differently to appeal to a variety of learners, honoring their stronger intelligences. Educators realize that unless they tap in to students' intelligences, students lack motivation and interest, detrimentally affecting lessons' outcomes.

Every lesson does not have to include all of the nine intelligences. Varying the intelligences associated with instruction and assessments throughout the year acknowledges different learners' strengths. Following is a list of Gardner's nine intelligences (alphabetically ordered; no one intelligence is more important) with a curriculum example of each:

1. Bodily-kinesthetic—manipulatives
2. Existentialist—open Socratic discussions
3. Interpersonal—cooperative learning
4. Intrapersonal—learning journals
5. Logical-mathematical—brainteasers
6. Musical-rhythmic—songs
7. Naturalist—scientific classifications
8. Verbal-linguistic—debates
9. Visual-spatial—graphic organizers

Consider passing out the Show What You Know list (page 42) and allowing students to explore their multiple intelligences through the application of different projects, whether the students are learning about Dr. Seuss or a double helix.

Sensory Modalities

Students interpret the environment through sight, sound, touch, smell, and taste. However, not all students possess the same sensory capabilities. For example, students with auditory processing difficulties may hear what is said during a lesson but have difficulty interpreting what was meant or applying the knowledge to other learning scenarios. Some students with ADHD or autism may overreact to too much stimulation, such as bright or flickering lights or the sounds of a fire alarm or even too many visuals on classroom walls. (Dimming lights, warning a student about a fire drill or offering earplugs to minimize the painful hearing sensation, and introducing visuals one at a time are viable and sensitive accommodations.)

Sensory modalities refer to how learners pick up environmental cues, and students usually favor one modality over another. For example, some students may prefer to listen to directions, while others prefer step-by-step visual outlines. Students with reading difficulties may favor tapping out syllables or color-coding them. Students with dyslexia may favor visual and kinesthetic/tactile over auditory approaches.

Related VAKT opportunities help students see, hear, touch, and move to the learning. Learning about environments such as the beach or forest comes alive when a child touches the sand, smells a leaf, or listens to the recorded sounds of waves crashing, birds chirping, or coyotes yelping. Forming nontoxic Play-Doh into different shapes and sizes with a rolling pin or a cookie cutter kinesthetically demonstrates the concepts of flat, thick, small, medium, and large. Students can form different shapes, letters, and numbers with salt trays, shaving cream, and Wikki Stix. The principle of buoyancy is better introduced through water centers with and without salt than through two-dimensional pictures alone. Spoons, watering cans, and straws can be used to demonstrate bubbles and waves. What better way to demonstrate the states of matter than through seeing and feeling water as a liquid in a plastic container, a solid ice cube, and H2O molecules that disappear into a gas?

Students of all abilities respond to musical experiences with finger plays, rhymes, and songs that teach about numbers, words, hygiene, body awareness, and more. Language skills can be reinforced when students write, scribe, or draw their answers to open-ended sentences, such as the following:

I saw _____ . It looked like _____.

I heard _____. It sounded like _____.

I touched _____. It felt like _____.

Some additional sensory options for inclusive classrooms are hopping to math multiples; using podcasts for lectures; communicating with Skype or blogs; showing online curriculum-related videos; using social bookmarking to highlight, share, research, and collaborate with peers; orally discussing and expressing ideas; creating an illustrated timeline; showing student videos or digital photos that model appropriate behavior during cooperative work; manipulating Unifix cubes to better understand place value; and creating or participating in online games in geography, science, or math. The VAKT possibilities are endless.

Technology

Technology offers many different avenues of exploration for students with different learning modalities and strengths. The general and special educators and other related staff and team members collaborate to figure out ways to provide students with the technology that will best promote learning.

IDEA (1990) defined technology rather broadly to include products commercially off the shelf and those modified or customized to increase, maintain, and improve specialized education, in addition to related services and supplementary aids. In 1997, IDEA amendments mandated that assistive technology be considered for each student receiving special education services (Lahm, 2003). According to the Assistive Technology Act of 2004, assistive technology services are defined as "any service that directly assists an individual with a disability in the selection, acquisition, or use of an assistive technology device." Under the Assistive Technology Act, each state, through a grant, has a fund for an Assistive Technology Act Project as a source of available technological possibilities for people with disabilities.

Multidisciplinary teams can conduct assessments to determine what technology devices or services will heighten students' needs and potentials. For instance, students may require wheelchairs, powered scooters, long white canes, portable keyboards, adaptive puzzles, closed-captioned TVs, note-taking outlines, computer simulations, triangular pens, and so forth. If the school has an assistive technology specialist, then he or she offers additional appropriate modifications, resources, and recommendations.

Educators can continually support students by being knowledgeable about technology that honors and maximizes their levels. QIAT (www.qiat.org) offers guidance on quality indicators for the implementation of assistive technology. There are many incredible opportunities offered by computer-assisted instruction. Also, the Center for Applied Special Technology, accessed at www.cast.org, has many opportunities that classroom teachers can explore, from creating online books to delivering universal design for learning.

Students with writing difficulties such as dysgraphia benefit from software with word-prediction capabilities or computer pens that write and record at the same time (www .livescribe.com/smartpen). Students with autism may need a picture exchange communication system (PECS) to express their thoughts or animated applied behavior analysis (ABA) programs (www.mousetrial.com). Augmentative and alternative communication (AAC) devices can range from manufactured communication boards to talking photo albums. A student who is nonverbal benefits from voice commands from digital audio communication devices. A screen reader will assist a student who uses Braille; a speech synthesizer orally reads the text. Technological services and devices must match students' capabilities and needs, enhance learning with more inquiry and access, and promote independence. The goal is to achieve maximum student access to the curriculum through appropriate assistive technology.

Technology with all of its devices and services offers endless possibilities for students with disabilities, but only if it is implemented and monitored properly. Regardless of the technology employed, educators should promote independence and individualization. No two students learn the same way. Everyone has strengths and weaknesses, but everyone also has dreams and aspirations that need to be acknowledged and matched with appropriate presentations and supports that deliver on the promises offered by technology.

Organizing Structures and Instruction

There is no specific inclusion template that fits every student. Each student has diverse needs that require differentiated forms of instruction; this includes students with and without specific classifications. All learners benefit from good teaching practices, extra attention, and opportunities for enrichment or practice. Good teaching methods shift among whole class, small group, and individualized instruction, depending upon students' levels, the complexities of given topics, and students' prior knowledge and experiences. The idea is to fill in the gaps with best practices that enhance the learning of all students within the general education classroom.

In an inclusive classroom, smaller groups may be more effective at disseminating content through direct skill instruction than a whole-group, one-size-fits-all approach that ends up frustrating both students and teachers. The goal is to continually investigate and determine how services can be efficiently employed to ensure increased understanding about the disciplines and social gains. Each child's progress must be monitored and viewed individually.

Quite often, the extra curriculum help that students with special needs receive in the general classroom benefits all students (Galley, 2004). For instance, organizational or study skills lessons can apply to and benefit many students, not just those with IEPs or 504 plans.

Students with learning differences who are instructed in a separate room as an interim step to increase literacy, numeracy, perceptual, communication, or cognitive skills with a lower teacher-student ratio, guided instruction, and more practice should be closely monitored and returned to the general education setting when progress warrants that return. Students with hearing impairments, visual impairments, or mobility differences may also require alternate ways to succeed with the lessons, allowing them to absorb the knowledge through their stronger modalities, and the respective help of a teacher for the deaf or hearing impaired, speech-language pathologist, or occupational or physical therapist. If a student has attention issues and does not respond to reading supports given in the general education setting, then the resource room with a lower teacher-student ratio may be an appropriate placement. It is imperative that the rules in the smaller setting teach the student productive ways to control his or her impulsivity. When the student's reading skills are strengthened and the student returns to the general education setting, he or she will not inappropriately call out but know how to wait his or her turn when responding to a question or asking for extra help. That smaller setting must model the same behavioral rules and act as a microcosm that mimics the structure in the larger general education classroom. If supplemental books are offered, appropriate parts of the classroom text should be used as a reference; students who are pulled out often feel inferior, and reading the same text boosts students' confidence levels.

No matter what interventions are used, school administrators and teachers need to be flexible in the way they organize instruction, allowing students to move between different groups and levels of learning based on the rate at which they progress. An infrastructure of staff training and support needs to be in place to ensure fidelity of implementation to programs and district directives (Adams & Carnine, 2003). It is often difficult to gauge appropriate time allowances for activities since students complete work at individual paces. At times, the work is too difficult for some, while the requirements may be too easy for others. Not all students learn the same way; consequently, students should be allowed to display their knowledge through varied types of assessments. For instance, some students with stronger visual-spatial abilities are excellent at puzzles and may prefer to doodle or sketch to show what they know rather than write a four-paragraph essay. If the student writes a caption for his or her picture and is then asked to expand on the caption, the educator is capitalizing upon stronger visual areas to improve weaker auditory areas.

Students also need help to develop study skills. Creating efficient learners requires giving students strategy instruction on how to think reflectively, how to integrate information, and how to then make sense of the learning when they apply it to other situations, settings, and grades (Steedly, Dragoo, Arafeh, & Luke, 2008). This includes reading directions carefully; extracting and understanding the big picture; increasing attention to details, both verbal and written; and organizing and sequencing thoughts. The U.S. Department of Education's website Doing What Works (http://dww.ed.gov) recommends research-based practices to help develop students' study skills (Pashler et al., 2007). Such practices include spacing learning over a period of time with reviews and quizzes and mixing up practice with alternate problem-solving and worked examples such as think-alouds. When students have better study skills, their confidence levels are increased.

Abstract concepts need to be delivered with concrete representations that include hands-on manipulatives and activities, along with simulations, stories, and visual representations. Educators who offer constructivist approaches know that most students need meaningful experiences and retain the learning by doing. Manipulatives and direct exposure to learning materials—such as counters, shopping circulars, guest speakers, and field trips—honor learners who need abstract concepts solidified with actual hands-on opportunities and materials.

Educators should assist students with above-average skills to continually expand their knowledge with enrichment activities and offer remediation and accommodations to help students with special needs understand the curriculum in different yet challenging ways. Standards in mathematics, science, literacy, history, art, music, health, and physical education must be connected to students' lives with relevant lessons. Yes, it is important to honor curriculum standards, but it is even more important to honor your classroom audience.

Question to Investigate

How can teachers deliver a lesson to the whole class to honor individual levels, modalities, and intelligences and still keep track of IEP, RTI, and 504 interventions and goals?

Collaboratively, student support teams decide upon interventions, problem solve, and then formally intervene with measures and ways to monitor effectiveness based upon individual student needs. Differentiation is applicable for those with both lower and higher skills, and this ensures that no one in the class stagnates.

Prominent educational psychologists Andrew Roach and Stephen Elliott (2008) report on several ways to assess fidelity to programs, including filling out self-reports, keeping checklists and logs, analyzing work samples, and documenting observations and data on software programs. Interest inventories such as a multiple intelligence survey can be completed for students of all grade levels. Active learning is then directly connected to students with accurate documentation as teachers keep consistent formative data on interventions implemented. If students have IEPs or 504 plans, then the progress toward meeting the listed goals can be documented each quarter and shared with parents through home mailings at the same time that report cards are sent home. The RTI Intervention Plan and RTI Progress Monitoring forms (pages 38 and 40, respectively) help educators monitor the effectiveness of specific classroom interventions every six to eight weeks.

RTI Intervention Plan

Subject(s):

Marking period: Week(s):   Date(s):

Whole-class interventions:

Small groups with targeted interventions:

Individualized, one-on-one, targeted interventions:

Role of general educator:

Role of special educator:

Role of instructional assistants/paraprofessionals:

Role of support teams/groups:

1 of 2

Role of administration:

Role of family/home:

Role of peers:

Role of guidance counselor:

Role of other personnel:

Related services:

Comments:

Source: Adapted from *Inclusion Lesson Plan Book for the 21st Century* by Toby Karten, 2010.

RTI Progress Monitoring

Fill in the data, taking into account observations, student monitoring, assessments, and input from team members. Indicate specific subject or skill interventions and students' interests and strengths. Identify the CBM (curriculum-based measurement), and record the initial testing results. Then select whether the student will receive interventions for remediation or enrichment and at which tier level. Indicate the remaining tests and dates at set weeks or months during the year. List members of the collaborative team, and include additional comments and recordings in reference to whole class, small group, and one-on-one interventions. Note other concerns, comments, or future plans about the chosen interventions or specific students.

Students	Subject/skill	Interests and strengths	CBM	1st testing level and date	Remediation or enrichment tier level	2nd testing level and date	3rd testing level and date

1 of 2

Collaborative team members who are planning and implementing the interventions:

Whole-class interventions:

Small-group interventions:

One-on-one interventions:

Other comments/concerns:

Show What You Know

Choose one of the options below to show what you know about what we just learned.

sing a song about the subject	answer a WebQuest about the concepts	create a poem
choreograph a dance that portrays the main idea and emotions involved	design a PowerPoint presentation on the concepts learned with graphics and custom animations added	draw a comic strip or storyboard that outlines the main concepts, people, and/or events
design a test on the subject	cooperatively write a skit, build props, design costumes, and act out the concepts in a script dialogue	classify and pantomime words or concepts into categories
create a board game or iMovie about the subject	create or take a survey about one of the ideas, issues, or concepts and then graph the results	sculpt a clay model about an important person, event, or object

THREE
Addressing Student Needs

"Is she kidding me? I can't believe that there's another test tomorrow. We just had a quiz yesterday, which of course I failed. I have no idea what she's talking about. I know that I'm going to fail that stupid test. The copies of the PowerPoints help, but she goes so fast that I'm lost, and she doesn't even let us ask questions. Maybe if I just act like I get it, they'll leave me alone. Fifty-eight more days until spring break."

A student who views school as a treadmill with no meaningful destination in sight only goes through the motions; he or she doesn't internalize the academics. However, students achieve gains when the teacher presents content in a way that acknowledges the diverse needs, attitudes, and levels of the learners present. Inclusion is a multidimensional, collaborative, and sequentially structured way of valuing everyone's potentials within classrooms to prepare students to successfully enter inclusive societies. Although each situation varies according to individual student needs, there are several important principles and strategies involved with implementing inclusion as a whole. Viable interventions apply evidence-based practices and fulfill the lesson's objectives on a daily basis. This includes effective and appropriate presentations, materials, and assessments. The strategies in this chapter help teachers create inclusive classrooms that benefit both students and educators.

Fourteen Points for Success

Within the successful inclusive classroom, educators advocate cooperation, confidence, and independence for students with special needs. Awareness and understanding encourage open-minded attitudes; physical inclusion is considered important, but emotional and cognitive supports are also in place and guaranteed for each child. The atmosphere empowers learners and guarantees every student the freedom to learn based upon IEPs matched with the appropriate interventions. Students with special needs thrive in this peaceful and safe environment. The following fourteen points are guaranteed in the successful inclusive classroom:

1. The absolute freedom and optimum opportunities to receive an education in a safe and productive environment that honors students' IEPs and provides academic, psychological, and social benefits

2. Assessments that are fair and appropriate, with instructional plans and curricular adaptations that yield viable information

3. Professionals who seek knowledge about different abilities along with the strategies to best implement evidence-based programs that value how students learn

4. Accommodations and modifications that allow students to perform to the best of their abilities yet lead them on the road to independence

5. Education in a collaborative atmosphere that values the input of all teachers, school personnel, and related staff in the fields of general and special education, as well as that of families and students

6. High yet realistic curriculum expectations

7. Opportunities to transfer and generalize learned skills

8. Treatment equal to that of peers without disabilities

9. Opportunities to achieve in all curriculum areas with outlined gains in literacy, numeracy, problem-solving competencies, listening skills, study skills, cognitive development, and functional academics

10. Ways that students' progress will be recorded and reported with efforts toward partial mastery acknowledged and future plans outlined

11. Environments that embrace and celebrate diversity and differences

12. Learner-oriented lessons that value all students

13. Respect for all abilities

14. Access to resources and services with the freedom to progress in ways that yield autonomous development that is transferred to life decisions

The Inclusive Educator Checklist, the Inclusive Classroom Checklist, and Ideal vs. Pseudo Inclusion (pages 60, 61, and 62, respectively) offer opportunities to put your inclusive practices to the test.

Strategic Learners

A strategic learner builds knowledge by using his or her critical thinking skills to engage and explore content areas. How the knowledge of a subject is gained and retained is more important than the focus on the content. Strategic learners take responsibility for their learning and are proactive in seeking methods of learning that work best for them. Students are not born as strategic learners; educators must help them become strategic learners.

In classrooms that value strategic learners, learning is not just about the lesson, but more about what each lesson *means* to each student; it is not just about an answer being right or wrong, but more about *why* one answer is the correct one as opposed to another choice. Strategic learners know that asking for help is a step forward, not a step backward.

Strategies

There are several ways that educators can create strategic learners. The following are some examples:

- Solicit inventories on how students like to learn by asking them to rank their learning preference. For example, are they a 5–4–3–2–1 or a 3–1–4–5–2?

    1 = I like to see it.

    2 = I like to hear it.

    3 = I like to write it.

    4 = I like to draw it.

    5 = I like to _____.

    I'm a ___–___–___–___–___.

- Discuss topics or concepts during morning or weekly meetings to help students in the primary grades develop simple conversation and listening skills, or facilitate debates and Socratic discussions with older students.

- Review concepts to solidify learning foundations.

- Ask students to paraphrase what was said: "Humor me and tell me what you think you heard."

- Ask the students to fill out self-assessment checklists to determine academic subskills.

- Distribute exit cards as quick assessments before automatically moving ahead. For example, an exit card may ask the students to write down one thing they learned today or to name something they need to be further explained.

- Take the time to divide the class into either enrichment or review groups, which vary in duration and student makeup, dependent upon topics and units.

- Frequently conference with co-teachers, related staff, students, and families to keep the lines of communication open—for example, provide lessons at least a week ahead of time to co-teachers if not planning together and send students home with progress reports that note both efforts and achievements.

KWL Charts and Reading Strategy Books

Two specific tools that help students become strategic learners are KWL charts and reading strategy books. KWL charts contain three columns: in the first column, students write down what they know or think they know about the subject; in the second column, students indicate what they would like to learn about the subject; and at the end of the lesson, students write down the knowledge that they have gained in the third column. Reading strategy books provide students with structured steps to help them identify unfamiliar words.

Examine KWL charts before, during, and after lessons or units. The KWL in table 3.1 shows incorrect prior student knowledge about the Middle Ages, which interferes with subsequent learning.

Table 3.1: Student KWL About the Middle Ages

Subject: The Middle Ages		
K	W	L
The Middle Ages happened about 200 years ago during the Roman Empire. There was a road made of silk.	How did people make money during this time? What did they do for fun?	

Instruction needs to clarify the correct time period and explain that the Middle Ages occurred after the Romans were in power, following the Barbarian invasions of Europe. Instruction on the Silk Road needs to define it as being a trade route linking the East (China) with the West (Europe). The teacher then needs to verify that the student later writes the correct knowledge in the L column. Similarly, economic and social activities of the Middle Ages could be investigated through readings, skits, and role-playing as knights, commoners, aristocrats, or monks to replace what the student thinks he or she knows with correct information.

In addition, students can be encouraged to keep strategy books across the content areas to help them tackle more difficult concepts or skills. Figure 3.1 is an example of an entry page in a reading strategy book.

Reading Strategy Book

Ways to read a word I don't know:

Break it up into syl-la-bles.

Look the word up in my electronic dictionary.

See if it has word parts, like a prefix or suffix.

Look at how the word is used in the sentence.

Highlight the word and go back to it later.

Figure 3.1: Entry page in a reading strategy book.

Attention and Motivation

Strategic learners pay attention and are motivated to learn. Strong evidence suggests that teachers can increase student engagement and on-task behavior by rearranging the classroom's environment, routines, or learning activities (Epstein, Atkins, Cullinan, Kutash,

& Weaver, 2008). Teachers can create constructivist learning experiences, implement direct instruction in whole groups, offer support in small groups, or help students with one-on-one interventions. Ultimately, the goal is for students to independently demonstrate their learning, but of course, good teaching strategies such as modeling and guidance precede independent practice.

Albert Bandura (1977), a prominent behavioral scientist, studied students' social learning and outlined four prominent factors: attention, retention, reproduction, and motivation. Whether or not students pay attention to lessons might depend on their given mood, internal or external distracters, and/or stimuli or situations within or not within their prior knowledge and experiences. Though video clips, curriculum songs, interactive whiteboards, and colorful charts or visuals captivate many students, novel material is usually more difficult to learn. Many teachers attest to the fact that just because students pay attention during a lesson, that does not always indicate that they will remember the learning. Lessons that are retained often include content-related concrete or semiabstract visuals that connect the concepts to students' lives. Learners often need to see an example or model before they can reproduce an action on their own. According to Bandura, this type of social learning has intrinsic factors as well, with students then internalizing or self-regulating their behavior. In addition, students who are able to imagine or envision their successes before actually applying a new behavior will then be able to perform it better. Bandura equates this to Olympic skaters who visualize successfully accomplishing a routine before the event takes place. The real-life success that follows has been motivated by their visions. He states that without the motivation or a reason to imitate a behavior, the behavior is not a lasting one.

Bandura's theory on social behaviors can definitely be applied to inclusive classrooms. Physical inclusion allows students multiple opportunities to model age-appropriate social thoughts and behaviors. It also certainly makes sense to honor students' multiple intelligences and preferred learning modalities. Students need to buy into the lesson, and teachers can accomplish this by providing motivating connections to students' lives, thus increasing interest, participation, and learning. Feedback is also effective at increasing student motivation. When teachers give immediate specific feedback to the students—for example, handing back quizzes and tests within the same week—that reinforcement increases student motivation. Timely feedback and communicating progress to students help to foster self-regulated learners who are cognizant of not only their numerical grade, but also the level and quality of the work completed.

Pacing and Complexity

Quite often, students with special needs are overwhelmed by the amount of the curriculum that is presented within a forty- to fifty-minute classroom period. Some teachers believe that they need to cover the curriculum at the same steady pace, regardless of whether or not the students are absorbing the knowledge. This consequently affects students with disabilities who cannot keep up with the rate of learning (King-Sears, 2008). Rather than repeatedly asking questions, some students prefer to pretend to know what's going on until the assessments reveal otherwise. Savvy educators circumvent this downward spiral toward student shutdown by periodically slowing down lessons with active discussion, with oral and written informal checks, and by intermittently asking students to paraphrase their understanding. Rapid deliveries need to be slowed down to achieve pacing that allows for more discussion, time for absorption, modeling, and appropriate scaffolding and guidance. Educators may also use pacing charts or map out lessons with general objectives throughout each quarter of the year to maintain curriculum pacing and a consistent focus on annual goals.

Effective educators create lessons that allow for varying degrees of representation, engagement, and assessment. Pacing that allows for differences has a setup of baseline objectives with gradual increments of difficulty for more advanced learners and learning opportunities for those students who require additional challenges (Karten, 2007d). For example, if the concept being taught is structural analysis through breaking up words into their parts, then giving students a list of words with different difficulty levels will differentiate for varying reading levels in a whole-class activity (see table 3.2). Students can work individually, ask for teacher guidance, or collaborate with peers in groups. Everyone is learning the same concept, just with different degrees of complexity.

Table 3.2: Differentiated Word Lists to Develop Structural Analysis

	Easier	Proficient	Challenging
Compound words	bathtub	household	meltdown
Words with prefixes	untold	reshape	telescope
Words with suffixes	funny	bluish	personable
Words with prefixes and suffixes	unfriendly	reappointed	incompatible

Curriculum demands are enormous. In some teachers' haste to move on and cover more, they fail to discover that less breadth or alternate approaches are sometimes better. The teacher's delivery must vary and be adjusted to meet the needs of the learners in the classroom.

Curriculum pauses, rather than maintaining classroom speeds that exceed students' limits and create frustrating cerebral traffic jams, are recommended. However, slowing a lesson down to benefit one or two students in whole-class instruction often disengages the other students. Options to avoid this problem include having group responses for lower-order questions, while allowing sufficient wait time for higher-order questions, or assigning individualized, short, structured tasks and providing frequent formative personal feedback.

Educators who provide centers with sponge activities (activities that soak up the time) and ongoing projects to review and absorb concepts are not concerned about the time it takes to finish the unit but about engaging students in meaningful learning opportunities. Students are involved in their own learning, not looking over each other's shoulders seeing who does what, while educators act as facilitators, not curriculum disseminators. A sponge activity or learning center can include activities that range from playing a game of Monopoly to designing a variation of Monopoly to coincide with a geography unit of study. Students can practice computational facts, conduct research, write poems or editorials for the school newspaper, or draw collages of what they learned. Sponge activities are useful during transitional periods and when the teachers are working with smaller groups or are busy with upcoming or unannounced administrative directives.

Sponge Activities (page 59) outlines ongoing learning experiences for inclusive students throughout the year. Sponge activities allow students to simultaneously work on various assignments at different paces and give teachers the flexibility to review concepts with smaller groups or offer other students enrichment. Students can work on skills independently or in cooperative groups.

All in all, students need sufficient time to digest the learning, allowing for more cognitive thought and practice. As with Aesop's fable *The Tortoise and the Hare*, slow and steady wins the race. Fast-paced lessons lead to curriculum losses. The curriculum and standards are important, but aren't the students' understandings more important? Learners supersede the curriculum; therefore, it is the students who should determine the lesson's pace. A lesson only has merit if it acknowledges the students as the audience.

Effective Co-Teaching Practices

More reforms are evidenced when teachers in inclusive environments work together to reach common goals for their students (Brownell, Adams, Sindelar, Waldron, & Vanhover, 2006). It is also essential that principals and other administrators offer guidance and ongoing support to their staff to foster the effective use of collaboration skills (Hines, 2008). Collaborative attitudes and practices should be a part of relationships with families, co-teachers, paraprofessionals, and other related staff.

Administrators lead their staff toward collaboration, but the educators are the ones who model positive collaborative interactions and set the classroom cooperative social tone that the students absorb (Causton-Theoharis & Malmgren, 2005). Therefore, the relationship between co-teachers within the classroom must be ongoing and productive. Co-teachers may not always agree on every aspect concerning lesson plans, objectives, accommodations, modifications, and assessments, but they do have to respectfully agree that it is OK to disagree.

It is no longer an option for a classroom teacher to do his or her own thing behind closed doors. Teaching is about sharing, and that includes time, ideas, lessons, worksheets, opinions, favorite books, and responsibilities. Within inclusive classrooms, co-teachers and instructional support staff who collaborate improve the learning scenarios for all students, both with and without disabilities. Collaboration is also about bridging the learning between grades and schools, so that each year's teacher replaces a blank slate with one that is filled with helpful strategies, social histories, and more.

Co-teaching and collaborative options include, but are not limited to, the following scenarios:

- Two teachers bouncing ideas off each other to model reflective thought and encourage more class discussion

- Two teachers dividing the class into two smaller groups and simultaneously teaching either identical lessons or lessons that vary in complexity, types of interventions, layers of learning, or accommodations (referred to as *parallel teaching*)

- One teacher leading, and one teacher assisting—one teacher circulates, while the other teacher monitors behavior, offers study skills tips, and just generally supports the lead teacher in multiple ways

- Co-teachers providing remediation or acceleration for academics or behavior to targeted groups while other groups or individual children are working independently

- Teachers and assistants using stations and centers to simultaneously offer remediation and enrichment to individuals or small groups within busy but productive inclusive classroom environments

Appropriate Interventions

Even though some students within inclusive classrooms share a disability classification, each child displays unique characteristics. Very generally speaking, there are appropriate interventions for particular categories of learners. However, keep in mind that the following categories are heterogeneous with variations under each heading. These labels denote possible characteristics of different groups, not descriptions of individual children. The overall objective of the following sections is to recognize the *gifts* of all students.

Above-Average Skills

If not challenged, students with above-average skills may learn the least in inclusive classrooms. Students with above-average skills need teachers to vary the depth, breadth, pacing, and complexity of instruction. Offer ongoing opportunities for students to creatively explore and manipulate concepts. Tap into their interests when possible. Strategies such as using contracts (outlining individual learning objectives) and compacting (eliminating objectives and curriculum material students already know and replacing it with enrichment activities) offer students challenging ways to expand their knowledge base (Hughes & Rollins, 2009). Be cognizant of expanding social interactions for these students as well as increasing their academic proficiency. Visit the Association for the Gifted at www.cectag.org and the National Association for Gifted Children at www.nagc.org for more information.

Asperger's Syndrome

Students with Asperger's syndrome may have significant difficulties with behavioral and social areas such as peer interactions. Cognitive and linguistic areas are usually stronger. Students often need help to understand the big picture rather than focusing on minute details (Atwood, 2005). Frequently check students for understanding. Model how to improve peer relationships with direct social skills training such as social stories and more monitoring during guided cooperative learning activities. Visit Online Asperger Syndrome Information and Support (OASIS) at www.asperger.org and the National Institute of Neurological

Disorders and Stroke (NINDS) at www.ninds.nih.gov/disorders/asperger/asperger.htm for more information.

Attention-Deficit/Hyperactivity Disorder

Attention-deficit/hyperactivity disorder is a condition that has varying combinations of behavioral symptoms. Students may be hyperactive and/or impulsive, be inattentive to sensory cues or details, or have focusing difficulties. Improved student attention and reduced disruptive behavior have been noted with *contingency management*—that is, providing reinforcement for desired behaviors and consequences for undesirable behaviors to help students better understand expectations. Academic interventions include peer tutoring and varying types of instructional materials and the way the subjects are introduced (DuPaul & Eckert, 1997). Parent training is an appropriate avenue of treatment for children with moderate impairments. Medication is given to those students with more severe ADHD. If this is the case, check with the school nurse for side effects, and communicate observations with families. Multimodal interventions, which combine home and school treatments with social skills training, help middle school and adolescent children (Young & Amarasinghe, 2010). Offer pragmatic ways to control impulses, such as jotting down a question or thought rather than impulsively shouting it out. Incorporate students' interests into lessons and offer frequent praise and constructive, immediate, specific academic, social, and behavioral feedback to students. Visit Children and Adults With Attention Deficit/Hyperactivity Disorder at www.chadd.org and the National Institute of Mental Health at www.nimh.nih.gov for more information.

Auditory Processing Difficulties

Students with auditory processing difficulties, such as a central auditory processing disorder, are not able to process the information they hear since their brains and ears do not coordinate the sounds. They have normal hearing but may have trouble with the following tasks: paying attention when other background noises are present, remembering information, following directions, detecting or discriminating differences between similarly sounding words or letters, completing tasks, and understanding verbal tasks requiring inferential skills. Offer more visuals, and frequently ask students to paraphrase their understanding. Use technology such as assistive classroom listening devices to amplify sounds. Increase students' awareness of progress, and encourage the students to ask for clarifications. Visit the American Speech-Language-Hearing Association at www.asha.org/public/hearing/disorders/understand-apd-child.htm, KidsHealth at http://kidshealth.org/parent/medical/ears/central_auditory.html, or Posit Science at www.positscience.com/braingames for more information.

Autism

Autism is a complex developmental disability that is typically evidenced during the first three years of life. Autism affects a person's ability to communicate and socially interact with others. Levels of cognitive need vary within this broad spectrum. Organized and predictable environments that outline rules, routines, and structures assist students with autism, for example, announcing changes and transitions and posting daily schedules. In addition, concentrate upon students' strengths and interests (Roberts, Keane, & Clark, 2008). Provide an array of materials with more opportunities to see, hear, and touch the learning. Offer structured academic, behavioral, communication, and social supports. Factors such as appropriate placement with teachers and paraprofessionals, parental involvement, professional learning, team approaches, and behavioral plans are crucial (Crisman, 2008). Visit the Autism Society of America at www.autism-society.org, Autism Speaks at www.autismspeaks.org, and Support Groups for Children with Autism, Aspergers, PDD at www.childrensdisabilities .info/autism/groups-autism-asperger.html for more information.

Childhood Apraxia of Speech

Students with childhood apraxia of speech, a motor speech disorder that affects the planning, executing, and sequencing of sounds, need assistance to decrease their articulation errors since their brains are not able to coordinate muscle movements of the tongue or mouth properly. Scaffold as necessary to help students say sounds, then syllables, and finally words. Students respond to intensive, structured, multisensory programs with coordination from speech-language pathologists. Use mirrors for visual cues and teach sign language for communication if warranted. Provide safe environments that value all forms of expression. Teach peers accepting attitudes by modeling appropriate attitudes and behaviors. See the American Speech-Language-Hearing Association at www.asha.org/public/speech/disorders /ChildhoodApraxia.htm and Speechville Express at www.speechville.com/diagnosis-destinations /apraxia/apraxia.html for more information. (Visit **go.solution-tree.com/specialneeds** for live links to the websites in this book.)

Communication Disorders

Communication disorders include difficulties with pronouncing, understanding, perceiving, remembering, and reasoning, and are divided into the categories of speech and sound, language, cognitive communication, stuttering (fluency), and voice disorders (volume, nasality, and hoarseness). Frequent consultation and collaboration with the school's speech-language pathologist is recommended for class and home practice interventions. Teach students' peers to patiently and nonjudgmentally allow the students to express their thoughts at their preferred rate and competency level. Provide additional practice with vocabulary, grammar rules, and sentence structure, and explain idioms. Use technology as appropriate with picture exchange communication systems and other augmentative devices. Visit the American Speech-Language-Hearing Association at www.asha.org for more information.

Deafness/Hearing Impairment

IDEA defines deafness as a hearing impairment that is so severe that the child is impaired in processing linguistic information through hearing, with or without amplification. Other hearing impairments will vary in degrees of severity and the usage of technological and medical devices that may enhance the residual hearing. Teach more complex vocabulary and comprehensions across the curriculum with additional examples, visuals, and models.

Frequently check for understanding, and be certain to speak in a normal tone, facing the student if he or she is reading lips. Offer accompanying visuals with graphic organizers and written outlines to clarify and solidify students' knowledge. Peer mentors can also help students with day-to-day interactions. Visit ASLPro.com at www.aslpro.com/cgi-bin/aslpro/phrases.cgi, the Hearing Loss Association of America at www.hearingloss.org, and the American Society for Deaf Children at www.deafchildren.org for more information.

Dyscalculia

Dyscalculia is a learning disorder that impacts students' competencies with numbers in math computations, time, spatial organizations, schedules, money, and budgeting. Guided modeling with practice and repetition is helpful. Use uncluttered worksheets, and encourage students to visualize or act out word problems. Employ more manipulatives to solidify abstract concepts. Try to relate the math learning to realistic practical applications such as comparison shopping, daily schedules, and opening lockers. Enlist peers to assist as appropriate. Keep in mind that people with dyscalculia can be highly intelligent and articulate (Spinney, 2009). Visit Dyscalculia.org: Math Learning Disability Resource at www.dyscalculia .org and K12 Academics: Students With Dyscalculia at www.k12academics.com/disorders -disabilities/dyscalculia/students-dyscalculia for more information.

Dysgraphia

Dysgraphia is a type of learning/writing difference that may be evidenced by characteristics such as illegible handwriting with poor letter formation, inappropriate spacing, incorrect spelling, poor pencil grip, and general disorganization or sequencing of written expressions (Learning Disabilities Association of Minnesota, 2005). Help students by offering advanced organizers for better note taking and copies of outlines such as PowerPoint slides. Early childhood instruction includes helping students by using multisensory approaches such as writing letters in salt or in the air. Peer note takers can assist students. Direct skill instruction is essential to improve writing mechanics, editing skills, and confidence through corrective practice sessions. If appropriate, offer learning options such as oral presentations instead of written reports. Technology options, such as those available from Franklin Electronic Publishers (www.franklin.com), Don Johnston (www.donjohnston.com), and Dragon Naturally Speaking (www.dragontalk.com), are worth investigating. Visit the LDinfo Web Site at www.ldinfo.com and Handwriting Without Tears at www.hwtears.com for more information.

Dyslexia

Dyslexia is a neurologically based learning difference evidenced by a reading disorder. Appropriate early interventions include direct skill instruction with phonemic awareness, word segmentation and fluency, and repeated reading and comprehension skill practice. Capitalize on students' preferred modalities with VAKT multisensory deliveries (for example, books on tape). Highlight students' strengths, allowing them alternate options as opposed to extensive readings (for example, creating a graphic novel or captioned picture as opposed to writing a five-paragraph essay). Accepting environments with structured reading programs help students maximize their capabilities. Visit Recording for the Blind and Dyslexic at www .rfbd.org, Bright Solutions for Dyslexia at www.dys-add.com/define.html, the International Dyslexia Association at www.interdys.org, and Orton-Gillingham Institute for Multi-Sensory Education at www.orton-gillingham.com for more information.

Emotional Differences

Emotional differences are complex and often misunderstood. Emotional differences can range from externalizing behaviors that involve conduct disorders to internalizing behaviors such as depression. Mood swings are evidenced in many students with emotional differences, from being compulsive and ritualistic as in obsessive-compulsive disorder to being defiant as in oppositional defiant disorders. At times, medication is prescribed for students, but it is also essential that students learn increased self-control. Functional behavioral assessments (FBA) determine the antecedent or reason for the behavior. Offer structured behavior incentives or behavioral report cards along with direct social skills instruction through social stories and role-playing. Be aware of children who are sometimes quietly crying out for attention through their dress or writings. Be sure to collaborate with the school guidance counselor and psychologist. Visit Mental Health America at www.nmha.org, the National Institute of Mental Health at www.nimh.nih.gov, the International OCD Foundation at www.ocfoundation.org, Internet Mental Health at www.mentalhealth.com, and the Anxiety Disorders Association of America at www.adaa.org for more information.

Epilepsy

Epilepsy, a disorder of the central nervous system marked by differences in electrical brain signals, has unknown causes in many cases. Some factors can include birth or head injuries and infectious diseases such as encephalitis or meningitis. Brain cells are affected by partial or general seizures, resulting in symptoms such as fidgeting, blank stares, loss of consciousness, confused memory, fatigue, different perceptions and thoughts about sounds, repetitive behavior, and the inability to stand. Students may have side effects from seizure medication. Students with epilepsy often feel stigmatized. If a student has a seizure, be certain that the student's head is protected, and reassure the student if he or she is in a confused state following the seizure. Offer assistance, such as an extra copy of notes, study guides, and peer mentors, with learning gaps that may occur if the student misses out on what was said in class. An accepting, academically stimulating environment with teachers and peers who are knowledgeable about epilepsy is essential. Qualified medical experts and families can share helpful first-aid information. Visit the National Dissemination Center for Children With Disabilities at www.nichcy.org/disabilities/specific/pages/epilepsy.aspx and the Epilepsy Foundation at www.epilepsyfoundation.org for more information.

Executive Dysfunction

Students with executive dysfunction have difficulties setting goals. Provide appropriate scaffolding and strategies such as study skills, ways to break up more complex directions, and organizational tips for short-term and long-term tasks. Students need to learn how to pick up environmental cues and sort knowledge from past experiences to gain more direction and metacognition. Help students develop more self-confidence through successful academic and social classroom experiences. Establish home–school communication that reinforces organizational strategies in both environments. Assist older students with transitional plans during IEP meetings. Visit Executive Dysfunction at http://home.comcast.net/ ~ kskkight/EFD.htm for more information.

Intellectual Disabilities

Students with intellectual disabilities (at the time of this publication, still labeled *mental retardation* under IDEA) have developmental differences with IQ scores usually in the range of 70–75. Areas affected include cognition, communication, and social and adaptive skills. Recommended interventions include accompanying abstract concepts with concrete examples. Complex directions and instruction need to be broken down into steps with a discrete task analysis approach. Instruction is often repeated to ensure retention and generalizations. When possible, relate academics to functional daily living skills. For example, if teaching the concept of classification, talk about food groups, types of transportation, or hygiene. Encourage peers to involve students with intellectual differences in all activities. Visit the Arc of the United States at www.thearc.org, the American Association of Intellectual and Developmental Disabilities at www.aaidd.org, the National Dissemination Center for Children With Disabilities at www.nichcy.org, and Think College! College Options for People with Intellectual Disabilities at www.thinkcollege.net for more information.

Physical Impairment

Types of physical disabilities vary in how they affect muscle movement and mobility. Teachers need to model attitudes that loudly state that students with physical disabilities are just as capable as their peers in terms of academics and socialization. Help students as needed, but always try to promote increased independence and self-determination skills. Accommodations will vary dependent upon each student's individual needs and strengths. Classroom arrangements and school environments need to allow students maximum access to all academic and extracurricular activities. Explore assistive technology for students, for example, word-prediction and voice-recognition programs and alternate keyboards. Collaborate with physical and occupational therapists for best classroom practices. Visit United Cerebral Palsy at www.ucpa.org and About.com: Special Education at http://specialed.about.com/od /physicaldisabilities/a/physical.htm for more information.

Specific Learning Disability (SLD)

Learning differences comprise difficulties in understanding or using spoken or written language. The ways a student listens, speaks, reads, writes, spells, does math calculations, and solves problems are affected areas. Learning problems that are directly related to a visual, hearing, motor, emotional, environmental, intellectual, or cultural or economic disadvantage are not classified as SLD. Increase students' self-awareness by allowing them to track their progress. Employ the principles of universal design for learning and multiple intelligences to help students shine. Offer students repeated application and review of learning to solidify concepts. Utilize multisensory learning strategies that capitalize on students' stronger modalities. Teach students to advocate for themselves in terms of letting teachers know which accommodations they need. Encourage peers to assist as mentors. Visit the Learning Disabilities Association of America at www.ldanatl.org, the National Center for Learning Disabilities at www.ncld.org, the Schwab Foundation at www.schwabfoundation. org, and the LDinfo Web Site at www.ldinfo.com for more information.

Tourette's Syndrome (TS)

Tourette's syndrome is a neurobiological disorder characterized by involuntary tics, rapid sudden movements, and vocal outbursts. Tics may include extra blinking and differing facial expressions. Students are usually classified as other health impairment (OHI) under IDEA. Their sudden movements in the classroom are often embarrassing to them; try not to seat them at the center of instruction. Allow students with TS acceptable ways to channel that motor energy, such as running errands. Some students may also need additional assistance to stay focused since attention issues and distractibility are associated with TS. Provide an accepting environment with educated peers who understand the needs of a student with TS, the characteristics that he or she may display, and how they can help. Visit the Tourette Syndrome Association at www.tsa-usa.org for more information.

Traumatic Brain Injury (TBI)

Traumatic brain injury occurs following a head injury, such as a blow to the head from a sports accident, a car accident, or a fall. Dependent upon the severity, students experience short- and/or long-term memory difficulties. Families need extra support to accept the sudden change in their children's abilities. Establish and coordinate home–school support programs that help students regain, relearn, and reinforce skills in both environments. Be sensitive to students' frustrations, and introduce learning in smaller steps that can be mastered, rather than overwhelm students with too many tasks at one time. Teach them how to chunk information and how to implement organizational strategies such as using calendars and sticky notes, and color-coding information. Enlist peers to be mentors. Involve students in all class activities on their instructional levels. Praise students for steps toward goals as well as mastery. Visit the Brain Injury Association of America at www.biausa.org for more information.

Twice Exceptional

Twice-exceptional learners are considered to be gifted students with disabilities (Hughes & Rollins, 2009). For example, they may have excellent literacy skills but be challenged in mathematics. Students who are twice exceptional have stronger areas that require enrichment activities with direct instruction and weaker areas that need remediation (Winebrenner, 2003). Like other groups of children, they display a wide range of abilities, strengths, and preferences that need to be tapped and nurtured. Encourage social growth through appropriate direct skill instruction and cooperative learning activities. Visit Uniquely Gifted at www .uniquelygifted.org for more information.

Visual Impairments/Blindness

This IDEA classification includes a broad range of students, from those who have low vision to those with blindness. Specialized services with the appropriate physical and human resources are required to meet students' needs. Skills taught need to parallel the general education curriculum with the addition of daily living and social skills. Technology may include but is not limited to the following: magnifiers, specialized Braille books, Braille label makers, talking websites, speaking calculators, and optical character recognition (OCR), which scans, speaks, and stores printed text. Infuse as many verbal and kinesthetic elements as possible into lessons, for example, lines of latitude and longitude on a map indicated with string and peers who act as verbal helpers to describe lessons and assist students. As with all disability groups, always assist, but promote as much independence as possible. Visit the American Foundation for the Blind at www.afb.org and Recording for the Blind and Dyslexic at www .rfb.org for more information.

Looking Past the Label

If teachers take the extra time to know their students, then they will be better able to assist their students in becoming better learners, regardless of differing abilities. In addition to increasing their knowledge about specific disabilities, educators must look beyond the disability and find ways to reach students on both academic and emotional levels—know what students like and dislike and then, if possible, infuse the likes into the lesson. That is the spark that entices students to listen and learn. For example, plenty of mileage can be obtained by relating physics concepts to something a student enjoys, such as a roller coaster ride or types of racing cars. The concepts of speed, inertia, gravity, friction, acceleration, potential and kinetic energy, and force then become enlivened with the loops and turns of a roller coaster or by watching the Indianapolis 500.

Educators who constantly observe their students figure out ways to help them sharpen their skills and grow individually and toward each other. This can be accomplished through such mechanisms as recognition envelopes, classroom awards, and private incentive charts. Positive social opportunities include cooperative learning with clearly defined student roles such as the encourager, focuser, and gluer (making sure the members of the group bond with each other) in addition to the more traditional roles of reader, recorder, and timekeeper. Teachers also need to always display a fostering attitude that accepts and respects all students as positive contributors, regardless of intellectual levels or behavioral needs, loudly and clearly stating that everyone is equally valued.

When teaching all students, it is also important to know that labels often have attached emotional, social, and behavioral implications, and students are often aware of the stigma associated with their labels. This applies to both students with visible differences, such as a physical disability, Down syndrome, or blindness, and students with less apparent differences, such as a learning or emotional difference, those considered twice exceptional, or perhaps a student with high-functioning autism or Asperger's. However, with RTI in the mix, interventions are moving away from the labeling paradigm as special education is evolving (Pereles, Omal, & Baldwin, 2009).

Question to Investigate

How can I quickly assess who is getting it and who needs extra help or different pacing?

Wise teachers circulate about a classroom to look over students' notes or answers during independent practice to monitor their students. If too much time passes before teachers assess what students know, then students' misunderstandings may be repeated or mistaken as facts. Informal assessments such as exit cards are great ways of figuring out who knows what before more summative assessments are given:

I now know _____

_____

_____ .

Students can also be given choices on practice tests or respond to oral questions in *Jeopardy!* or *Who Wants To Be a Millionaire?* formats.

Ask students to paraphrase directions or concepts learned or to write key facts in a graphic organizer to quickly discover who gets it and who needs extra help.

Sponge Activities

Introduce students to the idea that at certain times of the day or week, everyone will be working at a different pace on varied assignments. This work may be completed independently or cooperatively at classroom centers with subject-specific assignments or ongoing stations, providing an opportunity for co-teachers and instructional assistants to offer additional guidance, modeling, practice, review, reinforcement, or enrichment as they circulate about the inclusive classroom. The following table provides suggestions for sponge activities throughout the school year.

August–September	These back-to-school months are a wonderful time for establishing students' prior and baseline knowledge across the disciplines through informal interactive quizzes and fun activities such as crossword puzzles, computer games, bingo, and more. These activities are also an excellent chance to allow students to share their favorite summer activities with pictures, poems, journals, essays, songs, plays, debates, discussions, meetings, dioramas, and bulletin boards. Establish research centers with online curriculum-related sites, WebQuests, performance centers, artists' corners, writing centers, and math-related activities. Distribute interest inventories and people finders to get to know your students and to help your students get to know each other. Encourage your students to share their strengths and preferred learning styles. Celebrate Labor Day, autumn, grandparents, Johnny Appleseed, and Native Americans with fun centers.
October–December	Review what you have taught with cooperative and collaborative open-book quizzes that honor cognitive, affective, and psychomotor skills. Centers could ask students to retell a story in another genre or from another character's point of view, write a letter to a character, create a soliloquy for a protagonist, pretend to be a scientist who made a recent discovery pertaining to a lesson unit, perform a play set in a historical time frame or on another continent, or create a sculpture from clay or a collage. This is also a time of giving thanks, celebrating holidays with families, and sharing with those less fortunate. Students could write letters to soldiers overseas or seniors in local nursing homes or gather community collections to send to various charities. Celebrate firefighters, Columbus, literacy, the Statue of Liberty, veterans, the harvest, and the close of the calendar year with assignments that value visual, auditory, and kinesthetic elements.
January–February	It is time to make resolutions and honor people such as George Washington, Martin Luther King, Jr., and Abraham Lincoln. Sir Isaac Newton, Susan B. Anthony, Elvis Presley, Garth Brooks, and John Steinbeck are just a few famous people who were born in these months. Students can investigate these individuals by writing biographies, dressing in costume, and giving oral presentations. Remember groundhog and leap-year activities, too! Celebrate dental health and Valentine's Day, along with the Chinese New Year, black history, and the civil rights movement.
March–April	Students may be thinking school is almost over, but now is the perfect time to involve them in different sponge activities. March is a month to honor women, music, crafts, and the American Red Cross. Students could help each other with community projects and figure out ways to better their own school environments. Students could create a dance and song for a musical comedy, drama, mystery, or operatic performance with a cast of characters, instruments, scenery, and backdrops that relate to the curriculum. Students delve into higher-order thinking while reading, writing, and researching. They could perform for families or for students in younger grades. Collaborate with other classes and music and art teachers, too. Remember spring. Celebrate good nutrition and the accomplishments of women. Honor Dr. Seuss's birthday on March 2 by reading or critiquing a few of his books or having students emulate his style by creating some of their own stories, either independently or in cooperative writing teams.
May–July	Things are warming up as students in some regions think about diving into pools and visiting beaches. Create class environments that allow students to investigate the seashore with math, science, social studies, reading, and writing connections. Allow learners to cooperatively review and jigsaw topics in the table of contents of textbooks and then teach the concepts to the rest of the class. Lessons can include student-created tests, PowerPoints, videos, songs, dances, plays, collages, class debates, and more. Honor moms on the second Sunday of May and dads on the third Sunday of June. The first week of May is teacher appreciation week. Flag Day is on June 14, and June is National Safety Month. Don't forget that it is all about appreciating your pets the second week in June. Celebrate Cinco de Mayo, Memorial Day, summer, and the Fourth of July. Appropriate age-level projects and activities correlate curriculum topics with students' interests to develop literacy and numeracy skills and to strengthen peer relationships.

Source: Adapted from *Inclusion Lesson Plan Book for the 21st Century* by Toby Karten, 2010.

Inclusion Strategies and Interventions © 2011 Solution Tree Press • solution-tree.com
Visit **go.solution-tree.com/specialneeds** to download this page.

Inclusive Educator Checklist

Check off the appropriate column that best answers each descriptor.

Do I . . .	Definitely	Perhaps	Not really
Create a comfortable, accepting learning environment?			
Have a positive attitude with high expectations for all students?			
Keep an organized classroom?			
Establish students' prior knowledge?			
State my lessons' objectives?			
Respect my students' individual interests, strengths, and levels with different instructional deliveries?			
Believe in varying the types of assessments?			
Offer students timely feedback on their progress?			
Set up a system that monitors students' levels and progress at regular intervals throughout the school year (for example, each marking period)?			
Develop strategic learners who are aware of how they learn?			
Offer help but not enable the students?			
Share students' progress with their families?			
Regularly communicate with my grade-level colleagues, co-teachers, team members, and other staff?			
Continually research best practices learned from independent research, workshops, and conferences?			
Believe that learning is an evolutionary process?			
Admit that I do not always have all of the answers?			

Source: Adapted from *Inclusion Lesson Plan Book for the 21st Century* by Toby Karten, 2010.

Inclusive Classroom Checklist

☐ Student materials with modified levels of complexity, such as differently leveled texts on the same concepts or topics, are available.

☐ Strategy tables that all students can access are set up with resources such as extra pencil grips, graph paper, transitional word lists, calculators, electronic dictionaries, visual dictionaries, student-friendly graphic organizers, and models of acceptable work.

☐ Ongoing stations with sponge and enrichment activities are permanent classroom fixtures.

☐ School and classroom libraries have curriculum-related materials and appropriate resources, such as texts, journals, periodicals from professional organizations, and teacher magazines with viable lesson ideas.

☐ Furniture is arranged to allow all students easy access to materials and the learning. For example, clutter is removed to increase mobility for students with physical and visual differences, and desks are set to appropriate heights.

☐ Classrooms have setups that value students' varying sensory needs. For example, lighting and glare are considered, student is seated away from distractions such as an open window or door, or circular seating is used if a student is reading lips.

☐ Assistive technology, such as interactive whiteboards, Braille note-taking devices, portable word processors, word-prediction programs, voice-recognition systems, electronic dictionaries, augmentative communication, and amplification systems, is available.

Ideal vs. Pseudo Inclusion

Use the following table to keep on track with inclusion do's and don'ts. Space is provided at the end to add your own ideas of ideal and pseudo inclusions.

Ideal Inclusion	Pseudo Inclusion
Teachers honor students' instructional levels by giving them academic work that is within their zone of proximal development.	Assignments are standardized, despite students' prior knowledge or differing instructional, independent, and frustration levels.
Instructional goals, methods, and materials vary to match students' strengths and the data that reveal academic levels.	Identical instructional goals, methods, and materials are given to the entire class, regardless of data.
Students are inconspicuously part of the class, without being singled out as being different or less competent than their peers.	It is obvious who the included kids are by where they are seated and how they are treated by the teachers.
All students are integral parts of the classroom, both socially and academically.	There are limited times when students with disabilities socially or academically participate in the age-appropriate activities with their peers without disabilities.
Teachers share responsibilities with planning, instruction, and assessments.	The general education teacher is the main teacher, while the special educator has minimal input with the lessons.
Ongoing collaboration exists between administrators, school staff, families, and students.	Administrators, school staff, families, and students rarely share philosophies and objectives.

FOUR
Using Assessments, Accommodations, and Data

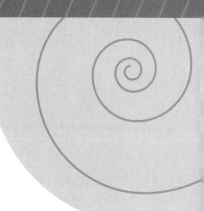

"I had the right answer, and he marked it wrong! The question asked what group fish belonged to. I knew it wasn't plants 'cause that's not even an animal group. I circled both a and b for vertebrates and invertebrates. The answer was vertebrates, but my teacher marked the whole answer wrong! I should've gotten at least half-credit."

Accountability is an important aspect of student progress. School successes are not defined by the numerical or letter grades students achieve, but by the knowledge that students retain and apply. Ongoing assessment data provide educators with valuable instructional information that can be used to create school successes. Teacher observations, quizzes, exit cards, reports, collaborative projects, unit tests, and standardized district tests are all forms of assessments that reveal important data.

In addition, accommodations and modifications must assist students and lead them on the road to independence. Sometimes, in our eagerness to help students, we encourage them to become overly dependent. Scaffolding may be needed, but the help offered must be realistic and individualized.

The Data

With more emphasis placed on accountability within school systems, standardized testing has consumed the lives of many educators, students, families, principals, administrators, and legislators, causing much anxiety and stress. As brain research notes, stress leads to discomfort and nonproductive environments for learning and teaching (Wolfe, 2008; Sousa, 2007). Some administrators and teachers are worried that the placement of students with disabilities within inclusive classrooms will negatively impact school and class scores (Voltz, Sims, Nelson, & Bivens, 2008). However, all parties must realize that assessments are valuable tools and should embrace, not fear, them.

Standardized test scores, while the most prominent, are not the only form of data. The following list includes various curriculum-based assessment options that provide valuable data:

- Academic/social journals
- Art projects
- Attention/behavior checks
- Chapter tests
- Cooperative projects
- Cumulative reviews

- Exit cards
- Graded homework
- KWL charts
- Learning contracts
- Musical projects
- Notebook checks
- Open-book or take-home tests
- Participation
- Portfolios
- Pretests and posttests
- Progress graphs
- Quizzes
- Self-assessments
- Student conferences
- Teacher observations
- Technological projects
- Unit tests
- Verbal projects

Assessments provide student data that can be used to guide instruction and curriculum decisions. Students with disabilities and exceptionalities require different presentations, accommodations, and assessments to promote learning gains. Inclusive classrooms incorporate more visual, auditory, and kinesthetic elements to tap in to students' multiple intelligences, and the assessments given ultimately yield valid student pictures beyond an assigned letter grade.

Inclusion is a work in progress, and data must be reviewed periodically. Keeping track of instructional strategies and progress toward goals is vital for producing curriculum gains. The inclusive players need to shed their anxiety and use the data to create effective instruction for student improvements.

Accommodations and Modifications

Data are valuable only if they offer realistic student portraits. If accommodations or modifications affect the validity of the data, then that skewed information serves no purpose. For example, if a teacher orally reads a passage to a student and then asks him or her to answer questions, the responses do not offer a realistic snapshot of that student's independent reading comprehension. However, a teacher may orally read math word problems as a realistic accommodation to ascertain math, not reading, skills.

There is a difference between an accommodation and a modification. An *accommodation* provides an adaptation for a student with special needs without setting different expectations for him or her. A *modification* requires that students with special needs perform objectives that are different from those of the rest of the class. Sometimes lesson or assessment modifications vary the quantity or depth of coverage—for example, a student may complete functional mathematics in lieu of an algebra course. An accommodation, on the other hand, sets the same expectations as those of the students in the general education class with adaptations such as a worksheet transcribed into Braille or the allowance of frequent breaks. Sometimes adaptations are as simple as paraphrasing oral or written directions for students with learning differences, facing a student with a hearing impairment who lip-reads, or enlarging the text on a worksheet for a student who has a visual impairment.

Accommodations

Accommodations correspond to individual student needs. A student with a learning or perceptual difference, for example, may need a more student-friendly format with less clutter or reworded directions.

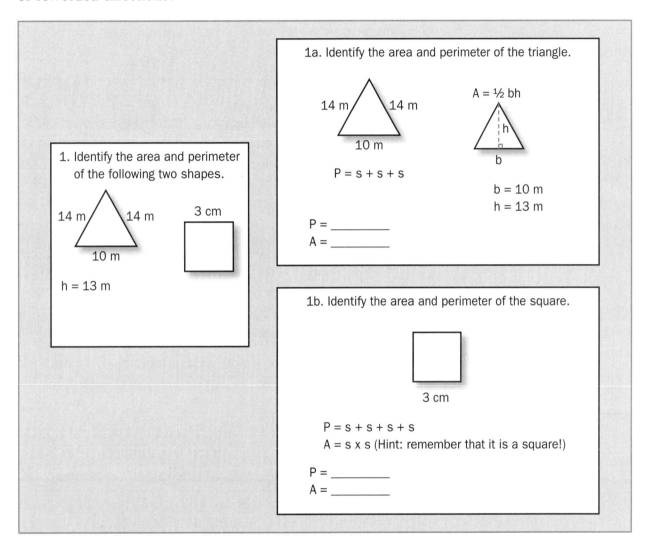

Figure 4.1: Adapted math question sample.

In figure 4.1, math question 1 requires prior knowledge of the applicable formulas and the ability to see that two distinct problems are presented. Questions 1a and 1b present the math formulas and break up the task into two separate problems. This would assist students with memory and perceptual issues. The student would still need to apply the formulas to each shape, but the complex layout is simplified, and each requirement is clearly outlined. The base and height are also labeled for the triangle, and as a hint, the student is asked to remember the properties of a square. There are also separate spaces for students to place their perimeter and area answers for each shape. Some students may require this additional scaffolding, while too much help enables other students. Discretion is necessary. The ultimate goal is to ease frustrations and complexities for students, yet still offer learning challenges.

Although the assessments in figure 4.2 appear similar in content, option II is less cluttered and offers fewer frustrations to students with reading difficulties. Option II breaks up the words into their syllables and offers the definition first. The text has less verbiage, a larger font, and bold and underlined key words. In addition, the second version allows the learners a chance to display their verbal-linguistic (paragraph writing) or visual-spatial (captioned picture) skills. It also offers students a chance to move beyond rote memorization to honor more critical thinking skills.

Classroom adaptations can be made in areas such as scheduling, quantity and quality of students' responses, settings, materials, and instruction. Testing accommodations include altering presentation, time, setting, response, and aids (Edgemon, Jablonski, & Lloyd, 2006). Very often, accommodations and modifications are specified in students' IEPs. Instructional accommodations and adaptations are never generic; they are applicable to some learners but not all students (Paterson, 2007). It is important for educators to offer appropriate scaffolding but at the same time offer challenges. The following are some examples of accommodation scenarios:

- Students with learning differences in an inclusive class may require repetition of skills to concretize and strengthen concepts. For example, one co-teacher can offer enrichment opportunities at centers, while another provides instruction in literacy, science, or math with other students. Always switch up groups so that one group of students will never be perceived by their peers as the needier group.

- Some students work better when there are no surprises. For example, if a student is required to write an essay for an assessment, he or she can practice sample essential questions at home.

- Many students need to have the vocabulary or directions paraphrased or simplified with less jargon if their prior knowledge differs. Offering students access to an electronic dictionary could be an appropriate accommodation.

- Some students do poorly on tests because they do not study the correct information. Frequent notebook checks, collaborative peer mentors, more student-teacher conferencing, and study guides would then be appropriate accommodations.

- If a student has a visual impairment, he or she may need a larger font on tests, a less cluttered worksheet, or perhaps a text-to-speech feature, without the content being simplified. A student may use headphones connected to a computer to hear the lesson instead of exclusively seeing it.

- If a student is visually overwhelmed by too much information on a page or cannot follow a line of print, then blocking off some of the text is a suitable accommodation. For example, a strategy table with reading trackers or page blockers does not alter the outcomes and requirements, but the presentation circumvents a student's perceptual difficulties from interfering with his or her understanding.

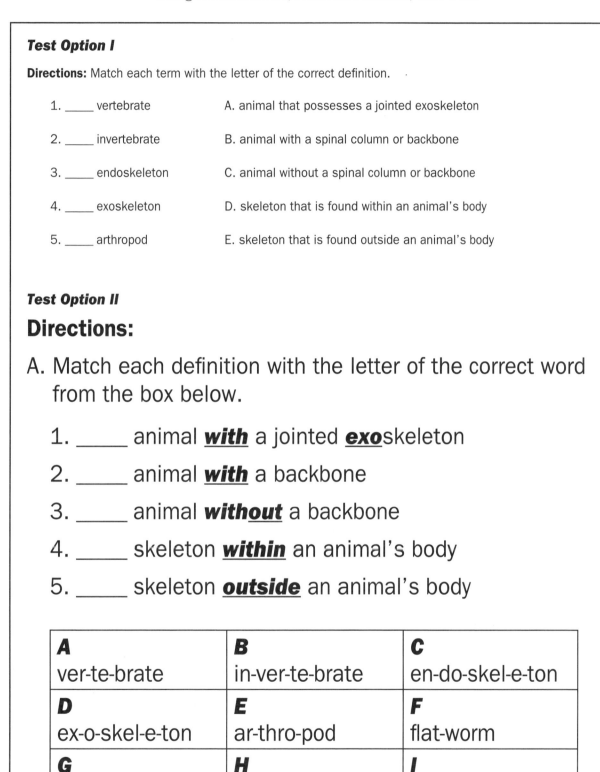

Test Option I

Directions: Match each term with the letter of the correct definition.

1. _____ vertebrate   A. animal that possesses a jointed exoskeleton

2. _____ invertebrate   B. animal with a spinal column or backbone

3. _____ endoskeleton   C. animal without a spinal column or backbone

4. _____ exoskeleton   D. skeleton that is found within an animal's body

5. _____ arthropod   E. skeleton that is found outside an animal's body

Test Option II

Directions:

A. Match each definition with the letter of the correct word from the box below.

1. _____ animal **_with_** a jointed **exo**skeleton

2. _____ animal **_with_** a backbone

3. _____ animal **_without_** a backbone

4. _____ skeleton **_within_** an animal's body

5. _____ skeleton **_outside_** an animal's body

A ver-te-brate	**B** in-ver-te-brate	**C** en-do-skel-e-ton
D ex-o-skel-e-ton	**E** ar-thro-pod	**F** flat-worm
G sponge	**H** par-a-site	**I** mol-lusk

B. Write a paragraph **_or_** draw a captioned picture with five vocabulary words.

Figure 4.2: Adapted science test sample.

- A student with dysgraphia who dictates his or her thoughts to a scribe or digital recorder is allowed a mode of communication without being penalized for incomprehensible handwriting.

- Students with hearing impairments may need additional visuals or tactile opportunities through manipulatives.

- A student with cerebral palsy may have issues with balance or physical dexterity but possess the same intelligence as his or her peers; he or she may just need more time with additional breaks to complete the same test. Set up a schedule with varied activities that honor his or her need to complete the work at a different pace.

- Students with ADHD may need the learning broken up into smaller bites, but do not draw attention to their deficits during classroom instruction. For example, offer private signals to the student to serve as a reminder for him or her to redirect attention on the instruction, and allow the student an opportunity to signal back if he or she needs a slower pace to keep up with the lesson.

Modifications

Like accommodations, modifications correspond to individual student needs. Even though modifications often alter the expectations and results, they are appropriate if they allow students to progress at their individual levels of independence without being frustrated by work that is too difficult or incorrectly leveled. For example, a student who completes the fill-in-the-blank questions but not the essay questions of a science assignment, instead of answering every single question like the other students, is completing modified work. A student who is allowed to use a calculator to solve word problems has been given a modified assignment. A student with poor handwriting who stamps his or her name, instead of writing it each time, is allowed an appropriate modification for his or her poor fine motor skills. Fewer repetitions of an exercise in gym class is a modification. The modifications educators employ are individual, student-based decisions. Together, the general education teacher, special education teacher, related staff, and families collaborate to modify the difficulty level, and they should always encourage increased independence and learning.

Table 4.1 provides more details regarding accommodations and modifications for both assessments and curriculum activities.

Avoiding Learned Helplessness

Accommodations need to be meaningful and realistic. They should not spoon-feed information to students, but give students the spoons, knives, and forks that they need to dig in to the learning themselves. Accommodations should also never be stagnant, but rather continually reviewed and tweaked by teachers, teams, families, and the students themselves. Otherwise, students might learn to depend upon adults or peers for answers rather than hone their skills.

Table 4.1: Accommodations and Modifications in the Classroom

Curriculum	Assessment
Location: quieter classroom area, study carrel, or different setting, such as a resource room or library	**Location:** quieter classroom area, study carrel, or different setting, such as a resource room or library
Preparation: establish baseline level of prior knowledge; have classroom strategy tables with items such as presharpened pencils, erasers, pencil grips, graphic organizers, transitional word lists, and other items that honor principles of universal design for learning; give out calendars at the beginning of the unit to pace students with the assignments	**Preparation:** inform students of types of questions, provide advance notice for quizzes and tests, encourage students to use personal or class calendars for both short- and long-range assessments
Quantity: smaller group instead of whole-class instruction, repetition of concepts, and deletion of questions, for example, only completing odd or even numbers in class or homework assignments	**Quantity:** testing in smaller group instead of larger whole-class setting, fewer questions on the test, more frequent testing to gauge understanding, and reducing number of test choices, for example, three multiple-choice options instead of four
Quality/Depth: monitor students more closely during independent assignments to ensure that vocabulary and concepts are on instructional levels, and apply individualized learning goals and objectives based upon prior knowledge	**Quality/Depth:** use observational checklists that are marked on a quarterly basis to denote progress within academic and social areas, review work samples in portfolios with frequent student conferencing to gauge levels and progress, and provide frequent yet realistic praise and feedback for not only mastery, but also for students' efforts and progress toward achievements
Time/Scheduling: extended time to write notes or complete in-class work and frequent or longer breaks if physical stamina or attention is an issue	**Time/Scheduling:** extended time, frequent breaks, and tests in the AM or before or after lunch
Materials/Resources: have larger font on worksheets or magnification overlays available; employ tactile graphics such as raised line drawings and relief maps; delete extra verbiage and use uncluttered formats, for example, number steps, color-coded sections, or more space between questions or problems; infuse additional graphic organizers, curriculum-related visuals, and student- and teacher-created study guides; use supplemental texts; add time for review sessions; allow usage of headphones to block out distractions; employ more manipulatives, for example, counting chips, calculators, number lines, and electronic dictionaries; employ sound amplification systems; and increase technology as needed	**Materials/Resources:** allow students to record answers in a test booklet rather than on a bubbled Scantron sheet; allow students to digitally record responses, dictate them to an adult or peer scribe, or write answers with a keyboard as a computer response; allow the use of headphones to block out distractions; and allow more manipulatives, for example, counting chips, calculators, number lines, and electronic dictionaries
Delivery: use audio amplification devices; vary multiple intelligences in lessons; offer sign language or total communication choices; provide Braille editions for worksheets, texts, and assessments; clarify directions for independent or cooperative projects with clear, concise language and modeling, for example, offer step-by-step directions and modeling on how to solve math problems, write essays, or fluently read passages; face students when speaking if the students are reading lips; and increase visuals, such as PowerPoint presentations	**Delivery:** honor multiple intelligences for assessment choices; offer sign language or total communication as needed; use audio amplification devices when delivering directions; provide Braille editions for assessments; reword directions; provide models, for example, rubrics; share acceptable work samples; use more instructions as appropriate; and offer ongoing, immediate, realistic feedback

Without the appropriate curriculum presentations, students with disabilities who participate in large-scale assessments and are exposed to more content from the general education curriculum will fall even further behind (King-Sears, 2008). Additional fine-tuning is required to ensure that students are not only exposed to the curriculum, but are also given the proper scaffolding with reasonable yet challenging accommodations or modifications.

Observe your students; they will guide you on the path to implementing appropriate interventions that connect to their needs. Visit your colleagues' classrooms and gain insights from them as well. In addition to communicating with colleagues in your school setting, it is important to belong to professional organizations, attend conferences, network with other professionals, and review evidence-based practices from a variety of resources.

Students benefit from the administration of assessments when the feedback from assorted evaluations is reviewed to yield proper instruction, services, and placements. Snapshots of what students know help gauge instructional scope and sequence by accurately measuring student progress. These data are then communicated to administrators, staff, families, and students. Educators who continually have high expectations for students with disabilities willingly and consistently offer realistic accommodations that allow students to show what they know. Proactive measures enhance, rather than thwart, student knowledge.

Sample Curriculum Lessons

Following are sample lessons that include appropriate objectives, procedures, accommodations, modifications, and assessments. Read through these samples, and then create your own using My Lesson Plan (page 78).

Percents

Curriculum Objective: Students will be able to find the percent of a number.

Procedure and Student Connections: Students bring in menus from their favorite local restaurants. In cooperative groups, students select what they would like to order, figure out the total restaurant bill, and then add tax and gratuity.

Accommodations/Modifications: Some students are allowed to use a calculator, while other students only use the calculator to check the computations. A checklist of steps required in the project is handed out to the students, and peer mentors partner with students to guide them through the steps. The teacher models a sample restaurant order with tax and gratuity before the class breaks into cooperative groups.

Assessments: Students are evaluated based upon both accuracy of the final product and presentation, along with observed collaboration with peers in cooperative groups.

Persuasive Letters

Curriculum Objective: Students will be able to write effective persuasive letters.

Procedure and Student Connections: During teacher-led class discussion, the students collaboratively compile a list of approximately ten things that they would like to see changed in their school, neighborhood, and world—for example, more books in the library, different school lunch choices, pets being permitted in a restaurant, famine and poverty eradicated, and no more wars.

Accommodations/Modifications: Students who need more time to respond are given the prompt the night before and asked to reflect upon the assignment with a family member at home. Teachers also paraphrase the assignment and ask students to list several things that are important to them and to then tell what would happen if someone were to take those things away. Different writing frames are offered to students to help them organize their thoughts into sentences and paragraphs. Some students are allowed to write their letters online with step-by-step technical assistance (http://readwritethink.org/materials /letter_generator). The teacher models the parts of a letter by distributing index cards listing the individual parts and then asking students to stand in the correct positions—date, address, salutation, body, closing, and signature. Students organize their thoughts on index cards before they actually write the letter, placing the topic sentence on the blank side and supporting details on the lined side. Students with poor fine motor control have an adult or peer scribe their dictated thoughts.

Assessments: Students are given a rubric of requirements and writing samples of excellent, good, fair, and below-par persuasive letters to review. Together the students and teachers grade the letters. The students are then asked to make corrections to revise their letters. The original letter and the revised letter are then averaged together and counted as one grade. In this way, the improvements are valued.

Functional and Alternative Assessments

Researchers point out that the way society views students with severe disabilities has changed from a developmental perspective (regarding mental/chronological age) to a functional perspective (regarding daily living) (Browder et al., 2004). Due to this, there is a strong interest in aligning alternate assessments for students with more severe disabilities with general education curriculum standards. When students with lower cognitive skills are given alternate assessment forms, applicable performance indicators blend the general education curriculum with a functional curriculum (Browder et al., 2004). Even though alternate assessments are modifications that are decided upon by families, general and special educators, and team members, the curriculum standards are always kept in sight. For example, if a student's class is learning about positive and negative numbers, and these algebraic concepts are too difficult, then allowing the student to learn about a thermometer and below-freezing temperatures instead would be a more functional way to teach that concept. Although objectives are aligned with curriculum standards, functional skills such as communication, self-care for daily living, and emotional regulation are not overlooked.

There are several options for accomplishing this. One is the delivery of a curriculum that is the same for all students in content but has different levels of achievement expectations or outcomes. Another way is to infuse the curriculum with functional and social skills. For example, when students are asked to share art materials within a cooperative group, they are provided with targeted social goals and outcomes in the major life domains of self-help, social, and communication skills. An alternate demonstration of knowledge allows students increased participation within the general education classroom.

Students with disabilities of all ages are to be included in assessments to obtain reliable and valid measures of their skills and strengths, thereby giving an accurate and accountable educational picture (Thurlow, Elliott, & Ysseldyke, 1998). If the focus is on outcomes, then all parties need to realize that efforts and progress toward mastery are also important (Iseminger, 2009). Valid assessments appropriately match the type of classroom instruction (Salend, 2005). For example, if the instructional lessons included class debates and discussions, then open-ended questions and position essays would be more valid assessment choices than matching or multiple-choice questions. Curriculum-based assessments such as exit cards, homework, notebook checks, and class participation encourage learners to be larger stakeholders in their education and to gain greater study skills and more metacognition of their levels. Assessments should not be used to rank students since this will lead to students who fail and fall further behind or simply stop trying; instead, they should be used to indicate the progress achieved (Stiggins, 2007).

Beginning with IDEA 1997 and reiterated in other legislation, such as IDEA 2004 and NCLB (2001), students with more severe cognitive disabilities are permitted to take assessments that are based upon alternate academic achievement standards, known by the acronym AA-AAS (Towles-Reeves, Kleinert, & Muhomba, 2009; Quenemoen, Rigney, & Thurlow, 2002). The alternate assessments on alternate achievement standards may include, but are not limited to, any combination of the following:

- Portfolios of dated work samples

- Anecdotal records

- Checklists of established skills or activities

- Performance assessments given on a one-on-one basis, for example, direct questioning and observations (Roeber, 2002)

In this age of accountability, no student should be exempt from testing. The AA-AAS is only given to those students who are not able to demonstrate their understanding with pencil-and-paper tests, even with modifications. That accounts for approximately 9 percent of students with disabilities, or about 1 percent of the entire school population (U.S. Department of Education, 2005). These alternate assessments must still be aligned to academic standards and grade-level content with indications of proficiency levels (Towles-Reeves, Kleinert, & Muhomba, 2009). Levels of complexity and the type of modifications administered will vary.

There are also other testing variations, including alternate assessments on grade-level achievement standards, known as AA-GLAS, and alternate assessments on modified achievement standards, known as AA-MAS. The modified standardized assessments may have fewer answer choices, simplified vocabulary, a reduced number of items, or perhaps shortened or fewer reading passages; however, the test is still aligned with grade-level standards. Standardized testing modifications range from students being tested in a smaller group to students being allowed to use a calculator or other manipulatives for math assessments. However, in order to accurately assess student levels, the modifications cannot circumvent the skill tested. For example, a student cannot have a reading test read to him or her, but having word problems read in a mathematics test would be allowable, since it is the math and not the reading skill that is being assessed.

Formative and Summative Assessments

Formative assessments, such as quizzes or notebook checks, are frequently given at intermittent intervals to gauge instruction, while summative assessments, such as chapter tests, standardized tests, and unit benchmark tests, are given at particular times, usually at the end of a unit of study. If frequent or formative testing is given as the curriculum increases with difficulty, then teachers are privy to students' understandings before a larger-scale summative unit test is administered. Informal observations, oral questions, notebook checks, more discussions, and student conferencing reveal just how much of the curriculum is getting through to the students.

Self-Assessments

Offering students instructional rubrics is another way to increase students' metacognition as they self-evaluate and compare their work to the assigned expectations (Salend, 2005). RubiStar (http://rubistar.4teachers.org) offers excellent rubrics in many areas, including music, art, reading, science, math, oral presentations, projects, and multimedia assignments, that can be tweaked for educators' use. Teachers distribute rubrics to the students before they complete the assignments to communicate the expectations. Afterwards, each student receives the same rubric with his or her grade highlighted in all of the categories. A sample rubric is depicted in table 4.2 (page 74) for the creation of a brochure about a literature piece.

Portfolios

A portfolio is a purposeful collection of work that showcases a learner's effort, progress, and achievement (Paulson, Paulson, & Meyer, 1991). Portfolios are often more valuable than a formal assessment, which only determines a final grade. Dated work samples in a portfolio offer a variety of tangible products to review and assess, allowing for increased dialogue with constructive feedback. Overall, this type of accountability considers the efforts involved, not just the numerical grade achieved. If learning is truly a process, then this type of reflection is crucial. Portfolios need not replace standardized tests, but they certainly belong in the assessment picture when considering students' progress and levels.

Table 4.2: Rubric for Literature Brochure

Student Name:

Category	4 Excellent	3 Good	2 Fair	1 Minimum Effort
Writing and Organization	Each section in the brochure has a clear beginning, middle, and end. All of the elements from the literature are included in sequential order.	***Most sections of the brochure have a clear beginning, middle, and end. At least 80 percent of the elements are sequentially ordered.***	Some sections of the brochure have a clear beginning, middle, and end, but fewer than 80 percent of the elements are sequenced.	Less than half of the sections of the brochure have a clear beginning, middle, and end, and the order is confusing.
Content and Accuracy	All facts in the brochure are accurate, and major story elements, depicting the setting, characters, plot, and resolution, are present.	***At least 80 percent of the facts in the brochure are accurate. Major story elements and details are included.***	Of the facts in the brochure, 70–79 percent are accurate. Story elements are present, but few details are given.	Fewer than 70 percent of the facts in the brochure are accurate. Many story elements are either inaccurate or missing.
Attractiveness and Organization	The brochure has an exceptionally attractive layout and includes well-organized information.	The brochure has an attractive layout and includes well-organized information.	***The brochure has well-organized information.***	The brochure's layout and organization of material are confusing.
Spelling and Proofreading	There are no spelling or grammar errors in the brochure.	***There are no more than five spelling or grammar errors in the brochure.***	There are more than five spelling or grammar errors in the brochure, but understanding is evident.	Spelling and grammar errors in the brochure interfere with the content.
Graphics	Graphics go well with the literature selection. There is a good mix of text and graphics.	Graphics correspond with the story, but there are so many that they distract from the text.	***Some graphics depict the story, but there are too few, and the brochure seems text-heavy.***	Graphics do not go with the accompanying text or appear to be randomly chosen without story connections.
Total	0 points	9 points	4 points	0 points
13/20 points = 65%				

Source: Created by T. Karten from http://rubistar.4teachers.org.

Both academic and behavioral gains are achieved through guided instruction and then meaningful practice. Teachers who also reflect on the lessons that did not go as well as they expected are active learners who improve their teaching repertoires. The old adage of how you get to Carnegie Hall is simply true: practice, practice, practice! However, without the corrective feedback, that practice involves repeated errors.

Functional Behavioral Assessments

Another area to consider is how to assess students who have discipline problems or have had a change of placement due to behavioral reasons. Functional behavioral assessments (FBAs) monitor behavioral data with the goal of positively influencing specific targeted behaviors (Stage et al., 2008; Chitiyo & Wheeler, 2009). This includes thinking about the task or situational demands and identifying the antecedents of the behavior. Specifically, was the task too hard, was the task not within a student's prior knowledge, was the student seeking more attention, or did a peer or staff member say or do something that unintentionally provoked the behavior?

The FBA approach effectively reduces the incidence of challenging behaviors. To promote positive change, it is important to conduct an FBA to find out why and when a behavior is occurring (Sasso, Conroy, & Stichter, 2001). Once the function of the behavior is known, a behavior improvement plan (BIP) can be created to address the student's needs. A BIP offers concrete, positive, structured behavior supports, with written plans of behavior that are stated in positive language, such as "I will attend to instruction by giving the teacher eye contact." Teachers then manage the student's behaviors and monitor daily and weekly progress toward specific agreed-upon goals, such as giving more positive self-references, offering realistic help to peers, or paying attention.

Teaching and monitoring social skills can follow systematic steps, starting with a general description and assessment of a student's current social functioning level (Bellini, 2006). This will then lead to a behavioral or social goal, specific strategies and interventions, and monitoring to determine the effectiveness of the interventions. Afterwards, revisiting the intervention is required to determine whether to continue, readjust, abandon, or possibly tweak, refine, or expand the goal or strategy.

BIP for Waiting Your Turn

A student is calling out in class without raising his hand.

Behavioral/Social Goal: This student will learn to wait his turn.

Strategies, Interventions, and Accommodations: Private signals are established with the student. Praise is increased when the student raises his hand. If the student does not raise his hand, he is ignored. Student writes down his thoughts in place of shout-outs.

Monitoring: Choices include student tallying, teacher observation, and student-teacher conferencing with the graphing of daily and weekly strides enforced (if available, an instructional assistant helps with tallying).

Revisitation: Behavior has decreased in frequency but is not extinguished.

Readjusted Goal: Student will appropriately increase contributions to class discussions.

BIP for Positive Peer Interactions

A student is aggressive during recess, hitting her peers.

Behavioral/Social Goal: This student will appropriately interact with peers.

Strategies, Interventions, and Accommodations: An FBA establishes the reason or antecedent for the behavior to see if there is a pattern. A BIP is set up with regularly scheduled student-teacher conferencing. Specific agreed-upon rewards are given for appropriate peer interactions—for example, extra attention, stickers, or computer time. Direct step-by-step teaching of social skills is conducted. The help of the guidance counselor is enlisted to talk to the student and class.

Monitoring: Staff monitor her daily and graph weekly progress. Digital photographs of the student are taken during recess to develop more self-regulation and to use as reflections and points of discussion during conferencing.

Revisitation: Rewards were given at fixed intervals for positive behavior; now weaning off these rewards is needed.

Readjusted Goal: Student will appropriately interact with peers with intermittent rewards.

The Merits of Mistakes

A perfect inclusive classroom does not exist. Inclusion is an ongoing learning process, and mistakes are made by students and educators alike. The key is to learn from those mistakes and use them to create positive experiences in the future.

Unconditional acceptance in school environments means that the educational staff communicate a message that there is nothing wrong with being wrong (McCrimmon, 2003). Learning is not defined by grades and final products, but by the process to reach those grades and completed works. Making mistakes and taking risks are part of active learning. Communicating that mistakes are welcomed and accepted creates a healthy, nonthreatening school atmosphere.

Professor Na'ilah Suad Nasir (2008) explains this point with a sports analogy. Even if a student misses a shot, has a bad run, or makes an incorrect move, what is learned from the mistake is perhaps more valuable than the score or points the student would have received. Mistakes are not only acceptable, they are to be expected if success is to follow.

Worldwide research values the consistent use of assessments as valuable tools to help students who struggle with the learning increase their achievements, instead of just monitoring and recording the results (Black & Wiliam, 1998; McNamee & Chen, 2005). People are not born as readers, writers, mathematicians, accountants, engineers, and scientists, but become such through the process of learning from errors and risks taken. Inevitable mistakes offer students opportunities to learn and achieve positive outcomes (Richburg, 2000). Carl Jung stated it best: "Knowledge does not rest upon truth alone, but also error."

Question to Investigate

How do educators administer assessments while implementing the best strategies and accommodations to assist students with special needs in mastering curriculum standards?

School is about the understandings achieved, not the grade, and assessments allow students to demonstrate their knowledge. Students' answers may be marked as right or wrong, but it is more important for both students and teachers to analyze the errors to determine which part of the learning needs additional review, turning the errors into learning opportunities. Assessments need to be linked to IEP objectives to impact daily instructional decisions (Towles-Reeves, Kleinert, & Muhomba, 2009).

Accommodations and modifications for students with special needs need to be realistic and value learning, not beating the system. On a level playing field, a teacher does not change his or her volume or emphasis to highlight one answer over another while orally reading a test with multiple-choice answers. Tests need to reveal useful data, not camouflage the results.

Some students with special needs or their families want additional accommodations as a means to receiving better grades, without the students actually deserving them. To provide such accommodations would be enabling the students, not assisting them to learn the concepts. When deciding upon appropriate accommodations, IEP teams, educators, and families must review the potential benefits and usefulness of the accommodations.

My Lesson Plan

Curriculum Objective: Students will be able to

Procedure and Student Connections:

Accommodations/Modifications:

Assessments:

Reflections:

STRATEGIES FOR EFFECTIVE
CURRICULUM PRACTICE

FIVE
Literacy and Communication

"What a stupid paragraph! I hate it that the rest of the class heard me read. I so did not want to read. Why did he call on me? I didn't raise my hand! Even when I held the book tight, the letters kept moving. I said, 'That pretty green bud is not really wide,' but the sentence was, 'That petty girl Deb is not always wise.' And there's no way I'm gonna do this dumb writing assignment. I hate reading, and I hate writing."

Reading, writing, and communication skills are important for daily living and thus need to be embraced by all students. Literacy is more than just the ability to read; literacy involves social and written communication through speaking, reading, writing with symbols (graphemes), gestures, pictures, technology, and more. Literacy skills are essential for success across school subjects (American Educational Research Association, 2009). However, more than one-fourth of eighth-grade students and one in three fourth-graders do not comprehend the main concepts from grade-level texts well enough to gain new knowledge (Roberts, Torgesen, Boardman, & Scammacca, 2008; Lee, Grigg, & Donahue, 2007). Statistics such as this call for the educational community to examine ways to improve literacy. Without effective literacy and communication skills, learning is devoid of meaning.

Reading Differences

Reading disabilities sometimes have overlapping characteristics but are generally divided into the following three categories of deficit:

1. Phonology (phonemes, syllables, sounds of language)

2. Processing speed or orthography (writing symbols)

3. Comprehension (Moats & Tolman, 2008)

Dyslexia is probably the best known learning difference. Dyslexia is a language/learning difference that affects the way people read, write, and spell. The brain of someone who has dyslexia interprets what it sees and hears differently than the brain of someone who reads with ease. The International Dyslexia Association (www.interdys.org) notes that many people with dyslexia are able to learn successfully but in different ways, such as listening to a book on tape while viewing the printed word or tapping out syllables. A child with dyslexia is not unintelligent; that child's brain is simply not wired to automatically read and needs extra help to break the written code.

Approximately 70–80 percent of poor readers have difficulties with fluency due to weaker phonological processing; another 10–15 percent of poor readers are able to decode but then cannot accurately comprehend what they are reading (Moats & Tolman, 2008). Some students decode and encode words with great ease but demonstrate other reading challenges. For example, some students read well at extremely early ages but are unable to understand or interpret the words, indicating signs of hyperlexia, a condition in which a person has advanced decoding skills but poor comprehension skills. Other reading differences may be evidenced with memory issues and difficulties processing both written and social cues.

Even though a reading difference such as dyslexia in no way defines intelligence, some students with reading differences believe that they are less competent than their classmates who are more fluent readers. Literacy spills over into many areas, with decoding, encoding, fluency, writing, and comprehension skills affecting students both academically and emotionally. Difficulties with the alphabet may lead to frustration and behavioral problems, and lower confidence levels are nourished by more mistakes. Students may display apathy after spending a great deal of time trying to succeed but remaining unsuccessful at deciphering more difficult texts and communicating written thoughts. If reading interventions are not offered, such students will wade through very murky reading waters throughout the grades.

Reading Strategies

It is imperative that all educators are apprised of effective research-based strategies that help students who are less-proficient readers (McLanahan, 2009). Help includes giving more remediation by preteaching vocabulary words, having visuals that accompany words, breaking words up into syllables, and teaching word identification and structural analysis skills. Direct instruction, modeling, and guided practice with decoding (sounding out words), encoding (spelling), and comprehension strategies are recommended.

The National Early Literacy Panel (NELP) report of 2008 examined the skills of young children and determined the factors that lead to higher reading, writing, or spelling outcomes: knowledge of the alphabet; phonological awareness; memory skills; rapid automatic naming of random letters, digits, and pictures of colors or objects; and name writing.

When students who struggle with reading are identified and given interventions in the early grades, the majority of reading remediation results are successful (Foorman & Al Otaiba, 2009, as cited in AERA, 2009). Skills such as writing one's name or being able to remember and repeat a sequence of letters, numbers, and pictures need to be monitored and strengthened in early learners. When students are older, they need structured systematic reading programs that include word study, practice with fluency, vocabulary, and comprehension skills to prevent continued struggling (Roberts, Torgesen, Boardman, & Scammacca, 2008). Early Literacy Skills (page 95) and Letters Mastery (page 96) can be used to keep track of progress and mastery throughout the year to ensure the retention of NELP's essential skills and to thwart regression with quick remediation.

Context and Meaning

Guided practice to make logical inferences and to decipher contextual clues to surmise the meaning of an unfamiliar word can be effectively delivered by creating meaningful connections. For example, if a child likes animals, let the new vocabulary words relate to that topic:

> The dogs were barking away, being quite loquacious!

> Cats are adamant about not budging to give their owners room to sit down.

> Those agile monkeys climb just about anything!

The reading process is a whole lot easier when the surrounding words act as contextual allies. Of course, not every vocabulary word can be related to students' interests, but every attempt should be made to make the learning—even in the content areas of social studies, science, and math—meaningful to the student.

Reading issues may result in the confusion of mathematical symbols, poor grades in other content areas, and task avoidance (Moats & Tolman, 2008). To create a more interesting context, math word problems could highlight a student's favorite movie star or other such interest to motivate him or her to solve the problems. Students can be drawn into social studies by reading about current events of interest, and increase their grade-level vocabulary by reading and writing topical articles such as those presented in *Weekly Reader*, *Scholastic News*, and *TIME For Kids*.

Chosen books need to reflect students' interests and reading levels, as well as offer a selection that respects diversity. Provide a variety of books in different genres in the classroom library that connect to the curriculum, diversity, and students' levels.

Structural Analysis

Structural analysis is another important component of reading strategy. Identifying word roots and affixes eludes many students with reading differences or those who have had limited exposure to higher-level vocabulary. Knowing the meanings of different prefixes can help students to better understand unfamiliar vocabulary. Accompanying visuals help to cement that knowledge. For example, an educator may use pictures of a tripod, a triathlon, and a triangle to illustrate the prefix *tri*, meaning three.

Teach the learners about word derivations. The word *prefix* itself is a perfect example; the first part, *pre*, means "before," while the second part, *fix*, means "to attach." By dissecting words, students can attach meanings to many words they have never encountered before. For example, the word *philanthropic*, when dissected, contains *phila*, meaning "love," and *anthro*, meaning "man." Knowing this then helps students to understand the actual meaning of the word: "a humanitarian" or "charitable nature." This knowledge could then be used to gain understanding of related words such as *anthropology* or *philosophy*. Seeing connections between words and organizing words into meaning categories strengthens students' vocabulary.

Vocabulary can be stretched to have meaning across the curriculum:

- Math—*geo*metry
- Science—*geo*logy
- Social studies—*geo*graphy

Systematic vocabulary instruction could involve teaching the meaning of one prefix a day. Literacy-enriched environments could have ongoing word walls on which students simultaneously maintain individual word lists. Cooperative groups could add words to each other's lists each day, throughout the week, and during monthly cumulative reviews. There could be an ongoing classroom vocabulary or word center all year long. There are several different ways to promote learning through structural analysis as opposed to memorization of new vocabulary.

Sounds and Syllables

It is essential that students receive direct skill instruction on the sounds of letters; the twenty-six letters create forty-four sounds. Additional essential skills include breaking words into syllables and chunking those syllables (Bhattacharya & Ehri, 2004). Figuring out word parts, segmenting syllables, and understanding letter sounds can easily be accomplished by using step-by-step direct instruction, modeling, and repeated practice to apply specific phonetic rules.

One descriptive study (Bernstein, 2009) emphasized that spelling errors involving vowels were more common with phonological errors, such as writing *fit* for *fat*, than orthographic errors, such as *pale* for *pail*. The study further revealed that the errors were evidenced more with nonsense words, indicating that context clues help with spelling. To help alleviate this problem, direct students to keep sound books with pictures associated with each letter, take notes, manipulate letter tiles, complete word puzzles and searches, and play word and sound games to notice the differences and similarities of the sounds of letters within words. *Fat* is not *fate* or *fit*, nor is a *cap* a *cape* or *cup*. Each letter counts!

Rather than insulting older students with inappropriately leveled words, such as *cap* or *dog*, teach them syllabication skills and incorporate closed syllables with short vowel sounds and the magic *e* with words such as *capsize* and *dogmatic*. Offering students literacy opportunities at their instructional levels acknowledges the students as integral members of the class without stigmatizing them or highlighting their reading deficiencies. Value think-aloud strategies, small-group collaboration, repeated modeling, and guided independent practice with relevant individual goals offered at students' instructional levels.

Researchers have investigated the academic achievements of secondary-level students and found that phonological awareness has an impact on not only reading, but also broader academic achievements in content areas such as science, social studies, and math. They also found connections between early literacy, speech and auditory processing, and memory (Shapiro et al., 2009). Hence, early interventions and direct skill instruction are important in the primary grades and cannot be overlooked in the secondary grades either. Coordination with speech-language pathologists also increases chances for greater reading successes.

Multisensory Approaches

When a multisensory approach to learning a language combining visual stimuli with touch is used, the auditory connection is heightened, and the words are better understood (Fredembach, de Boisferon, & Gentaz, 2009). A literacy-enriched inclusive classroom often includes a multisensory reading and language program to increase student proficiencies with explicit systematic instruction. Such a program capitalizes on the pathways of seeing, hearing, and feeling the sounds and concepts.

Multisensory reading materials include items such as picture books, salt trays in which to write letters, tactile letters, books on tape, and interactive computer software and websites that allow students to listen to the spoken word. Oral and written language skills are nurtured and developed with rhymes, songs, puppets, dramatic plays, daily readings, pictures, computer keyboards, labeled school objects (for example, window, chair, desk, and door), and functional school and community signs (for example, stop, walk, and deer/bear/moose crossing).

Multisensory reading deliveries include learning the letters by feeling cut-out sandpaper or magnetic letters, writing letters and words in shaving cream or salt trays, or tapping each letter sound with fingers (as is required by the Wilson Reading Program, www.wilson language.com). Singing vowel, consonant blend, digraph, or diphthong raps or color-coding syllables on index cards are fun and memorable ways to strengthen reading skills. Associating visuals with letter sounds and word parts or clapping or jumping to each syllable applies to a host of modalities. Feeling the breath of air and shape of the mouth as sounds are made also reinforces reading skills. Enlarging fonts on laminated pages allows students to mark the vowel sounds or segment syllables. A label maker is a fun way to learn and reinforce words as labels are placed on classroom items.

Students also have different perceptual abilities with stronger and weaker senses that impact their reading. It is important to offer younger students opportunities to visually track the left-to-right progression of letters across a printed page to improve phrasing and fluency. The following two exercises are examples of such opportunities. While being timed, a student circles letters or words in order from left to right and line to line to follow the model in the first row:

abcdefghijklmnopqrstuvwxyz

AcbnnjicdutremfjkkgopehiqazmjlklncoewjmoPnhwqowspuiexclfgteqwpsieurjuweazxn
BlvpsutmncunmopwqvMeiwogdlwnXmoepyndslaoenqpwatzrtyoudiditwell

We went to the movies last night.

I you We the go saw went the at to the store movies yesterday last Monday morning afternoon friends night fun time

Collaborative Reading Approaches

The structured approach of collaborative reading strategies allows peers to read together comfortably, producing both social and academic gains. Collaborative reading strategies are therefore beneficial for students with special needs. Approaches include reciprocal teaching or collaborative strategic reading, partner reading, and peer tutoring or peer-assisted learning strategies.

Reciprocal teaching or collaborative strategic reading is an approach that includes the steps of prediction, question generalization, summarization, and clarification of vocabulary and main ideas (McLanahan, 2009; Palinscar & Brown, 1984; Klingner, Vaughn, & Schumm, 1998). First, students brainstorm what they know about the subject of the assigned reading. Next, they preview articles, looking at the titles, subheadings, illustrations, charts, and graphs, and form predictions about what they will read. Then the students begin reading and identify vocabulary. Following this, they distinguish the main ideas and the important people and events, and write topic, or main-idea, sentences. Finally, the students elaborate upon the main-idea sentences with details from the article and create longer summaries. Throughout the reciprocal or collaborative process, the students continually ask each other questions to affirm or clarify understanding.

Partner reading (Bryant, Vaughn, Linan-Thompson, Ugel, Hamff, & Hougen, 2000) pairs a weaker reader with a stronger reader. The stronger reader models how to read a passage, while the weaker reader listens. The weaker reader repeats the same passage and is corrected by the stronger reader. Reading is repeated and timed to determine the words read per minute (WPM). The partners ask and answer comprehension questions.

Peer tutoring or peer-assisted learning strategies (Fuchs, Mathes, & Fuchs, 1995; Mastropieri, Scruggs, & Graetz, 2003) are similar to partner reading, with many variations, but often include these steps:

1. Students abbreviate shared readings into ten- to twelve-word sentences.

2. Students make predictions about what will be read in the next section.

3. Students read the material to see if predictions were on target.

4. Students write a short summary.

Just as adults participate in book clubs to sharpen their thinking skills through discussion, students can do the same with their reading partners. Of course, not all reading can be collaborative, but setting aside periods during the week for collaborative reading allows students to look forward to reading as a fun activity.

Writing Strategies

Educators in successful inclusive classrooms acknowledge that writing is one of the most powerful communication, instruction, and assessment tools at their disposal by devoting the necessary time to honor and practice this discipline. Written communication is sometimes difficult for students with special needs, and many students would rather draw a picture or just voice their thoughts instead of writing them on paper. Model and guide students through the process in fun ways that exhibit your own writing pleasure, encouraging students to enjoy the whole writing process, rather than viewing it as mandatory drudgery necessary for a test. Engage students by allowing them to write within different genres—poems, jokes, travel brochures, letters, or blogs. Writing is fun. Students just need more successful, interactive, and meaningful writing experiences to believe that.

Writing Accommodations

Some students will not be able to complete all written assignments. In those cases, establish a baseline level and work from there. For example, the main topic may need to be identified with pictures, A–Z lists, or graphic organizers before students free-write their thoughts and then organize them into sentences. Some students may find it helpful to pre-write their thoughts on three index cards labeled *beginning*, *middle*, and *end* before they enter the computer lab to write.

Each student is different and may require a variety of writing accommodations. To honor visual-spatial learners, allow students opportunities to illustrate their writings. Students with visual differences may need enlarged assignments, magnification pages, or text-to-speech programs. If students have learning differences, they may require additional scaffolding with modeling and guided practice to brainstorm writing ideas and to increase their vocabulary fund.

Students with speech and language impairments or cultural differences may know what they want to express but have difficulties with the semantics, grammar, organization, word choice, and fluency in both oral and written communications, requiring more guidance with revisions or class presentations. Access to portable electronic dictionaries would also be helpful. Ask your school's speech-language pathologist to share strategies and teach mini-lessons as needed, such as the past tense of verbs, subject-verb agreement, figurative language, and idioms.

Students with fine motor and other physical differences labor at holding a pencil, writing legibly within the lines, or keeping a paper steady. Offering slant boards and taping a paper to a desk are simple accommodations. If students cannot write legibly across a page without lines, marking the page with a highlighter provides concrete parameters within which they can write. Technological accommodations or the services of an instructional assistant as a scribe may be required. Collaborate with the occupational or physical therapist for additional ideas.

Weaknesses such as dysgraphia need to be recognized by allowing students to work with a variety of mediums and scaffolding. This includes accommodations such as thicker pencils, pencil grips, prediction software programs, writing frames, graphic organizers, planners, and scribes to more efficiently communicate their thoughts.

Writing is a process that can be mastered with appropriate scaffolding and the visual assistance offered by graphic organizers. Appropriate scaffolding may include the provision of word lists (for example, transitional word choices) or word walls, writing frames, letter samples, rubrics listing graded requirements, and detailed feedback on writing improvements. The Story Element Planner (page 97) and Story Frame (page 98) can be used to help students map out information before they begin writing. Some students will complete these writing organizers independently, while other students will require more assistance from teachers and peers. After completing these organizers, students then rewrite the frames and expand their thoughts with more audience awareness, sensory elements, and vivid vocabulary.

Some students may need lists of transitional or sensory words to refer to during the writing process. The Transitional Word Lists (pages 99–100) and Sensory Word Lists (pages 101–102) can be passed out to your students. Of course, the ultimate goal is for these students to internalize the concepts, but in the interim, this type of scaffolding is a necessary accommodation that moves them in the right direction.

Revisions

Encourage students to view the writing process as if they are artists completing their first works of art. A picture is not ready to be framed until the artist completes several sketches and studies concerning composition, perspective, shading, colors, and lines. Neither is a written piece ready to be published without many revisions. Effective writers use three recursive stages in the preparation and completion of their written work: planning, writing, and revising (Luke, 2006). Share some sloppy copies of your own to further illustrate this point.

Encourage your students to revise. Direct them to skip lines when they write their drafts, allowing room for corrections. In addition, conferencing with students increases dialogue and guides students on the path toward meaningful revisions. This can be accomplished while other students are working at cooperative stations or during independent seatwork.

My son, who was in seventh grade at the time, came up with the following mnemonic, *Ed's Car*, for the major aspects of revision.

Expand

Delete

Substitute

Combine

And

Rearrange

The following sequence shows a science-related writing sample that applies Ed's Car. The original sentence is *Plants grow a lot*.

1. Expand by asking questions such as: When? How? Where? Why? Revised sentence:

    Plants grow big, tall, and strong when near sunlight and when they get water every day.

2. Delete words that are not necessary or are restated. Revised sentence:

    Plants grow tall and strong near sunlight when they get water every day.

3. Substitute overused, vague, or wordy phrases with more exact wording. Revised sentence:

    Plants grow tall and strong near sunlight when watered every day.

4. Combine and rearrange the words in the sentence. Revised sentence:

    When watered every day and kept near sunlight, plants grow tall and strong.

Once students have mastered Ed's Car, they can then learn to tweak writings for different audiences.

Some students might not understand what writing for an audience means. They might just assume that the people reading their writings know exactly what they are talking about and fail to include full introductions, explanations, transitions, and connecting details. Such students should be given direct instruction and thought-provoking questions they can ask to reflect upon their writing, such as those found in the Writing for an Audience exercise (page 103).

IEP Narratives

Explicit writing instruction is connected to self-determination with the GO 4 IT NOW strategy; middle school students learn to write paragraphs as they write goals for their IEPs. Using this strategy, students write a topic sentence and then provide four objectives or supporting details for that topic sentence. The students name the focus IEP goal or topic, order the details, and then wrap it up, or restate the topic in a concluding sentence. Then their thoughts about their IEP goals are organized into paragraphs. Thereby, writing and self-determination skills are taught simultaneously (Konrad & Test, 2007).

The Persuasive Letter

Students today are so attuned to writing informally that they find it quite difficult to write a formal letter. Communicating thoughts in written form is an important practical skill that requires direct instruction for all students. Students often find it helpful and less stressful to work from a loose outline, such as the following. An outline provides organization and structured guidance:

Heading and Salutation

Paragraph 1: Introduction of the topic. Statement: "We should _____."

Paragraph 2: Reason 1

Paragraph 3: Reason 2

Paragraph 4: Reason 3

Paragraph 5: Restate and sum up ideas.

Closing: Signature

Some students may require a teacher to set up the paragraphs or write the beginning lines of each paragraph. If students use a writing frame, afterwards require those students to rewrite the entire persuasive letter to gain a coherent view of writing. Hopefully, the organization and revisions will then be internalized after several practices.

Interdisciplinary Writing

Interdisciplinary writing approaches advance critical thinking skills in all curriculum areas. This type of writing can establish prior knowledge, be part of the lesson delivery, or act as an assessment of knowledge through open-ended student responses, essays, narratives, poems, and more. Some students will write on a semiabstract level, giving captions to curriculum pictures, while other students will write more details about concepts studied.

Following is a writing acrostic for a social studies lesson on Julius Caesar. This example involves writing skills but also offers students a chance to demonstrate their knowledge of the curriculum:

> **C**aesar, a famous Roman, was born in 100 BC. **A**lthough he started out as a Roman patrician, he soon became a popular general and conquered many lands. **E**ven Gaul was conquered by Caesar and his unbeatable army. **S**oon afterwards, he traveled to Egypt and helped the Egyptian queen defeat her brother, the pharaoh. **A**fter that, Caesar conquered Rome and became the dictator. **R**oman senators grew angry at Caesar's dictatorship and killed him in 44 BC.

Math, physical education, art, music, reading, science, and social studies journals or learning logs offer chances for students to express their understanding of both baseline and more advanced curriculum objectives, as well as opportunities for students to reflect upon what they know, don't know, or, in some cases, think they know, thus increasing their metacognition. Monitoring and feedback given to learners while they are performing a task increases their metacognitive knowledge, allowing them to change strategies (Garner, 2009) and obtain command of the concepts.

Communication Strategies

In this day of technology, many students prefer to interact through nonverbal communications such as texting or emailing rather than face-to-face conversations. Although technology is a wonderfully expedient way to communicate, it cannot totally replace face-to-face forms of communication. Regardless of language differences or developmental levels, all students must learn to socially interact with others. Meaningful communication involves many skills, from the actual spoken words to actions such as listening, responding, and sharing.

Promoting Communication in the Classroom

Teachers can establish environments that allow and encourage opinions to be expressed, heard, and respected. A regularly scheduled morning meeting with an open classroom forum is one way to honor student communication. Students can talk about their favorite foods or what they did over the weekend, or respond to a read-aloud.

Educators can continually promote communication through many class activities, whether students are conducting laboratory experiments, solving geometric proofs, or learning about the Age of Enlightenment. For example, teachers can ask students to discuss and explain what they learned to each other in pairs, in small groups, or through classroom presentations. Inclusive classrooms value face-to-face interactions and provide activities that allow students to communicate, explain, and reinforce learning concepts through increased conversation.

Interacting, talking, and hearing language modeled helps students to develop language and social skills and promotes vocabulary skills. Such interactions are offered in conversation stations (Bond & Wasik, 2009), where students have the chance to talk and listen to their peers. Primary-level conversation station examples include the Food Place, the Animal Place, the Outside Place, the Number Place, and the Letter and Word Place. Secondary-level station examples include How to Act at the Mall: Shopping Etiquette, What to Say or Not to Say on Facebook, Communicating With My Parents, How to Solve This Geometric Theorem, and What Benjamin Franklin Would Have Said.

Stations or centers are used to highlight weekly, monthly, and annual curriculum objectives to promote individual academic and functional skills along with language development. Activities at each station will vary and are dependent upon individual students' interests and levels. Language tasks could range from identifying the names and sounds of letters or animals to creating dialogue for a college interview.

Educators should present the curriculum in a way that allows optimum access to information with nonthreatening universal classroom designs. Lesson objectives to improve communication skills include the building of interpersonal relationships, increasing learning, and assisting with daily functions.

Accommodating Communication Differences

Inclusive classrooms reflect the fact that students with communication and language differences are a diverse group. Some may have difficulties due to language barriers, while other students cannot understand concepts whether they are presented in their native language or the language spoken in the classroom. The basic interpersonal communication skills (BICS) of some students with cultural differences may be OK, while their cognitive academic language proficiency (CALP) levels are weaker. Idioms, sarcasm, figurative language, and higher-level cognitive thought are lost to some students whose language differs from the language of the delivered instruction and assessments.

Students with lower cognitive levels may need directions repeated and reworded with concrete applications. These students benefit from specific language and communication skills being directly taught and modeled. Educators can break down the steps required to help them achieve communication strides.

Students with hearing impairments and those with attention or auditory processing differences often increase listening and focusing skills when sound-field amplification systems are installed in their classrooms. Ask the school's speech-language pathologist to come into the classroom to observe, offer suggestions, and conduct mini-lessons with individual students or the whole class for pragmatic language, articulation, and receptive and expressive skills.

Students with autism, hearing disabilities, and more severe developmental disabilities may require communication choices that include nonverbal language with gestures or picture exchange communication systems (Spencer, Petersen, & Gillam, 2008; Tincani, 2004b). The content of picture exchange communication systems should be student specific with pictures of the student's favorite things or people he or she knows, such as his or her pet, house, classroom peers, or family members.

Augmentative and alternative communication (AAC) refers to nonverbal messages through such forms of expression as gestures, symbols, and pictures. AAC may be investigated as a way to replace or supplement natural speech to maximize learning and social, behavioral, emotional, and communication skills for students who do not communicate through oral language. Gestures, finger spelling, and concrete objects to represent abstract thoughts come into play (American Speech-Language-Hearing Association, 2002).

The cognitive academic language learning approach offers specific strategy instruction for students with language differences, including more self-regulation of learning and tapping into prior knowledge and cultural experiences with the academics through hands-on, cooperative, and inquiry-based tasks (Luke, 2006).

Creating a Communication Profile

When students possess differing communication skills, the setup of a communication profile by speech-language pathologists for teachers, support staff, and families is essential (Cascella & McNamara, 2005). Such a profile provides the following:

- Outline of what methods the student uses to communicate
- Outline of the reasons the student communicates
- Specific descriptions of all current verbal and nonverbal communications, noting both positive and negative—for example, a smile or a tantrum
- Correlation of speech to functional activities—for example, classroom routines, procedures, curriculum, and daily social interactions with peers, adults, and families
- All communication progress—for example, shifting from pointing and nodding to vocalizing or giving eye contact

After the profile is established, IEP groups decide upon communication goals to include in areas such as articulation, voice, fluency, and receptive and expressive language. Also included are functional goals that involve daily living skills such as academic classroom responses or social dialogue during lunch. Examples of specific communication goals include identifying the names of common objects and people; requesting help to perform a task; indicating preferences with vocalizations, gestures, or signs; imitating sounds; following directions; improving verbal reasoning skills; identifying people's feelings from photos or interactions; and so on.

Communication is a lifelong functional skill that enhances students' lives in schools, careers, and community activities and is therefore an important aspect of a child's education.

Strategies for ELs

Like all groups of learners, ELs are a heterogeneous group that displays varying communication and academic levels. Instructional choices vary and may range from labeling classroom items to speaking in both languages until proficiency and comfort are evidenced. If students speak in both languages, switching from one to another, the teacher needs to increase their awareness of their linguistic choices. Concise direction with less verbiage is also helpful.

A nonthreatening, accepting atmosphere encourages students to take chances with their speech as they develop increased proficiencies through independent reflective work as well as cooperative work that promotes interpersonal skills. Improving conversational skills through daily social and academic interactions and hypothetical situations, such as social stories or simulated conversations, is important. Gradually introduce, explain, and illustrate idioms and figurative language, such as "It's raining cats and dogs." Accompany written work with more visuals or oral modalities, such as talking websites, books on tape, video clips, electronic translating dictionaries, and podcasts. Provide bilingual and visual dictionaries (http://visual.merriam-webster.com) and curriculum-related clip art (www.clipart forteachers.com). Educate peer mentors to help students with notes, homework, independent and group assignments, test preparation, and such. Frequently check for understanding by asking students to paraphrase, observing, reviewing homework, checking notebooks, and administering informal and formal tests.

Lesson objectives should go beyond remediation and challenge students to improve their communication skills. It is the school's responsibility to communicate lessons on a level that allows all students to achieve maximum strides. For some students, this may require picture exchange communication systems (Spencer, Petersen, & Gillam, 2008) or foreign language translators.

Parents and families of ELs or students with disabilities should be encouraged to fully participate in their children's education without their cultural or other differences impacting that involvement. This includes complete access to school activities such as parent-teacher conferences, IEP meetings, screenings, assemblies, conferences, school plays, and testing sessions.

Literacy and communication skills open up many doors for students, both in the classroom and in the real world. Reading, writing, speaking, and listening are verbal-linguistic tools that allow students to negotiate the curriculum, interact with peers and adults, and gain familiarity with their community. Inclusive classrooms that address these areas communicate loudly and clearly that everyone's voice needs to be developed and included.

Question to Investigate

How can educators boost the self-efficacy of a student who has literacy, writing, or communication differences?

Students with literacy, writing, or communication differences must realize that their competencies are not defined by their reading, writing, or speaking abilities. Inclusive educators can allow students to be privy to their improvements and acknowledge progress, not just mastery. This can be accomplished by establishing timetables and graphs that concretely indicate how reading, writing, and language competencies have improved. Students' self-efficacy gets a boost when they realize that it's not a question of whether or not they will become better readers, writers, or communicators, but a question of *when* that will happen. Students should be offered continuous reassurances and strategies on how to improve reading, writing, and expressive competencies, putting the controls in their hands. Overall, students need to realize that they are not defined by their weaker areas.

Early Literacy Skills

Keep track of students' skills by checking off the columns below. Retest on all skills at a later date to ensure mastery.

Student	Knows names of letters	Knows sounds of letters	Writes own name	Sequences numbers	Sequences letters	Sequences pictures	Speaks in simple sentences

Letters Mastery

If students haven't mastered the names and sounds of all the letters, use the following form to indicate which letters need more review.

Student:
Name of Letter A B C D E F G H I J K L M N O P Q R S T U V W X Y Z
Sound of Letter A B C D E F G H I J K L M N O P Q R S T U V W X Y Z

Story Element Planner

Name _____

The title of the story is _____ ,

by _____ .

Some characters are _____ .

The story takes place in the (circle one) past / present / future in the year _____ ,

in (location) _____ .

First, _____ .

Then, _____ .

After, _____ .

The main problem is _____ .

It gets really interesting when _____ .

Next, _____ .

Finally, _____ .

This makes me think about _____ .

I (circle one) liked / did not like this book because _____

_____ .

Story Frame

Title of story:

Author:

Genre:

Characters:

Settings (where and when):

Plot (main idea):

Problem/conflict:

Rising action:

Ending/resolution:

Theme/message:

This reminds me of:

Opinion:

Transitional Word List for Primary Grades

first	how-ev-er	as an ex-am-ple	as a re-sult	on the oth-er hand
next	be-fore	again	for this rea-son	mean-while
la-ter	then	name-ly	be-cause	sud-den-ly
af-ter	once	since	since	for in-stance
fi-nal-ly	in ad-di-tion	there-fore	due to	in con-clu-sion

Transitional Word List for Secondary Grades

initially	specifically	on the contrary	beyond	generally
consequently	notwithstanding	correspondingly	incidentally	similarly
equally important	accordingly	for the time being	particularly	in contrast
comparatively	in essence	conversely	moreover	despite the fact
simultaneously	nevertheless	furthermore	ordinarily	ultimately

Sensory Word List for Primary Grades

The last rows provide space for the teacher or students to add to the list.

Sight	Sound	Touch	Smell	Taste
bright	noisy	slimy	sweet	sweet
small	quiet	damp	stinky	bitter
big	silent	silky	stale	salty
short	hissing	smooth	fresh	spicy
tall	tinkling	cool	clean	peppery
narrow	whispering	hot	strong	mild
wide	crackling	soft	burnt	sour

Sensory Word List for Secondary Grades

The last rows provide space for the teacher or students to add to the list.

Sight	Sound	Touch	Smell	Taste
angular	rustling	fleshy	rancid	acrid
distinct	rumbling	leathery	putrid	tangy
portly	piercing	spongy	fragrant	tart
glistening	melodious	prickly	pungent	savory
unsightly	reverberating	satiny	musty	tasteless
translucent	deafening	velvety	sterile	gingery
quaint	thundering	oily	odorous	bittersweet

Writing for an Audience

Questions	Answers
Who will be reading my paper?	
What age is my audience?	
Do I explain things enough?	
Do I explain things too much?	
Do I write things in the correct order?	
Do I include accurate details?	
Have I used descriptive words?	
Are my sentences interesting, with different beginnings and vocabulary?	
Did I say what I wanted to say?	

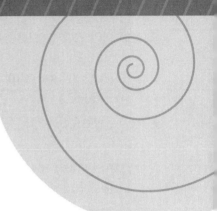

"I had the right answer; I wrote 200. I did 18 ÷ 9 and then added two zeros. Why isn't that right? Oh, I did it again. The problem was 81,000 ÷ 90, not 18,000 ÷ 90. For sure, the kid who sits next to me, the one I hate, had the right answer, 900. The way I see things, especially letters and numbers, is just different. It's not fair!"

Quantities, arrangements, patterns, and symbols involving shapes, whole numbers, fractions, and decimals can be confusing to students. However, if students are given appropriate scaffolding during mathematics, the advanced skills they learn will not only help them to better understand and sort out these aspects of math but also to negotiate everyday situations. Mathematics is not exclusively about numbers. The National Council of Teachers of Mathematics (NCTM) advocates a comprehensive curriculum for math with thinking, problem solving, and reasoning as the focal points. Students in prekindergarten through grade 8 need a core of knowledge to be successful in mathematics. The high school curriculum builds upon the skills learned in the lower grades with courses such as algebra, geometry, statistics, probability, and discrete mathematics. The curriculum framework for mathematics spirals throughout the grades, from basic math skills to algebra to probability to proportions and beyond to achieve solid long-term mathematics curriculum goals and standards. Conceptual understanding, procedural fluency, and automaticity of facts all are crucial and interrelated (U.S. Department of Education, 2008). Effective educators of inclusive classrooms deliver the math curriculum in a way that acknowledges and addresses different rates of learning and positively alters negative student attitudes toward mathematics.

One way to improve students' attitudes toward math is by applying it to the context of their lives. NCTM emphasizes that students need to know how to apply logical reasoning to justify procedures and solutions and to devise and examine different representations to connect mathematics to everyday life activities. Systematic instructional approaches advance math skills (Steedly, Dragoo, Arafeh, & Luke, 2008); innumerable skills are gained with the delivery and solidification of curriculum standards through structured instructional goals and objectives for students of all ability levels.

Math Representations

Concrete representations of abstract concepts help students gain understanding. For example, listening to a presentation about the value of coins and bills is quite different from actually holding a penny, nickel, dime, quarter, and dollar bill in your hand. If students then manipulate base-ten blocks that represent the value of decimals in money, they make additional gains in understanding.

Students often better understand concepts in mathematics when manipulatives are used to explain those concepts. First, the objects are introduced. Then pictures to represent those objects are added. Finally, the abstract mathematical symbols are given. This mode of presentation is applicable for all grade levels. As examples, an abacus can be used in the primary grades to represent place values, while virtual manipulatives and visualization software such as Geometer's Sketchpad can be used in the upper grades to explore geometry.

A study of sixth- and seventh-grade students with learning disabilities investigated the effect of different levels of mathematical presentations (Witzel, Mercer, & Miller, 2003). One group was taught mathematical concepts with approaches that used both concrete representational and abstract deliveries, while the other group received a delivery that exclusively used an abstract presentation. There were improved results for both groups, but the students who received the explicit instruction with the concrete representations performed higher on posttests than the students who exclusively received an abstract delivery.

A variety of concrete, semiconcrete, and semiabstract presentations assists students in better grasping math concepts. Concrete presentations allow students to hold and maneuver manipulatives, such as counting actual objects. Semiconcrete presentations might use pictures to represent objects or terms. Semiabstract presentations might allow students to use tally marks to count. Fraction bars, Unifix cubes, pizza math, or a grapefruit divided into its sections can teach the concept of breaking a whole into its parts. Decimal problems can be introduced using a whiteboard with a cookie magnet as the decimal, allowing students to move the decimal while working out the problem. Students can color-code place value—for example, underline hundreds with green, tens with blue, and ones with red. Place-value charts with separate slots allow students the opportunity to see that each digit represents a value. Unfamiliar vocabulary can be explained with visuals such as math glossaries. Of course, modern technology offers many opportunities for students to explore math, from graphing calculators to virtual manipulatives.

Moving Math Beyond the Worksheet

Because math is quite an abstract concept, students find it easier to comprehend math instruction when it relates to their prior knowledge and the world around them. Learning isolated mathematical facts has low enduring value. It is essential that students learn to process information and develop conceptual understanding beyond worksheets that only offer skill and drill (Silva, 2004). Direct guidance to engage students in rich mathematical tasks beyond exercises from the textbook helps students to develop critical thinking skills (Ollerton, 2009).

Without guidance, students may not understand how the math lesson is connected to their everyday lives. For instance, students may find the topic of decimals rather dull and believe that there is no reason to learn the concept. However, when decimals are equated with money, they suddenly take on new meaning—and interest. Students better understand decimal values when the importance of a tenth of a second in winning an Olympic gold medal is explained. Students learn to line up decimals by creating a visual image of buttons lined up on a shirt. Students learn and retain knowledge when they can connect that knowledge to the world outside school.

Students can skip-count, make up songs, create illustrations, and work on software programs to learn while honoring their stronger intelligences, if the logical-mathematical intelligence is not their preferred one. If students love cooking, cars, sports, or dinosaurs, then think of word problems that include those topics to better draw students in to the lesson. Counting actual coins at a school store, the book fair, or at lunchtime strengthens money concepts beyond the designated math periods or textbook pages. The meaning of perpendicular or parallel lines can be found on bookshelves, bulletin boards, window blinds, and in nature, not exclusively on a math worksheet.

The reproducibles at the end of this chapter offer assignments that connect math to students' lives. The Math Interview Assignment (page 111) asks students to reflect on math outside the classroom and then interview a friend and family member about how they use math and what they like about it. Living the Math (pages 112–115) offers exercises that take math into a kitchen, ball field, store, and restaurant.

Math skills can also be strengthened when connected to other subjects, such as science, literature, world languages, social studies, music, and art. Projects in other disciplines involving measurements, graphing, tessellations, probability, beats, time, distance, and map skills utilize math concepts. Teachers in all subject areas can write grades as fractions, such as $\frac{15}{18}$, encouraging students to figure out their scores. Logic is a primary component of mathematics, and doesn't logic belong in every class?

RTI Math Recommendations

The following eight recommendations (Gersten et al., 2009) are intended to help teachers, principals, and school administrators use RTI to identify and address the needs of students who require assistance and interventions in mathematics:

1. Screen all students to identify those who are struggling or at risk.

2. For students receiving interventions, provide instructional materials that have been selected by a committee. Focus on whole numbers in kindergarten through grade 5 and on rational numbers in grades 4 through 8.

3. Provide explicit systematic instruction and interventions that include problem-solving models, verbalization of thought processes, guided practice, corrective feedback, and ongoing cumulative review.

4. Provide interventions with word problems to help students see the underlying structures or types of problems and direct skill instruction on how to figure out the solutions, such as setting up an equation, finding a simpler problem, or working backwards.

5. Offer visual representations of mathematical ideas.

6. Conduct ten-minute daily reviews of basic arithmetic facts at all grade levels to build fluency.

7. Monitor progress of struggling students.

8. Incorporate motivational strategies for Tiers 2 and 3.

Interventions and scaffolding help students accept and embrace math. Modeling and step-by-step explanations may be beneficial and even required, but students also need to explore the concepts on their own to increase understanding. As these RTI recommendations point out, the instruction needs to be delivered in a structured way that monitors and motivates the students.

Math Strategies

In a mixed-ability classroom, some students will require instruction with an emphasis on basic skills, while other students need more challenging, higher-level mathematical instruction to retain interest. Always think about students' levels and the prerequisite skills required. Mathematics, as with all subjects, must be taught within students' zones of proximal development (ZPD) as outlined by Vygotsky, which includes learning by imitation, instruction, and collaboration (Kearsley, 2009). Concepts within a student's ZPD are at a level just above the student's current understanding but still connected to what that student already knows, drawing the student toward new learning. Educators must provide the appropriate scaffolding that allows for achievement without the frustrations of a mismatched instruction level not within the student's prior knowledge. For example, if a student cannot distinguish *same* from *different*, he or she cannot achieve the mastery or identification of acute, obtuse, or right angles or lines of symmetry. If one-to-one correspondence and seriation skills are below par, then these weaker skills will negatively impact upper-grade-level math skills.

Learners with mathematical misunderstandings and weaker numeracy skills often lack the confidence that they hold the key to strengthen their math skills. Educators can combat this by offering realistic praise about progress and consistent detailed feedback about errors—instead of just marking a problem as right or wrong—allowing students to analyze their work. For instance, you can help students solve word problems with cognitive strategies that teach them to break down the steps with guided practice and corrective feedback (Cole & Wasburn-Moses, 2010). Weaker reading skills influence but should not interfere with word problem solving if teachers appropriately provide necessary accommodations, such as reading the problem aloud, deleting superfluous vocabulary, or paraphrasing the original problem.

Students with cognitive differences, traumatic brain injury, ADHD, and learning differences have difficulties in math since visual memory and spatial perceptions influence the understanding of concepts and fluency with operations and procedures. Their strategic mathematical competencies to formulate, represent, and solve math problems are thereby impacted (Kilpatrick, Swafford, & Findell, 2001). Mathematical instruction that is sequentially organized with cumulative reviews helps to strengthen prior knowledge.

Perceptual differences often interfere with mathematical understanding. Some students with dysgraphia will have errors because their numbers are illegibly written. They may mistakenly think a 4 is a 9 or vice versa just because they cannot decipher their own handwriting and then get the whole problem wrong because of their perceptual difficulties, not their mathematical competencies. If students have handwriting issues or poor fine motor control, using graph paper or holding horizontally lined paper vertically for separate columns is a way to assist these students in better organizing numbers to correctly solve computations. Some students with perceptual or visual difficulties may come up with the right answer but then transfer or transpose it incorrectly to the final answer sheet on an assessment. The same holds true for students who reverse numbers (for example, who see the number 24 as 42). More perceptual training with visual discrimination activities such as identifying, sorting, and tracking numbers is beneficial to these students. Also, encourage students to highlight operation signs, so they do not mistakenly add instead of subtract, or vice versa, and minimize visual distractions with fewer problems or less clutter on a page.

In addition, as mentioned before, incorporate visual images and manipulatives to solidify concepts. Since listening skills, attention, and motivation vary, math must first promote interest before raw facts are delivered. While demonstrating a lesson on mixed numbers and improper fractions to a class of diverse learners, divide several oranges into sections to concretely demonstrate this abstract concept. This added tactile component relates to a familiar object, an orange, rather than meaningless problems that students see on worksheets or in PowerPoint presentations. Illuminations (http://illuminations.nctm.org), a website from NCTM, interactively demonstrates fractions, decimals, and percents, allowing students a way to better grasp these abstract concepts through virtual manipulatives.

Sometimes math requires too many sequential steps for students to remember and apply. Mnemonics are great tools to use in this case. For instance, FOIL, representing first, outer, inner, and last, is a well-known mnemonic applied to multiplying binomials in algebra class. MAD (multiply, add, and [put it over the] denominator) might help students remember how to convert a mixed number to an improper fraction.

Allow students to talk out the math. When think-aloud opportunities are offered, understandings are strengthened while misconceptions are diminished. Also, allow some students to work on enrichment activities to advance their levels, while other students receive additional remediation, rehearsal, repetition, and guided practice. Students do not have identical mathematical competencies; therefore, educators' rates, types of delivery, and breadth of curriculum should vary. With the right instruction, all students can do the math.

Strengthening Computational Fluency

Computational fluency needs to be continuously strengthened through guided programs. Low-tech options such as number lines, abacuses, and hundreds charts are valuable ways to teach and strengthen basic addition, subtraction, multiplication, and division. Teachers can duplicate multiple copies of the Hundreds Chart (page 116) and ask students to highlight numbers as they skip-count and discover patterns. Concepts such as place value, base-ten patterns, fractions, and decimals are strengthened with handheld visuals in fun ways as students discover patterns and internalize the numbers. Collated stapled packets of multiples highlighted on hundreds charts can be used as multiplication study guides for students as young as second-graders.

Some students with special needs have become almost fearful of math. Other students claim math is boring to mask their incompetence. Students may require frequent repetition to master the curriculum and truly own it. Even though the curriculum spirals, when teachers periodically repeat and rotate units, it often solidifies the mathematical learning.

Math expands students' thinking skills. As students have varying strengths and weaknesses, they will require a variety of supports through appropriate accommodations and modifications. Allowing a student to use a calculator, number line, or geoboard is not taking a step backward, but allowing that student to see and feel the math in a way that has more meaning.

Question to Investigate

How can educators help students with special needs gain competency with mathematical concepts?

Students of all levels, including those with learning disabilities, are capable of gaining competencies with math skills and concepts (Maccini, McNaughton, & Ruhl, 1999). Alternate deliveries with step-by-step explanations, multiple concrete representations, repeated modeling, guided practice, and frequent feedback assist students who have difficulties with mathematics. Recognize that students with learning differences require organized formats and deliveries that highlight their strengths, not their weaker areas. For example, if a student loves art, allow him or her to illustrate the math concepts by drawing diagrams to capitalize on his or her visual strengths. Always try to connect the math to students' lives to increase their motivation. Teach students study strategies along with the lesson's mathematical objective.

Math Interview Assignment

Question	Family	Friend	Myself
What math skills did you use this week (other than those used in class or for homework)?			
What is your favorite math topic?			
Describe a way that math makes your life easier.			
Draw a picture of something mathematical on the back of this page. Describe your picture with a caption.	Caption:	Caption:	Caption:

Living the Math: Sports

Consult your teacher for the number of items to complete and the due date.

1. Calculate the number of baseball hits of your favorite team or player for one game, a week, and a month.

   Player/Team: _____

   Game hits: _____

   Weekly hits: _____

   Monthly hits: _____

2. Calculate your favorite player's batting average for a game. (Hint: divide the number of hits by the number of at-bats—for example, 20 hits ÷ 60 at-bats = .333.)

   Batting average: _____

3. Make a graph that compares the number of hours that you watch sports on TV to the number of hours that you play or practice a sport.

   What I discovered from the graph: _____

4. Compare the circumference of a baseball to the circumference of a basketball. (Hints: C = circumference; π (pi) = 3.14 or 22/7; r = radius; C = π × diameter or 2r)

   Circumference of baseball: _____

   Circumference of basketball: _____

5. List the different shapes that you see at a stadium, gym, or ball field—for example, sphere, triangle, or rectangle.

   Shapes I saw: _____

Living the Math: Cooking

Consult your teacher for the number of items to complete and the due date.

1. Figure out the cost of what you ate in one day. (Hint: keep a food diary, and then find the cost of each item to find the total.)

   Breakfast: _____

   Lunch: _____

   Dinner: _____

   Snacks: _____

   Total: _____

2. Double and then halve the ingredients for a favorite family recipe.

Ingredient	Original Measure	Doubled	Halved

3. Calculate the average time that is spent preparing meals for your family for five days. (Hint: divide the total hours by five to figure out the average.)

   Day 1: _____

   Day 2: _____

   Day 3: _____

   Day 4: _____

   Day 5: _____

   Average: _____

4. Calculate the number of calories you ate in one day.

   Calories consumed in one day: _____

5. Find examples of parallel and perpendicular lines in your kitchen.

   Parallel: _____

   Perpendicular: _____

Living the Math: Shopping

Consult your teacher for the number of items to complete and the due date.

1. Compare the cost of three different bags of potato chips or pretzels, and decide which is the better buy per ounce. (Hint: divide the total cost by weight to figure out the cost per ounce to compare bags.)

Bag 1	Bag 2	Bag 3
Cost:	Cost:	Cost:
Ounces:	Ounces:	Ounces:
Cost per ounce:	Cost per ounce:	Cost per ounce:

Best buy: _____

2. Choose a clothes catalog, and pretend that you have $100 to spend. Select items and find your total with shipping charges. How much money will you have left over after your purchases?

Total with shipping charges: _____

Money left over: _____

3. Estimate the cost of ice cream for your family. Then compare your estimate with the actual cost when you go to the store.

Estimate: _____

Actual cost: _____

Difference: _____

4. Figure out the number of shelves in five aisles of a grocery store.

Number of shelves per aisle: _____

Number of shelves in five aisles: _____

5. Choose five of your preferred foods and calculate the cost of one serving of each.

Food	Cost per serving

Living the Math: Eating Out

Consult your teacher for the number of items to complete and the due date.

1. While your family is ordering at a restaurant, estimate the cost of the bill. After your server brings the check, compare your estimate with the actual cost.

   Estimate: _____

   Actual cost: _____

   Difference: _____

2. Using the total from the bill in the previous exercise, figure out the tip. (Hint: First, figure out 10%. Double it for 20%. Halve it for 5%, and then add that to the 10% to get 15%. For example, if the bill was $25.00, then 10% would be $2.50. Double it to get 20%, $5.00. Halve it to get 5%, $1.25, and then add that to the 10%, $2.50, to get 15%, $3.75.)

   What would a 15% tip be? _____

   What would a 20% tip be? _____

3. With a few friends, review a restaurant's menu and decide what you would order. Figure out what each of you would pay if you divided the total bill evenly. Include an 18% tip.

   Price per person: _____

4. You visit a bakery to purchase cookies to take to a friend. You intend to purchase 2 pounds of cookies, which are $3.99 a pound. However, you see a sign that says 3 pounds of cookies are $11.00. Explain why you choose to purchase 3 pounds instead of 2 pounds. Also, explain why someone might not want to purchase the extra pound.

   Reason for purchasing 3 pounds: _____

   Reason for purchasing 2 pounds: _____

5. You are eating out at a local restaurant with a friend, and the bill comes to $33.00 before tax. Your friend has a coupon that allows for 30% off the total bill. How much money will you save? What is the new cost of the bill with 8% tax and a 17% gratuity? Please attach all scratch paper.

   Money saved with coupon: _____

   New total: _____

Hundreds Chart

1	2	3	4	5	6	7	8	9	10
11	12	13	14	15	16	17	18	19	20
21	22	23	24	25	26	27	28	29	30
31	32	33	34	35	36	37	38	39	40
41	42	43	44	45	46	47	48	49	50
51	52	53	54	55	56	57	58	59	60
61	62	63	64	65	66	67	68	69	70
71	72	73	74	75	76	77	78	79	80
81	82	83	84	85	86	87	88	89	90
91	92	93	94	95	96	97	98	99	100

SEVEN

Social Studies and Science

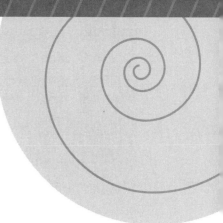

"My teacher has no sense of humor. She didn't find it funny when I wrote HIJKLMNO as the formula for water; I wrote the letters H to O. Just what's her problem? Another time, when my class was doing research on the colonies, I was looking up stuff about Jamestown on the computer, and she nearly flipped out when she came by. Jamestown was big on tobacco, right? So, what's the big deal about me Googling cigarettes?"

Misunderstandings can occur when specific instructions are not provided for clarification. Some lessons require specific instructions as well as more planning, frequent monitoring, and modeling to ensure understanding. Social studies, with its many facts and distant places and time periods, and science, with its higher-level thinking skills of observation, hypothesis, research, and analysis, are often viewed as difficult courses in inclusive classrooms. Students with learning and developmental disabilities often do not have the same prior knowledge as students without disabilities, and each of these subjects builds upon that prior knowledge to increase understanding. Some teachers also lack the necessary training and resources to adequately teach science to students with varying abilities and special needs (Irving, Nti, & Johnson, 2007). However, with increased preparation and different strategies, teachers can enhance the scientific and historical knowledge of the students and show them that social studies and science bring the past, present, and future to life in the classroom.

The Social Studies Curriculum

The social studies curriculum spans thousands of years, from the Early Stone Age to modern times, and different grade levels emphasize different courses of study. Because of this extensive curriculum, educators often present one unit in depth, missing opportunities to see the greater picture. For example, it is important to discuss the American Revolution, but there should also be time to discuss the Civil War and the Great Depression in order to get a bigger picture of American history. Failure to do so causes important information to be lost, and consequently, some students will lack basic knowledge of geography or historical timelines of important events. Was it really important enough to memorize the names of twenty explorers from European countries when doing so caused the class to run out of time to talk about civil rights? Why not jigsaw the explorers through cooperative stations or have students do independent research projects by dividing up a timeline of civil rights events?

When students are able to see the big picture, more prior knowledge is established with increased conceptual understanding. The National Council for the Social Studies (NCSS, 2002) recommends thematic strands that include cultures, time, continuity, changes, people, places and environments, individual and group identities, power and governance, production, distribution and consumption, civics, communities and global arenas, and technology and science, indicating what students should know to create a big-picture view of each theme.

Maria Montessori valued exploration and discovery and was a strong advocate for students with special needs. Montessori schools encourage students to explore the history of the Earth through investigations with a holistic approach. Montessori methods teach students about future scientific and social impacts in relation to the past or present. Visit Teaching History's Big Picture (www.fossils-facts-and-finds.com/history.html) for additional information. Students in today's inclusive classrooms could learn a lot from such explorations.

Including more frequent formative assessments is a good idea, but don't rely on just the number of assessments. *OK, I'll assign chapter 5, lessons 1 and 2, then quiz the kids on that. Then I'll assign lessons 3 and 4, and quiz the kids on that. Then I'll give a whole-unit test on all of chapter 5.* Take into consideration what the students are learning about the overall picture. How does chapter 5 relate to the earlier and later chapters? What is its topic's importance in the grand scheme of the curriculum?

Researchers Laura Dull and Delinda Van Garderen (2005) talk about how many textbooks are strictly narratives that are not suspenseful or engaging, creating comprehension difficulties for many students. This is another problem with the social studies curriculum. Texts definitely need more compelling dialogue to draw students in. There are several ways to make the text more appealing. Students can investigate primary documents to hear the voices of the past come alive, act out docudramas or mock interviews, rewrite portions of the text as dialogue instead of narration, read appropriately leveled historical fiction, or create PowerPoints that depict the main concepts with appropriate visuals.

To get the most from the social studies curriculum, students need to experience the lessons beyond the pages of a textbook. As Dull and Van Garderen point out, the stories need to come alive for the students. Social studies is more than just what is found in a textbook; it is an ongoing and evolving story.

The Science Curriculum

What students are taught in science is given more credence by legislation. Science was addressed in the No Child Left Behind Act, with the grade reporting of progress in science mandated beginning with the 2007–2008 school year (Spooner, Ahlgrim-Delzell, Kohprasert, Baker, & Courtade, 2008). The National Science Education Standards affirm that science is an active, complex process. The nature of the discipline requires professional knowledge and continuous teacher preparation since the field never remains static in this ever-changing world. The pedagogical emphasis is threefold: learning the science, learning how to teach the science, and helping students learn how to learn. Science may involve other disciplines, such as literature, media, technology, and mathematics, to better understand the world around us. Teachers who have solid knowledge of the science curriculum can then offer their students well-designed lessons that value inquiry-based learning through cooperative, engaging activities that allow students to increase their prior knowledge and make observations and connections as they manipulate science-related materials.

The learning cycle of science involves exploration, concept development, and application (Olson & Mokhtari, 2010). For example, when teaching about force and acceleration, involve students in activities such as hitting a golf ball or baseball before words such as *momentum* or *mass* are introduced. This allows Newton's second law to be experienced before it is memorized. Educators need to plan science lessons that allow students to observe a phenomenon, experiment, and draw conclusions based upon that data.

Social Studies and Science Strategies

Students need accommodations and support for instruction and assessment in both social studies and science. Educators need support as well. For instance, science teachers reported that they require extra help to teach students with special needs, including instructional methodologies and more professional development on content (Irving, Nti, & Johnson, 2007; Kirch, Bargerhuff, Turner, & Wheatly, 2005). This section offers strategies to support both students and educators in inclusive classrooms.

Engaged Learning

When teachers implement a constructivist, inquiry-based approach, students become empowered learners who employ the five Es: engage, explore, elaborate, explain, and evaluate (Miami Museum of Science, 2001). Guided inquiry, group work, assistance with investigative processes, and more monitoring and facilitation with cognitive thought and reasoning help students who are typical learners, low achievers, and students with learning differences achieve gains in heterogeneous science classes (Palincsar, Magnusson, Collins, & Cutter, 2001). If students are asked to solve problems rather than just spew out memorized facts in both science and social studies, then they are engaged in their learning on a higher level that promotes more critical thinking skills.

Both science and social studies often have heavy vocabulary loads with abstract concepts (Mastropieri et al., 2005). This renders many of the texts, lab assignments, and written work problematic and less motivating for students with language and literacy difficulties. Educators may need to reword directions and reduce the verbiage in assignments or offer alternate texts that propose the same concepts but have fewer reading requirements.

Effective teachers use ongoing creativity to teach abstract concepts in concrete representational ways before jumping to a conceptual level. Students with differing cognitive levels sometimes require concrete examples to clearly understand concepts such as connections between past, present, and future events; how the choices of people in different regions are impacted by geographic and climatic influences; and implications of scientific discoveries. As an example, if the class is learning about pollution, then ocean biomes in bottles serve to show how varying contaminants such as oil, grease, and detergents impact water's purity. Observing and discussing the results and implications lead to understanding at the conceptual level.

Take any opportunity to allow the learning to jump off the textbook page. Multimedia tools, cooperative learning activities, learning logs and journals, demonstrations, modeling, dramatic presentations, and hands-on activities yield more *minds-on* science and social studies. Perhaps students act out the building of a LEGO car to demonstrate the concept of an assembly line during the Industrial Revolution or use skeins of yarn to show lines of latitude and longitude or food webs. If learning about the Revolutionary War, enlist volunteers to act out the parts of colonists, Loyalists, French, and African and Native Americans. Reenactments of events, plays, debates, videos, historical fiction, relief maps, hands-on experiments, and communications with online pen pals are all mediums through which to concretize concepts and accomplish more curriculum gains.

Personalizing these subjects helps students to realize that social studies and science are not fragmented topics that solely exist on their textbook pages or as part of an assessment. Social studies and science can be portrayed through the lives of people such as Marie Curie, Benjamin Franklin, Benjamin Banneker, Amelia Earhart, and Francisco Vasquez de Coronado. For example, a discussion of great military leaders could provide a terrific opportunity for the class to jigsaw and prepare presentations on the lives of Genghis Khan, Alexander the Great, Napoleon, and George Washington.

Both subjects offer great stories that can be taught through plays, first-person accounts, simulations, debates, and more. Why not allow a guest speaker—such as a lawyer, war veteran, architect, engineer, biologist, science or history teacher, politician, social worker, psychologist, paralegal, doctor, astronomer, environmentalist, radiologic technologist, or researcher—to share his or her real-life experiences with the students? This would certainly give the respective subjects more credence. Prepared educators offer students enriching experiences that enliven their subjects with real-life connections.

Graphic Organizers

Graphic organizers allow students to compartmentalize the many facts and concepts of their lessons under the proper headings, helping to organize concepts, delete curriculum overload, and increase understanding. There are several types of graphic organizers, such as outlines, storyboards, concept maps, and concept webs. Visually organizing pages of information, notes, and facts allows students with learning differences to relate the many details and concepts to the bigger picture or essential questions. Following are examples of different types of graphic organizers and how they can be used effectively.

Mind Maps

A mind map is a visual representation that diagrams data, allowing several concepts to be linked together around a central topic. Many pages of notes can be organized in a student-friendly way. Figure 7.1 is a geography mind map to help students better understand continents and countries.

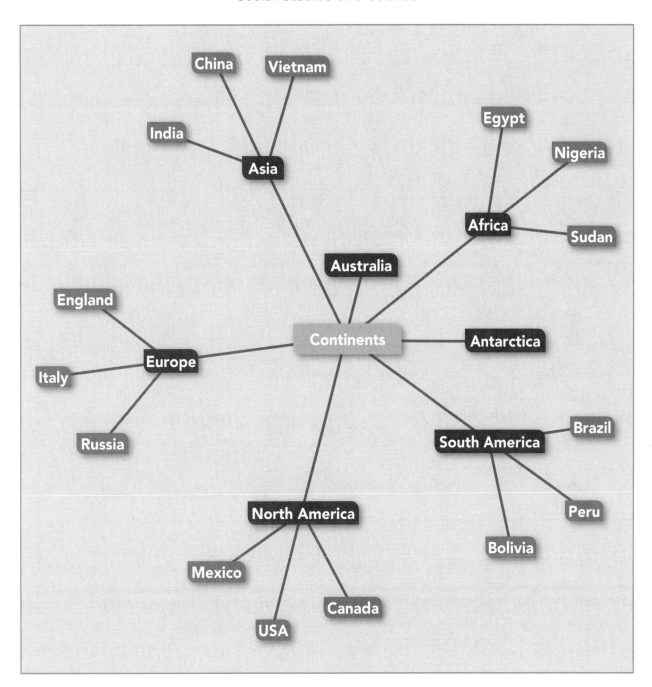

Figure 7.1: Mind map.

Source: Created by T. Karten at www.text2mindmap.com.

Outlines

An outline divides topics into their subtopics with supporting details or attributes. Figure 7.2 (page 122) is a different version of the same information provided in the mind map.

I. Continents

   A. Europe

      1. Russia

      2. Italy

      3. England

      4. _____

      5. _____

   B. Asia

      1. India

      2. China

      3. Vietnam

      4. _____

      5. _____

   C. Africa

      1. Egypt

      2. Nigeria

      3. Sudan

      4. _____

      5. _____

   D. Australia

   E. South America

      1. Brazil

      2. Peru

      3. Bolivia

      4. _____

      5. _____

   F. North America

      1. Canada

      2. USA

      3. Mexico

      4. _____

      5. _____

   G. Antarctica

Figure 7.2: Outline of the continents.

The geographical lesson in figure 7.2 about continents can include assignments that honor diverse student levels, interests, preferred modalities, and multiple intelligences. For example:

- Students add countries to the outline and create individual mind maps about specific countries by referencing political maps, atlases, gazetteers, texts, and approved online sites.

- Students write details about different continents, countries, states, provinces, and cities in paragraphs, essays, poems, or captioned pictures.

- Students create a game or PowerPoint about one of the continents.

- Students trace the boundaries of and color in the continents on a world map.

Inspiration Software (www.inspiration.com, www.inspiration.com/kidspiration) allows you to create concept webs that with the click of an icon are transformed into outlines with topics narrowing down to subtopics. In addition, its clip art library includes several images that illustrate abstract concepts and vocabulary for students in grades K–12.

PEPs

A self-questioning technique called PEP (Harmon, Katims, & Whittington, 1999) helps learners focus on the person, event, and place of the lesson to extract relevant information and raise comprehension. Table 7.1 is an excellent graphic organizer that serves to emphasize key facts and establish basic prior knowledge. Students can use PEPs as discussion notes or as study guides and later expand upon them as they learn more.

As an option, some of the entries in the PEP can be totally or partially filled in ahead of time for students who need such an accommodation, minimizing the simultaneous tasks of listening and writing. Table 7.1 is an example PEP for John Rolfe.

Table 7.1: PEP Example

Person	Event	Place (and Time)
John Rolfe	sailed for colonies	England, 1609
	planted tobacco	Virginia, 1612
	married Pocahontas	Jamestown, Virginia, 1614
	returned home	England, 1616
	lived in a colony	Virginia, 1617–1622

Boxed Timeline

Many students find it beneficial to have user-friendly guides that juxtapose many facts. Table 7.2 (page 124) is a boxed timeline that helps students to see the big picture of Russia's history.

Table 7.2: Boxed Timeline Example

1200 BC	200 BC	0
Balkans settle in Ukraine as powerful chieftains.	Samarians bring Greek and Roman ideas.	Jesus Christ is born.
200 AD	370	800
German Visigoths enter.	Attila the Hun is a ruthless leader.	Eastern Slavs and Czechs settle here.
1200s	1547	1682
Mongols (Genghis Khan) invade Russia.	First czar is Ivan the Terrible.	Peter the Great rules, and Russia is viewed as a great European nation.
1762	1853	1894
Empress Catherine rules.	Crimean War with the Ottomans takes place.	Nicholas II is czar.
1898–1905	1914–1918	1929–1953
Marxism-Leninism philosophies are spreading, and Bloody Sunday takes place.	WWI takes place. Communists take over following the Bolshevik Revolution in 1917. Beginning of the USSR (Soviet Union). Lenin is the first leader.	Stalin is dictator. Khrushchev comes to power following Stalin's death.
1939–1945	1957–1977	1978–1982
WWII takes place. Berlin falls to Russia. Berlin is divided into East and West Berlin.	Brezhnev comes into power through numerous posts in the Communist party; he becomes president in 1977. Sputnik is sent into space as a satellite.	Soviet Union invades Afghanistan.
1989	1990–1991	1999–present
Mikhail Gorbachev is leader of the Soviet Union. The Berlin Wall is destroyed.	The Russian Federation is formed, and Boris Yeltsin is elected president. Fourteen former Soviet Union lands become independent, including Russia.	Russia invades Chechnya. Medvedev is elected president after Vladimir Putin. Russia invades Georgia.

Educators can use this boxed timeline for assignments that honor diverse student levels, interests, preferred modalities, and multiple intelligences. For example:

- Students receive blank copies of this timeline with only the dates and fill in the events by conducting research.
- Students are given the timeline filled in and one that is blank on which to rewrite the facts or paste cut-up strips to match the completed one.
- As an enrichment activity, a sponge activity, or a follow-up, the class cooperatively jigsaws these events and explains more through student-created quizzes, crossword puzzles, Jeopardy! games, PowerPoint presentations, skits, posters, poems, and songs to honor their multiple intelligences.

Enlightening Details

Enlightening Details compartmentalizes the abstract knowledge and thoughts about a topic and also acts as a study guide. The first column, labeled "Topic," offers a broad view of a unit of study. The second column includes the "Enlightening Details." (Add a graphic of a light bulb to this column as a fun way to dress up this organizer!) The third column makes a direct connection between the student and the topic. Vocabulary words can be broken into syllables, phonetically spelled, and defined on the same page to act as an easy reference for those students with reading difficulties. Tables 7.3 and 7.4 are examples of Enlightening Details.

Table 7.3: Enlightening Details, Example 1

Topic: Pollution	Enlightening Details	Me
Pol-lu-tion is un-healthy to life on land, air, and sea. There are different kinds of pollution like light, noise, water, and *ther-mal.*	Pollution is hurtful to fish in rivers, streams, oceans, and lakes. Oil spills and garbage dumped into the water can cause water pollution.	If we eat *con-tam-in-a-ted* fish, it can be harmful to our health.
	What we do to the air can cause problems for people, plants, and animals. Examples of air pollution include fumes from cars and factories that affect the *at-mo-sphere* in a bad way, causing smog and other harmful effects.	Breathing unhealthy air can cause problems to our *lungs.* My uncle was a firefighter who helped out at the World Trade Center on 9/11, and now he coughs a lot.
	Pollution can be inside buildings or outside in the environment.	I hate the smell of burnt toast, of cleaning stuff, and when my dad smokes cigarettes in the house.

Vocabulary:

at-mo-sphere (at-moe-sfear). Air or gases in space that surround the Earth.

con-tam-in-a-ted. Tainted by pollution, making things im-pure (not clean).

lungs. Two or-gans (like a heart or brain) in our chest that let us breathe in ox-y-gen as a good gas for our blood and breathe out the gas car-bon di-ox-ide, which plants use to grow but we need to get out of our bodies.

pol-lu-tion (pul-loo-shun). Makes the en-vi-ron-ment (our sur-round-ings, air, land, and water) dirty and sometimes dangerous.

ther-mal. Heat.

Table 7.4: Enlightening Details, Example 2

Topic: Pollution	Enlightening Details	Me
Pollution in our atmosphere, water, and grounds is often caused by the production, distribution, consumption, and disposal of environmentally harmful products and wastes that negatively affect air and water quality.	Issues such as smog, global warming, ozone depletion, acid rain, deforestation, and soil contamination endanger life on Earth, causing problems for living things.	I need to cut down the amount of garbage I produce and convince other people to do the same to protect our environment, reduce pollution, and create a healthier world.
	Too many gases in the air create an imbalance that causes a greenhouse effect with extreme heat that can destroy plants, which in turn affects animals and humans.	The greenhouse effect reminds me of getting into a car on a hot day when all the windows have been shut. The car traps the sun's heat and light, just like the Earth's atmosphere.

Notice that the topic of the two examples is identical, but the breadth of knowledge on each table differs. The two levels of learning account for students with varying background knowledge, reading levels, language skills, and vocabulary.

Students can easily create this graphic organizer by folding a piece of paper into three columns and heading them as shown, or you can provide students with a blank Enlightening Details table (page 128) to be filled in.

Question to Investigate

How can educators teach social studies and science to students in inclusive classrooms who have varying prior knowledge and abilities?

Educators can divide more difficult concepts into levels of understanding that offer baseline knowledge first. This knowledge then spirals in the weeks that follow as individual, small-group, and whole-class competencies are shown. Younger students first must gain a greater awareness of their own place in the world before they branch out to learn about other families, cultures, and communities. As students advance in the grades, the learning expands to states, provinces, territories, countries, and continents. The same holds true with science. Before students learn a detailed unit about arthropods, for example, they need to understand the differences between living and nonliving things along with basic characteristics of vertebrates and invertebrates. The disciplines should be broken up into components of knowledge for some students, while other students may work in centers or on other projects to advance their knowledge.

Educators must reevaluate their lessons to figure out how students with different developmental, cognitive, physical, communication, or behavioral levels can be better engaged to gain a breadth of knowledge. Accommodations could include providing alternative tools in lab experiments (a turkey baster rather than an eye dropper, for example), enlarging fonts for printed directions, facing a student who is lip-reading, or lowering the height of a lab table. Students with behavior differences and visual impairments need to know and follow safety rules in laboratory environments, which might require additional monitoring or the help of a peer or instructional assistant. Advance organizers help students with attention issues to keep pace with the lesson. When vocabulary is pretaught, the interrelated concepts are easier to understand. In addition, educators who offer realistic praise and feedback to students increase their confidence.

Observations are not only part of the scientific process, but the inclusive one as well. Observations yield realistic accommodations that are delivered in that laboratory we call the classroom. After all, teaching is a science! Together, educators create a learning environment that honors the differences and interests of their students with lessons and strategies that value auditory, visual, and more hands-on experiences.

PEP

Person	Event	Place (and Time)

Enlightening Details

Topic	Enlightening Details	Me
Vocabulary:		

EIGHT
Art, Music, and Movement

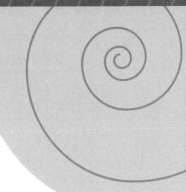

"I can't wait until Thursday. That's when we go to gym. It's so much fun to play with the parachute, capture the flag, and just run around with my friends. I wish we could move around more in class. I hate sitting still and taking so many boring notes."

Students with learning differences often have difficulties paying attention, controlling impulses, and remaining focused for long time periods if the level of presentation does not honor their diverse sensory modalities and multiple intelligences. Art, music, and movement increase students' engagement, concentration, and overall willingness to learn. Quite often these subjects offer students with learning differences a chance to shine beyond restrictive traditional worksheets and lectures. This, in turn, creates interest, resulting in increased understanding. Art programs for students with special needs help them to improve their observational, perceptual, and cognitive skills (Guthrie & Su, 1992). Music is a distant cousin of art that provides students with a form of expression that is not only soothing to the ears, but is also connected to fine motor dexterity, self-discipline, listening, and thinking skills. It yields improved interpersonal, logical-mathematical, verbal-linguistic, bodily-kinesthetic, and, of course, musical-rhythmic intelligences. Physical education and other movement activities also enhance the curriculum. Brain research supports the idea that lessons that have the students moving about in the classroom to gain knowledge are better retained (Wolfe, 2002; Sousa, 2007). This chapter shows you how to make learning a moving, visual, and resounding experience.

Artful Education

Art is a feel-good discipline that often has therapeutic value, whether students are creating their own art or appreciating the creations of others. Art can be used as a nonthreatening medium by which students of all abilities communicate their thoughts.

Students often need guidance to realize that art is an individual process that takes time to develop and that they should not compare their work to that of other students. Assure students that not every picture needs to be worthy of a mat and frame and that it is OK to ask for more modeling and guided practice. Like other disciplines, teaching art is a step-by-step process. Before students draw an item, they need to see the basic overall shape. For example, rather than concentrating upon drawing the details of a flower, a student has to first see that the flower has a circular or elliptical shape.

Art Across the Curriculum

Whether students are creating finger paintings, silhouettes, portraits, political cartoons, or abstract pieces, perceptual and critical thinking skills are used in the process. Researchers Patricia Guthrie and Chun-Min Su (1992) trained young children in perceptual skills and explain that the same skills used in other disciplines are used in art as well:

- Cognition—what is known about the object
- Perception—what is seen
- Graphic production—mark-making

For example, cognition, perception, and graphic production are connected to literacy and numeracy as students associate sounds with the letters of the alphabet, exhibit one-to-one correspondence, and learn how to write sentences. Cognition involves establishing prior knowledge; perception includes accurate observations; and graphic production involves written expressions that reproduce what was learned and perceived—skills that are involved in art and most other disciplines.

Art is not just a feel-good type of expression; it is an integral part of the curriculum and can be connected to math, science, literacy, and history objectives and goals. When learning about other civilizations and time periods, students can see how the artists expressed themselves through the various mediums. For example, what better way to learn about the post–Civil War exodus of African Americans in the South than through the drawings of Jacob Lawrence in the *Migration Series*? A picture prompt can be used to initiate conversations in a variety of subjects. For example, *Starry Night* by Vincent van Gogh lends itself to discussions that can range from astronomy to the circumference of a circle to types of landforms. If students are learning about Egyptian culture, share that information with the art teacher, who can then infuse Egyptian art, architecture, paintings, hieroglyphics, and sculpture into art projects to relate to the social studies curriculum. Art can be used in several ways to connect the students to the lesson topic—drawing geometric shapes, creating map scales, storyboarding, diagramming science experiments, investigating artifacts produced by diverse cultures, and so on.

Also, keep in mind that art is sometimes a great way to release thoughts or energies while learning about any subject. For example, students can honor their visual-spatial intelligences by creating collages, dioramas, or posters to show what they know.

Accommodations

Some students within inclusive classrooms may need extra help to develop and refine fine motor, matching, discriminating, and classifying skills. Engaging students in art projects that require manipulating objects of different shapes, sizes, and textures is a good way to encourage the development of these skills.

Some students who are more impulsive may need additional structure and guidance to realize that each step in the art process contributes to creating a whole. Educators can help such students create a checklist with long-range dates and the necessary objectives for each art assignment. Art also requires students to refine their skills and sometimes slow down to complete assignments.

Students with different physical and sensory needs may benefit from accommodations such as slant boards to work with blocks or coloring activities or desks adjusted to an appropriate height. Some students will require pencil grips or paper secured to a desk with masking tape if coordination is difficult. Other students may require precut templates if cutting or freehand tracing is too difficult. Fine motor skills can be fostered through mediums such as chalk, paints, shaving cream, salt, pudding, JELL-O, pipe cleaners, Wikki Stix, and more.

Art is not exclusive to those who can see but can be experienced through other senses as well, such as through verbal descriptions, the touch of lines, and use of Braille to make abstract representations more concrete. Many mediums and materials such as clay, textured paints and papers, differently scented markers, Wikki Stix, raised glue, templates, string art, and rubber bands on geoboards offer students with special needs ways to both appreciate and create art.

There are definitely many values, shades, and hues involved in artful inclusion. However, it is most important that teachers focus attention on the individual first, then the art (James, 1983).

Music Matters

From thumping paintbrushes on a bucket to creating music with computer programs, educators can use music to tap in to students' interests. Music can be used to improve attention, memory, concentration, and retention of concepts in every discipline.

Structured musical settings foster peer interactions and collaborations. Listening to music while doing work helps to create a classroom climate and mood that often soothe students' spirits. If some students in the class are distracted by the extra stimuli, then headphones may be a good option. Many students with autism are responsive to music instruction (Hourigan & Hourigan, 2009). Music also enhances emotional regulation for students with severe emotional differences (Foran, 2009).

There are a variety of curriculum-related songs that teachers can use to help their students connect with the concepts being taught. For instance, songs like "Head, Shoulders, Knees, and Toes" reinforce knowledge about body parts, while songs like "We Didn't Start the Fire" or "The Night They Drove Old Dixie Down" enhance American history knowledge. Music can even be applied to math as musical notes can be related to fractions. Music can enliven subjects ranging from invertebrates to patriotism. Keep the music teacher informed of the current lessons; perhaps he or she can help the students create curriculum-related lyrics to remember times tables or the principles involved with the forces of friction, gravity, and magnetism.

Feeling and understanding the music is essential, even when students do not have excellent auditory or comprehension skills. Offer students with hearing impairments opportunities to feel the vibrations, rhythms, and beats. Remember that signing music is OK, too. Use a picture exchange communication system if needed. Some students with learning differences need help to understand the stories conveyed through musical pieces.

As Henry Wadsworth Longfellow astutely stated, "Music is the universal language of mankind."

Moving Beyond the Pages

Prior knowledge regarding students' physical skills and experiences informs educators about the adaptations that may be required to allow students access to safe but stimulating physical education programs. Necessary accommodations, modifications, and supports can be found or written into students' IEPs or 504 plans.

Active students often need movement to yield increased focus and to facilitate learning (Cloud, 2009). A study of students with ADHD revealed that a walk in the park helped the students pay attention when they returned to classroom lessons (Taylor & Kuo, 2009). Increased play has been revealed as a healthy creative outlet and a way to manage impulsivity (Chmelynski, 2006).

Strategies

Of course, not every class can just stop work to play or take a walk in the park, but there are other ways to advance the learning with movement. Students can cooperatively make sentences with words held on index cards, find partners with matching vocabulary words by moving about the classroom, or touch their heads for agreements and toes for disagreements. Students can hop while skip-counting or stretch their arms to imitate compass directions. If teaching about plate tectonics or the solar system, have students act out the concepts—for example, coming together for convergent boundaries and then moving apart for divergent boundaries, or spinning on an imaginary axis to imitate rotation. Ask a student to skip across the room to emphasize skipping every other line in first drafts of written expression. Students can indicate their knowledge of a clock by moving to times posted on the walls of a classroom. Teachers can write curriculum facts or vocabulary words on paper plates, which students then step, hop, or jump on to show their knowledge. Students can form concentric circles and face one another to study or talk about curriculum topics. Students can toss a soft foam ball around to ask questions of each other as a fun way to catch the learning. The list of possibilities is endless.

Brain breaks are another way to allow students acceptable movement activities in all disciplines. Brain breaks do not mean that students' brains are on vacation; they are simply ways for students to break from longer periods of classroom sitting to be actively engaged. Quite often, students in inclusive classrooms need time away from instruction for a brief minute or two to better attend to a lesson. Brain breaks improve concentration, attention, and listening skills. Examples include Simon Says, hallway hopscotch, seventh-inning stretches, and vocabulary beach ball toss.

Physical education teachers, coaches, occupational therapists, physical therapists, school nurses, and families are excellent resources to tap for information on how to allow students the opportunity to use their bodies better in the classroom. This may involve adapting lessons for students with fine or gross motor limitations, encouraging and defining good nutrition and exercise habits, or maybe training students how to be team players.

Accommodations

Students with physical differences may require alternate visual and auditory adaptations for assignments as appropriate, for example, a beeping or blinking ball or a target that makes noise when it is hit. Of course, allow appropriate rest periods between activities or shorten time requirements as necessary. Be creative with your ideas and use a variety of adaptations, such as larger or smaller equipment, lowered volleyball or basketball nets, or modified grasps, and modified rules, such as allowing a ball to bounce before striking it.

Offering students with physical impairments the necessary support is important, but an overreliance on adult support can thwart the independence and autonomy of a child. In addition, the modifications must honor the student's strengths. Allow the student the necessary space to safely try out activities without automatically diluting the objectives. For instance, an assistant should maintain a proximity that permits the student to experience an autonomous feeling (Egilson & Traustadottir, 2009). If a child cannot physically participate in a lesson, then still try to include that child in an integral way, for example, as an encourager, coach, or scorekeeper.

Nutrition

Quality physical education programs also include teaching students about good eating and exercise habits. Teachers can enlist the help of families as partners by establishing communication reports that record exercise and food intake to encourage healthy lifestyles that extend beyond school settings. This can be accomplished with interactive nutrition books or with communicated home–school messages about nutrition (Blom-Hoffman, Wilcox, Dunn, Leff, & Power, 2008).

Life Skills

During the course of instruction in each of these disciplines, students learn important life skills without even realizing it. Students who lack organizational skills are encouraged to keep neater work areas and are provided with guidance on how to care for equipment, such as cleaning paintbrushes, maintaining a musical instrument, or putting away gym equipment. For the students who have developmental needs, the curriculum relates to functional skills, such as using scissors safely, creating patterns and designs with their own names to promote recognition, taking turns, or following safety rules. Students with emotional needs benefit from safe opportunities to express their thoughts, without judgmental eyes or ears critiquing their works. Students with emotional and behavioral differences receive guidance and monitoring to foster positive relationships and to productively be part of a group, such as band, orchestra, or chorus.

Offer students chances to express their imaginations and feelings—and learn important life lessons along the way—through art, music, and movements by valuing these subjects as integral disciplines and allotting them the time, resources, and respect they deserve.

Question to Investigate

What is a people finder?

A people finder gets students up and about to move to the learning. It is a bodily-kinesthetic, interpersonal, and intrapersonal avenue that connects students' lives to the curriculum and is applicable for students of all ages. Students are given a list of descriptors. They then circulate about the classroom to find people who can sign their names next to the descriptors. Table 8.1 is a sample people finder that utilizes descriptors relating to a variety of subjects across the curriculum.

Table 8.1: Sample People Finder

Find someone who . . .	Signatures
knows five words that begin with s	
can tell the perimeter of his or her desk	
rode his or her bicycle this week	
ate a fruit today	
knows the names of the seven continents	
can estimate the product of 58 x 12	
sings in a chorus	
plays a musical instrument	
has a pet or wants one	
knows the Spanish word for "happy"	
read a book for fun this month	
can describe the types of clouds	
loves to write poems	
saw a great movie	
knows oxygen's properties	

NINE
An Interdisciplinary Approach

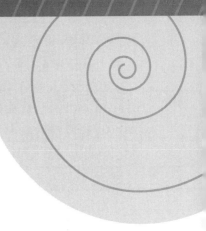

"'You'll see; things will click.' That's what I've heard since I was little. 'You'll be fine,' my third-grade teacher said, 'just wait until you are older, and then things will really click.' Now we're learning about the Renaissance, a time of rebirth in Europe, a gazillion years ago. Just what does that mean? I leave this class and then go to algebra and chemistry. No rebirth there, just dead things floating around in my brain. Nothing 'clicks.'"

Often students view school as a series of fragmented subjects that are disconnected and irrelevant to their own lives. In contrast, interdisciplinary units offer learners a chance to establish "aha insights" that connect the concepts, allowing for a deeper exploration. Interdisciplinary units, built around common themes, empower educators with fun and creative ways to delve into the curriculum. Subjects connect to each other as skills are taught across the disciplines (Gardner, Wissick, Schweder, & Canter, 2003; Northwest Regional Educational Laboratory, 2001).

Setting up these units involves outlining which core curriculum standards will be addressed, eliciting students' interest, and collaborating with other teachers and staff. For instance, if the students love cars, then that could be a theme of study. Explorations may include writing a biography of or business letter to Henry Ford, examining the scientific aspects of combustion, investigating the pricing and quality of cars from decades ago to now, creating a medley of songs about cars, comparing and contrasting economy and luxury cars, designing an advertisement featuring a favorite car, and creating a car prototype, to include the disciplines of language arts, science, math, social studies, art, and music.

Establishing connections between fragmented subjects also allows students the opportunity to form associations and apply what they learn in one subject or year to the next. Teachers help by linking the learning to students' lives and establishing connections with the real world by applying concepts to daily tasks in jobs and life. Both teachers and students gain knowledge about the classroom audience and the subjects in stimulating and enriching ways (Lee, 2007).

Lesson Strategies

Educators should be certain that when students work in interdisciplinary groups within the general education classroom that the groups are heterogeneous, not segregating. Resources and instruction will vary according to students' interests and levels. Teachers can easily adapt units according to individual student needs, making the curriculum fun and meaningful for all (Jenkins, 2005).

Educators can start with one broad topic and then brainstorm related concepts and skills within different subjects (Jenkins, 2005). For example, if the topic is nutrition, students can read stories on their instructional levels, answer comprehension questions, define specific terms, divide a list of words into syllables, create poems, and measure ingredients of products to honor math, reading, and writing objectives. If the students were to create a healthy menu for the school cafeteria, then many of these mentioned skills would be embedded in the assignment along with independent research and collaborative group work that matches standards and replaces boring worksheets. Technology could come into play with graphic designs of menus or advertisements, word processing, databases, research, and more. This assignment could link to the objectives in students' IEPs along with curriculum standards.

A group of third-grade teachers collaborated on a unit to teach their students about trees (Shaw, Baggett, Daughenbaugh, Santoli, & Daughenbaugh, 2005). The lesson involved the disciplines of literature, social studies, art, technology, and science. The students investigated trees, shared research, asked questions, and increased their knowledge about trees, while bettering their skills as reflective learners. Students tackled a series of demands across the curriculum to learn about related products and concepts. In social studies, there were discussions about forestry and physical environments and about renewable versus nonrenewable resources. Technology was explored as students used computers to research more information, viewed animated online clips about trees, and used Inspiration Software to create tree diagrams and outlines. The students created art rubbings, read books like *The Giving Tree* by Shel Silverstein, and wrote sensory poems on trees for the class book *Po-e-tree*.

While designing a unit on colonial America, teachers discovered that the alignment of assignments to students' individual IEPs and interests across the curriculum was easy to achieve (Jenkins, 2005). Students marched in formation as soldiers; created and sang songs from the perspectives of the British, American colonists, and Native Americans; analyzed paintings; constructed graphs to compare the colonies' populations; and created PowerPoints of the colonial time period. Literacy, math, physical education, and music objectives were then graded with rubrics for oral and written assignments.

The next three interdisciplinary examples show how topics can be connected to an assortment of subjects and at the same time offer differentiated objectives that honor students' levels.

Primary Level Example

Topic/Concept: Time

Academic Goal: Students identify time on a clock.

Functional Goal: Students follow class and home schedules.

Baseline Knowledge: Students tell time hourly and at the half-hour.

More Advanced: Students note time of quarter past and quarter before the hours, with more intermediate minutes noted.

Knowing Beyond: Students create and solve word problems and functional classroom scenarios involving elapsed time.

Reading/Writing Objective: The teacher reads *The Grouchy Ladybug* by Eric Carle. Students respond to oral and written questions and then summarize what they heard with student-made clocks and short paragraphs.

Math Objective: Time problems with clock pictures are solved in small groups. Co-teachers observe and monitor students to assist as needed.

Science Objective: Students investigate different types of clocks such as analog and digital. After teacher modeling, students cooperatively create sundials, using measurements of shadows and materials such as plates, straws, pencils, rulers, scissors, and tape.

Social Studies Objective: Students identify time at different locations around the globe.

Perceptual/Musical Objective: Students move clockwise and counterclockwise to song lyrics and time directions.

Study Skill Objective: Students keep personal logs to identify the time of the day for home and school activities. Other possible activities include Bingo games, BrainPOP and BrainPOP Jr. (www.brainpop.com and www.brainpopjr.com), short stories, art projects, movement activities, songs, and skip-counting.

Middle School Example

Topic/Concept: *The Lion, the Witch and the Wardrobe* by C.S. Lewis

Academic Goal: Students read, discuss, and write about the novel.

Functional Goal: Students identify and apply character education skills.

Baseline Knowledge: Students compare and contrast fantasy and realistic fiction.

More Advanced: Students understand the book's theme of good versus evil through character analysis.

Knowing Beyond: Students discuss self-sacrifice and temptations.

Reading/Writing Objective: Students read chapters, identify synonyms and antonyms for selected vocabulary, write detailed summaries, and answer oral and written comprehension questions.

Math Objective: Students create and solve algebraic word problems involving Lewis's characters. Some students create a scale drawing of the professor's house.

Science Objective: Students investigate the seasons through student-created models of the Earth and sun using an activity found on the Exploratorium website (www.exploratorium.edu /ancientobs/chaco/HTML/TG-seasons.html).

Social Studies Objective: Students create a timeline and map of London and Europe during this period.

Perceptual/Musical Objective: Using www.puzzlemaker.com, students create and solve cross-word puzzles. They also research songs popular during the WWII era.

Study Skill Objective: Students collaborate to create a test with multiple-choice, matching, and open-ended questions.

High School Example

Topic/Concept: The Holocaust

Academic Goal: Students answer document-based questions and read novels on the Holocaust.

Functional Goal: Students collaboratively complete assignments.

Baseline Knowledge: All students identify and share what happened during the Holocaust by reading one of the following books in literature circles (assigned according to interest and reading levels): *The Boy in the Striped Pajamas* by John Boyne, *Number the Stars* by Lois Lowry, *The Book Thief* by Markus Zusak, *The Upstairs Room* by Johanna Reiss, or *Six Million Paper Clips: The Making of a Children's Holocaust Memorial* by Peter W. Schroeder and Dagmar Schroeder-Hildebrand.

More Advanced: Students investigate the cultural, social, and economic conditions in Germany from World War I to the 1940s.

Knowing Beyond: Students compare the Holocaust in Germany to the events in Darfur and Rwanda.

Reading/Writing Objective: Students read and critique the following primary documents (assignments based upon students' reading levels): the Kristallnacht Order (www.jewish virtuallibrary.org/jsource/Holocaust/kristallnacht_order.html), "Life in the Warsaw Ghetto" by Emanuel Ringelblum in Yad Vashem Documents (www.jewishvirtuallibrary.org/jsource /Holocaust/life_in_warsaw.htm), a Ghetto ration card, an excerpt from *The Diary of Anne Frank*, or *I Never Saw Another Butterfly*. Students pair up to create poems, essays, and illustrations based on their documents.

Math and Science Objectives: Students record their calorie intake per day and then estimate their total calorie intake for a week and year. The students then compare their calorie intakes to the starvation that existed in the concentration camps and ghettos. Students investigate the health and psychological effects of the diets of those who were imprisoned.

Social Studies Objective: Students compare and contrast political maps of Europe during the 1940s to current political maps of Europe.

Perceptual/Musical Objective: Students visualize their stories' elements and depict them in a collage. Students choose a song that depicts the mood of their primary document.

Study Skill Objective: Students collaboratively jigsaw the Simon Wiesenthal Center's 36 Questions About the Holocaust (www.jewishvirtuallibrary.org/jsource/Holocaust/36quest1 .html#2%22) and share correct answers.

Thematic Planning

Time to plan interdisciplinary lessons is often an issue as teachers have many administrative, curriculum, family, and student-generated demands. However, thematic lessons can be accomplished in professional learning communities, at grade-level meetings, during district in-services, or by sending lesson plans as email attachments. Filling out the Interdisciplinary Thematic Planner (page 140) for each interdisciplinary theme will help you to organize the lessons quickly and painlessly. If an ongoing collaborative system is set up, then this thematic approach becomes a collegial routine, rather than one that burdens teachers.

Connecting concepts to a multitude of subjects grounds those concepts in students' minds. It basically makes both the teaching and learning more fun, less subject-specific, and more student-oriented. This, in turn, increases the generalization, application, and synthesis of concepts to be cemented into long-term memories.

Question to Investigate

What benefit do interdisciplinary lessons have for students with special needs?

Some students with special needs need a reawakening to negate stagnation and to point them in new directions that yield many academic, social, artistic, and personal benefits. Interdisciplinary lessons that are creative and fun, while providing connections across the curriculum, create such a reawakening. Interdisciplinary instruction also helps students form associations that are needed later on in life (Gardner et al., 2003). Project-based learning with the blending of ideas and disciplines helps students who lack organizational skills to achieve increased understanding (Northwest Regional Educational Laboratory, 2001).

Interdisciplinary Thematic Planner

Topic/Concept:

Academic Goal:

Functional Goal:

Baseline Knowledge:

More Advanced:

Knowing Beyond:

Reading/Writing Objective:

Math Objective:

Science Objective:

Social Studies Objective:

Perceptual/Musical Objective:

Study Skill Objective:

Other Objective(s):

Accommodations or Modifications:

TEN
Transitional Plans

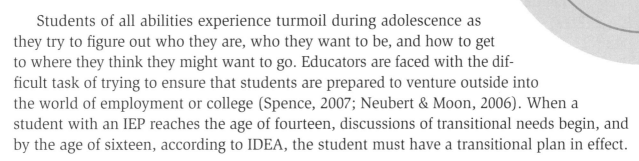

"My parents keep telling me that I should start thinking about what I want to be. I have no clue. I'm only in seventh grade. I don't care, so stop asking me. I just want to download a new song on my iPhone."

Students of all abilities experience turmoil during adolescence as they try to figure out who they are, who they want to be, and how to get to where they think they might want to go. Educators are faced with the difficult task of trying to ensure that students are prepared to venture outside into the world of employment or college (Spence, 2007; Neubert & Moon, 2006). When a student with an IEP reaches the age of fourteen, discussions of transitional needs begin, and by the age of sixteen, according to IDEA, the student must have a transitional plan in effect.

A transitional plan outlines specific measurable goals for a student to prepare him or her to transition to the world after high school. The plan considers specific steps toward college, other postsecondary training, employment, or necessary adult services. The general and special educators, team members, families, and students create these individualized transitional plans together.

At age fourteen, or younger if appropriate, the statement of transition service needs in a student's IEP often includes types of transitional assessments, a discussion of environmental barriers, and future goals. Transition services include goals related to community involvement, employment, and other functional and adult living skills. After these transitional goals are set, inclusive classrooms then prepare students to be active and viable participants in the inclusive world beyond school walls.

Setting Goals

While change can be intimidating for anyone, transitional plans are designed to avoid the unnecessary emotional duress of leaving school and entering unprepared futures. Students with special needs can create proactive plans that allow them to think ahead and set goals, thus helping them to smoothly transition from one situation to the next. Setting goals to reach targeted outcomes is an important life skill.

Educators can find out students' interests and strengths with increased class discussion, individual conferencing, and written or online inventories. The Interests and Strengths Questionnaire (page 146) offers a structured writing frame that will help educators to discover interests that could lead to future plans. Once students' interests are identified, then goals can be set, and course selections and skills taught can be tailored for their individual paths.

School staff, families, and students should constantly collaborate to encourage the achievement of the students' goals. Ongoing home–school communication is beneficial. Share portfolios of students' works with the students and their families, and highlight strengths, accomplishments, and avenues worth pursuing. Set up transitional meetings with support teams, case managers, general education and special education personnel, families, and the students themselves when students move from one building to the next. Communicate with other staff members and arrange programs and related services based upon students' needs, such as meetings with a guidance counselor. Apprise students and families of local agencies and organizations that may assist, such as the Association for Higher Education and Disabilities, vocational rehabilitation agencies, and independent-living councils. The Higher Education Act allows students with intellectual disabilities to apply for and possibly receive Pell Grants and Federal Work Study if they meet specified criteria.

Strategies

Educators of all grades need to proactively think ahead about how lessons relate to life opportunities. For example, logical thinking in mathematics, inference in literature, and observations in science are all applicable life skills. By relating lessons to life, educators help learners realize that the skills and concepts that they are taught in school prepare them for many choices and experiences after school. Bridging the learning objectives to outside situations and individual interests is essential in achieving transitional goals. For example, if a student is hesitant to write a résumé for himself or herself, ask the student to first write a favorite music or movie star's résumé to learn the proper format.

The summary of performance (SOP) is completed in the last year of a student's high school education. It describes the student's academic achievements, functional performances, and recommendations that will assist with the achievement of postsecondary goals. Often linked to the student's IEP, the SOP includes descriptions of the accommodations, modifications, and assistive technology the student received in high school and allows room for student input. This information is then communicated to postsecondary agencies to ensure continued achievement. The ultimate goal is to help each child achieve success as an independent productive adult, while focusing on skills and preferences.

Study skill strategies mixed with the curriculum teach many life skills, such as organizing information, self-regulation, and how and when to ask for help. When educators organize cooperative groups and collaborative projects, students learn important skills in getting along with others and working as a team to complete agreed-upon or assigned goals. These are skills that have huge merits in the workforce and in life.

Curriculum and transition programs must highlight students' strengths and abilities, not their weaker areas or assumed characteristics of their labeled disabilities (Karten, 2008a;

British Columbia Ministry of Children and Family Development, 2001). For example, if a student shows interest in writing but has weaker fine motor and physical skills, then appropriate technology is required, such as a portable keyboard or word-prediction program. Encourage this student to be part of the school newspaper, or have him or her submit an article or editorial to a local newspaper as a junior writer in training. Help this student acquire an internship to make real-life connections. If a student with autism has strengths that include an affinity for animals and a sharp eye for detail, then perhaps the student should be encouraged to volunteer at a local animal shelter or help inventory books in the library.

If intellectual disabilities are evidenced, the student would benefit from additional courses that offer more literacy and numeracy lessons that are essential for daily functioning, such as reading a subway map or online bus schedule, shopping in a store, preparing a budget, telling time, or responding to emails. Students with intellectual disabilities need concrete experiences in the community to understand more about functional daily living (Hartman, 2009). Trainings and preparations include helping students develop self-determination, advocacy skills, and professionalism—communicating, dressing appropriately, and being punctual. Practice hypothetical conversations to mirror actual scenarios such as how to act during an interview, while traveling on a bus, or when watching a movie in a theater. Collaborate with outside agencies such as personnel on college campuses or possible employers to allow students to visit the actual sites. Guest speakers in the classroom offer insights, increase familiarity, and dispel fears. Students should also be exposed to the academic skills that will help them with their postsecondary placements, such as learning how to use computer tools or make a bank deposit. The bottom line is that literacy, numeracy, and thinking skills need to be sharpened through practice and discrete task analysis.

If a student has emotional or behavioral differences, then more practice with socialization through hypothetical situations and role-playing would be advantageous. This includes learning how to diffuse volatile situations, exhibit self-control and anger management, and respond appropriately to unexpected events. Students with learning differences may be overwhelmed with information or writing requirements in the transitional planning stage. Give these students a visually pleasing template to fill in instead.

The curriculum needs to illustrate how students will use the knowledge gained later in life. The more positive experiences students have in school settings, the more successful the transitions.

Overall, the purpose of transitional planning for youth with special needs is to identify opportunities and experiences during their school years that better prepare them for life as an adult (Johnson, Brown, & Edgar, 2000). Transitional plans that are well thought out review personal achievements and strengths and provide insights into future accomplishments to help students realize their potential.

Question to Investigate

How can educators help students with disabilities develop more self-determination?

Educators can conference with students and offer more reflective learning opportunities. Increased discussion with ongoing encouragement helps students to continually be cognizant of their own strengths and weaknesses. Students should outline personal and academic goals along with the barriers that would stop them from achieving those goals. If a student views himself or herself as capable of achieving strides, then, with school and family support, progress becomes a reality. If educators incorporate the following five steps identified by authors Sharon Field and Alan Hoffman (1996) into lessons, then more self-determination will be modeled, absorbed, and applied:

1. Know yourself and your environment.
2. Value yourself.
3. Plan.
4. Act.
5. Experience outcomes.

Inclusive educators can offer lessons on study skills, give specific and constructive feedback, teach listening skills, and guide and coach students to believe in themselves. The present levels of academic achievements and functional performances (PLAAFPs) in students' IEPs and the narrative statements in 504s should include information about students' self-determination levels and goals. Those levels and goals should be used to create transitional plans and support students in navigating school, home, and the community with confident future plans. Following is an example of part of a hypothetical PLAAFP that connects academic skills, functional skills, and self-determination.

Ebony Wright, a seventh-grade student, currently receives in-class support for the subjects of reading, language arts, science, and social studies in the general education classroom. Her current Developmental Reading Assessment (DRA) level is 50, and she received a C- on her second marking period report card in English, science, and social studies. She benefits from the inclusion and scaffolding that include modeling, guided practice, preteaching of vocabulary, high-interest readings, and repetition. At times, Ebony becomes frustrated with work that is above her fifth-grade reading level and seems to tune out the teachers if the lesson is not within her prior knowledge. She also needs gentle reminders concerning the accuracy of the assignments and frequent monitoring to complete assignments by given due dates. Ebony productively works with peers in cooperative groups and responds well to multisensory presentations. She excels at mathematics but needs some of the word problems orally read. Steady improvements in reading, social studies, science, and language arts are evidenced by quizzes, unit tests, observations, and work samples in her portfolio. She loves reading activities from online sites and has a reading peer coach to help her with some of the difficult vocabulary.

Her mom is also given a list of the upcoming curriculum words a week ahead of time for Ebony to preview. Ebony is continually encouraged to record her strides, value improvements, and make plans to move ahead by reflecting on feedback.

Ebony loves music and singing in the chorus. Her music teacher and English teacher collaborate with the sharing of lessons. Sometimes, Ebony even creates lyrics with curriculum songs about characters in stories that she has recently read. This transfer of skills has now helped improve Ebony's word decoding skills. She even indicated that one day she might want to become a music teacher herself.

Ebony was invited to attend this year's IEP meeting but said that she is not ready yet. Ebony is beginning to experience positive academic outcomes and increased self-determination. Her mom wants to discuss and explore further transitional plans and services at our next scheduled meeting.

As students transition to life beyond school, they face increasing pressures and demands that must be proactively addressed. Transitional services map out students' current levels, accommodations, supports, future aspirations, and successes achieved. With transitional plans in place, students continue to make strides when they graduate and enter their communities.

Interests and Strengths Questionnaire

What I like about myself and others:

What I'd change about myself and others:

Favorite subjects and activities:

Least favorite subjects and activities:

Best friends:

Songs, books, and movies I like:

A job that I might like to do one day:

Skills that would help me to do that job:

What might stop me from doing what I want (people, my weaknesses):

Who could help me achieve my goals:

Other things I think about:·

MAINTAINING THE
INCLUSIVE CLASSROOM

ELEVEN
Professional Collaboration

"OK, I have no idea what this math teacher is talking about, but I don't think he does either. One minute he tells the class one thing, and then the next minute he says, 'No, that's not right.' How am I supposed to get it when he doesn't even get it? I don't think he really cares if we learn the stuff or not. My English teacher is different, though. She loves books and writing and always gives us cool things to do from a workshop or conference she just went to or a book she just read."

Teachers owe it to their students to deliver the best curriculum possible, whether it is the first day of the school year or last year of their teaching career. Research-based interventions are now offered to students with and without disabilities to help catapult all learners into the 21st century. That means that ongoing professional learning experiences are part of both general and special education teachers' schedules.

Inclusion is a collaborative effort that requires the input of school team members, co-teachers, families, and, of course, the students. The school team is comprised of general and special education teachers, related staff, and other appropriate individuals who determine a student's strengths, educational needs, necessary resources and materials, and recommended educational programs. All of these people play a part in creating a successful inclusive classroom; therefore, it is important that they work together effectively.

Inclusion Players

Inclusion players include those involved in writing IEPs and intervention and data groups who act as teams with labels such as *child study teams*, *instructional support teams*, *student support teams*, or perhaps *multidisciplinary teams*. These group members gather information and data on students who evidence individual needs and convene with teachers and family members. Teams decide whether or not an IEP is warranted based on observations of the student, the student's functional performances and academic achievement, psychological testing, review of past educational records, behavioral assessments, emotional and social functioning, current and past program history, and responses to interventions. The players on these educational teams may include learning disabilities consultants, school psychologists, social workers, principals, guidance counselors, special education teachers, general education teachers, occupational therapists, speech-language pathologists, physical therapists, mobility trainers, advocates, and others. Input from families concerning a student's early history, home background, interests, and such is important as it allows school teams to view the whole child, including how he or she behaves outside of the school setting.

Local Education Agencies

LEAs ensure that students with special needs are getting the appropriate services, such as a mobility trainer for a student who is blind, language services for a student with autism, physical therapy for a student with cerebral palsy, or transportation for a student who is deaf to a school outside the school district for more specialized services.

LEAs must advertise their services to the public, through newspapers and other local and state sources, so that children who are in need of special services at crucial early ages, before school, can receive the necessary early intervention services. This is in conjunction with the early intervention program and preschool services of IDEA. Infants and toddlers with developmental delays benefit from such services at early ages, and, of course, children of all ages must be provided the appropriate services. As a component of IDEA, Child Find (www.childfindidea .org) identifies students with disabilities who need help from birth to age twenty-one.

Families

Inclusion is most effective when families, including caretakers, are honored as integral partners. Their crucial input and support affect the effectiveness and implementation of many of those written documents and lesson objectives and plans. It is important for teacher candidates to learn how to develop positive collaborations and partnerships with families (Patterson, Webb, & Krudwig, 2009). When everyone is on the same inclusive side, then the students gain double support, from home and school environments.

Families of students with disabilities experience a wide range of emotions, from guilt to denial to acceptance, that must be heard, acknowledged, and respected by the school. Keep in mind that if you have not raised a child with a disability, it is difficult to fully understand the dynamics involved. The gamut of family needs requires appropriate services and supports and ongoing consideration to improve the family's and student's quality of life, resulting in better outcomes (Wang & Brown, 2009).

IEP teams apprise families of their rights. When parents do not agree with IEP decisions, mediations with hearing officers try to resolve conflicts before more formal due process hearings occur. The best scenario occurs when the middle ground is reached and everyone effectively communicates and advocates for the students. Once a program is in place, the special education teacher is usually the one who documents students' progress and regularly communicates with the families via quarterly reports, conferences, phone calls, emails, and so on.

Related Staff and Services

Related services include, but are not limited to, the domains of transportation, recreation, rehabilitative counseling, augmentative communication, speech and language, orthopedics, vision, orientation and mobility, deaf and hard of hearing, audiology, autism, social work, psychology, parent counseling and training, nursing, and medical services. Evaluations are conducted to determine students' developmental and functional levels and to identify the types of services needed. The nature or type of service, frequency, duration, and location need to be discussed and specified by IEP teams. Qualified personnel then deliver these services.

Indirect services may involve obtaining consultation from other parties, such as a behavior therapist helping a teacher or parent with understanding a student with conduct differences who may need intensive monitoring with an applied behavior analysis approach. Sometimes a related service provider such as the speech pathologist or the occupational therapist offers therapy in the classroom or in a separate therapy room within the school. Communication and collaboration with all staff, families, and students is essential to ensure that the appropriate services continually match students' levels and needs.

Staff must collaborate with each other as a team to communicate how goals can be enforced across settings. As an example, the occupational therapist can offer the general or special educator strategies for handwriting while the speech-language pathologist can offer ways to foster better expression within the inclusive classroom. This same collaboration and communication is then extended to families and other special subject teachers who need to be privy to IEP goals and present levels of academic and functional performances.

Administrators

Administrators are often affected by legislative mandates, which trickle down to classroom teachers and students. Principals require preparation, training, and ongoing home, district, and staff support to effectively handle many of the special education scenarios they will likely confront and to assume an effective leadership role in their building (Angelle & Bilton, 2009).

When administrators value inclusive agendas, the structures to support proper scheduling, co-teaching, RTI, and instructional support teams are in place with respect to equity and excellence for all students (National Association of Secondary School Principals, 2009; National Association of State Directors of Special Education, 2010). If all parties maintain an attitude that their ultimate goal is students' successes, then no matter what issues arise, they will be effectively handled.

Communication

Teachers in inclusive classrooms need to work collaboratively with team members, families, co-teachers, and support staff—that means communicating effectively, sharing information, offering respect, listening to each other, and sometimes guiding one another as well. The latter is sometimes a difficult task for teachers who are more comfortable and prepared to teach students than to tell colleagues what to do (Carnahan, Williamson, Clarke, & Sorensen, 2009).

When communicating with administrators, document what extra inclusive supports are required, such as hiring an inclusion or behavioral specialist to enhance the learning conditions within the general education setting. Be realistic about your concerns based on data such as student work samples, chapter and unit tests, and observation records about how the student works both independently and cooperatively. If you would like to attend a professional workshop, then communicate why you wish to attend and perhaps offer to share the information gained with the rest of the staff. Remember that everyone is on the same side.

Honor the concerns and input of families in your communications. Some families believe in full inclusion, while others think that the personnel in the general education setting lack the proper training and appropriate strategies to best meet their children's needs and, therefore, advocate for separate classrooms. Perhaps they believe that the physical setting is ill suited due to a lack of resources and appropriate programs (Tomsho, 2007).

It is important to remember that schools and homes are inclusive partners who direct children to become independent, self-regulated thinkers. A plan for monitoring the effectiveness of the educational programs and communicating that progress to families is important. Monitoring may include, but is not limited to, teacher observations, quizzes, pre- and post-tests, graded homework, class participation, portfolios, and reading and math inventories. Communications can be offered at set time intervals, such as quarterly report cards, weekly teacher emails, and conferences outside of the annually scheduled IEP meetings. Also beneficial are positive phone calls to the family indicating that all is fine. It is important for educators to remember how much mileage is obtained when families and schools consistently communicate and collaborate.

Communicating and collaborating with the students in the inclusive classroom can be accomplished in various ways. Solicit oral inventories from younger students or ask older students to complete informal written questionnaires that give them a nonthreatening medium through which to reveal more about themselves. Know what students view as their competencies (stronger intelligences), and capitalize on those strengths. Offer your students valuable, realistic, and timely feedback on their progress and steps toward mastery. Always allow—and encourage—students to ask questions and continually communicate their concerns.

Sometimes co-teachers who work side by side in inclusive classrooms end up finishing each other's sentences. Other times, the situations may be less than harmonious, with teachers fearful of a loss of authority, territory, control, or input. The Co-Teaching Planner (page 157) will go a long way toward encouraging positive and effective communication among teachers in the inclusive classroom and focuses on central co-teaching issues that can be discussed in weekly meetings.

Exact language is an important element of effective communication. For example, instead of saying to an instructional assistant or paraeducator, "Matty can't add," say, "Matty needs to use these counters or a place-value work mat when adding." Vague statements are often misinterpreted. Exact language deletes the guesswork and provides specific guidance.

It is also helpful for co-teachers to attend workshops and staff development opportunities that present "what if" scenarios, such as the following, to increase their own knowledge and to practice, collaborate, and share with their colleagues:

- If a student is calling out, I will _____.
- If a lesson goes wrong, I will _____.
- If extra help is needed, I will _____.

Overall, collaborative attitudes and practices include ongoing productive relationships with families, co-teachers, paraprofessionals, other related staff, and families. Authors Marilyn Friend and Lynne Cook (2009) eloquently define *collaboration* as an interpersonal relationship that develops when parties equally share in decision-making toward a universal goal. Inclusion with ongoing collaboration should be a universal goal for all schools and communities.

Professional Development

Professional development strengthens the entire school staff, from lunchroom aides to administrators. For instance, instructional assistants or paraprofessionals could attend workshops that teach them how to monitor the social skills of a student with autism without creating overdependence, focusing on how and when to fade out support. Bus drivers could learn more about specific physical or emotional disabilities and how to properly address possible scenarios while in transit. Knowledge about disabilities yields increased sensitivities that can positively impact students' educational experiences.

Teachers who join professional development committees to jointly plan for the application of evidence-based practices yield higher educational outcomes for students in their classrooms (Boscardin, 2005). Students prosper when teachers proactively prepare lessons and healthy environments based upon what they learn through workshops, conferences, in-services, independent research, and collegial discussion and planning sessions.

Quality induction programs for new teachers and ongoing professional development for veteran teachers, administrators, and staff are important. This can range from reflective discussions to professional book clubs focusing on specific topics, such as assessments, multiple intelligences, or a type of disability. Sharing ideas with colleagues paves a road of excellence for all learners.

When administrators foster professional learning communities (PLCs), school climates are positive and productive for staff. A PLC focuses more on learning than teaching, emphasizes working collaboratively, and values accountability for results (DuFour, 2004). PLCs often include in-class strategies for students who need help before more intensive remediation is mandated.

If time is an issue, teachers can learn together through digital tools that close the gap between cities across the country, and countries across the world (Ferriter, 2009). Educational wikis and teacher blogs offer collaboration tools for teachers to learn and share expertise, strategies, and experiences across content areas.

Just as students benefit from active learning experiences, teachers also benefit from practicing, sharing, and absorbing content and knowledge on how to teach students through ongoing collaborative, collegial, hands-on learning (Darling-Hammond & Richardson, 2009).

Interventions

As noted earlier, RTI services are offered in appropriate tiers with intensive interventions. The tiers, or levels of support, require much communication and collaboration within the general education classroom among teachers, co-teachers, learning consultants, and other support staff. Collaborative teams write IEPs, 504s, and intervention plans in such a way that clearly emphasizes accountability of outcomes with students' individualized goals, objectives, and programs. Students in all tiers are intended to derive benefits from these collaboratively planned interventions, which often occur in an inclusive classroom.

Effective teacher preparation programs train educators with collaborative and instructional skills to effectively implement Tier 2 and Tier 3 RTI instruction (Brownwell, Sindelar, Kiely, & Danielson, 2010). Following a review of progress, the team makes decisions about whether to offer fewer or more intensive interventions. RTI offers good teaching strategies to students regardless of classifications or labels, but to be effective, these interventions must be collaboratively planned and documented by all personnel involved.

Inclusive interventions start at the top with administrators who listen to and appropriately plan for and respect staff, student, and family needs. Supervisors who offer curriculum strategies, release time to plan, and constructive assistance on ways to disseminate best practices are also vital players who help the interventions connect to the staff, families, and students. Curriculum gains only occur if the staff expand their knowledge of evidence-based practices and learn how to apply them to classroom lessons. Ultimately, the teachers and school staff are the daily educational protagonists whose voices and concerns determine what form inclusion and interventions will take.

Some educators are ill prepared to deliver the appropriate instruction to students with disabilities (Jenkins & Ornelles, 2009; Kamens, Loprete, & Slostad, 2003). Before such teachers can offer appropriate accommodations and modifications, they need to know more about disability classifications and the needs of their students. In-house, district workshops can be both data driven and based upon surveyed teacher needs concerning specific disabilities, management ideas, and appropriate inclusion interventions to sharpen students' skills.

High-quality teacher preparatory programs are important in assisting future educators in the inclusion of students with disabilities in general education settings (Winter, 2006; Mintz, 2007). All educators should embrace professional development and collaboration as means to better serve their students with appropriate interventions and inclusive strategies.

Question to Investigate

How do you collaborate with a colleague who would prefer to do things his or her own way?

Start small, proceed gently, and value the evolutionary element of change. Offer the colleague time to learn and experience outcomes. Always listen to the co-teacher and find something redeeming in the way that he or she is proceeding, and then offer a different slant or perspective. Always offer professional resources or research on good practices that validate your points. Respect each other's differences and create a collaborative atmosphere that says, "Let's do this together."

Lesson Review

Both general education (GE) and special education (SE) teachers can use this sheet to reflect on the success of specific lessons. Check off those items that pertain to this lesson, and provide comments to elaborate.

Lesson Date: Topic: Overall rating for the lesson (using a scale of 1 to 5, with 5 as the highest rating):			
	GE	**SE**	**Comments**
Objective was achieved.			
Ideal support was provided.			
Too much support was provided.			
Majority understood the lesson.			
Co-teaching was effective.			
Student knowledge varied.			
Tasks were too complex.			
Additional help, materials, or support were needed.			
Whole class needs to revisit this topic.			
Some students need to revisit this topic.			
Enrichment activities are required for some students.			

Co-Teaching Planner

The following sheet is to be filled out by both general education and special education teachers to promote collaboration.

Lesson/unit objective:

Materials:

Time needed:

Step-by-step procedure:

Co-teaching choice (for example, one teacher leading and one assisting or parallel teaching):

Technology:

Curriculum-based assessment:

Homework:

Follow-up:

Accommodations needed:

Modifications needed:

Related staff needed:

Family contact:

Administrative support:

Other interventions:

Collaboration Checklist

☐ General educators are given planning time with their co-teachers and instructional assistants to figure out the week's lessons and how to best deliver the curriculum.

☐ Special educators who implement the strategies are offered opportunities for appropriate pre-, inter-, and postplanning with their co-teachers, instructional assistants, related staff, and team members.

☐ Instructional assistants and paraprofessionals are treated as integral inclusive members of the classroom whose input is respected and needed. Guidance is given to them on how they can help the students, such as checking notebooks, monitoring time on task, scribing, and offering encouragement.

☐ Administrators and supervisors listen to and collaborate with their staff and build time into teachers' schedules to effectively problem solve and communicate with each other throughout the week.

☐ Instructional student support or multidisciplinary teams offer ongoing support beyond the scheduled IEP meetings or testing dates. For example, they observe and plan with the teachers, discussing teachers' and students' efforts, progress, and concerns.

☐ Related staff are inclusive members who offer their input. For example, the speech-language pathologist helps students gain conversational skills, and the occupational or physical therapist gives students handwriting tips or helps them to increase other motor functions.

☐ Families are regularly informed on the progress of their children and offered ways to assist in the school's efforts.

☐ Students are aware of daily, weekly, and monthly lesson objectives and are offered realistic feedback on their progress.

TWELVE
Honoring Inclusion

"I'm glad I'm included!"

This succinct sentence represents the most important aspect of the inclusive classroom: the student. The overall purpose of this book is to offer academic interventions that include students' goals and passions. Educators who offer their students ways to recognize and then better capitalize on their preferred intelligences, learning styles, passions, and goals teach students first and their disciplines second.

Disability Awareness

General education teachers need to continually heighten their disability awareness, attitudes, and confidence levels to effectively teach students who have disabilities. Even when educators believe that students with special needs belong in inclusive settings, if they view the students from a deficit paradigm, highlighting what they cannot do, then the results for those students are lowered (Campbell, Milbourne, & Silverman, 2001). The learning environment and school atmosphere have a strong influence on how students perceive their value (Tomlinson, 2003). Therefore, teachers need to let their students know that they are an integral component of the learning process regardless of what IDEA label or RTI tier they may be categorized with.

Though the following poem by Dick Sobsey was written in 1976, it still speaks to educators and students of today.

The Ballad of Special EDDIE

Part I

> This is a story about special Eddie,
>
> Diagnosed as a bowl of neuro-spaghetti
>
> His mother sat with her friends and cried
>
> While his father kept it all inside
>
> (If you think you have heard this tale before
>
> You will know for sure when you read some more)

---

continued ➲

When he was five his mom took Eddie
To school, but they said, He's not ready—
He will wet his pants, he will get in fights
He will freak out under the fluorescent lights.
It's for his good, we have got to spare him—
A special preschool might prepare him.
So that day in warm September
Was one for Eddie to remember,
For that decision really led
To ten more years of Special Ed.
Special teachers, special books,
Extra special dirty looks.
BD, LD, TMR?
How we wonder what you are!
Though Eddie's social life was plain,
He had more names than kings of Spain.

The school psychologist declared,
He's neurologically impaired
With overlays (coincidental)
Social and environmental.
Although the problem just might be
His unilaterality.
The case is really so pathetic—
The cause is probably genetic.

Eddie never did deny it.
He just sat back and he kept quiet.
Year by year, the time went past.
In special seventh grade at last,
His sixteenth birthday finally neared,
Then Ed dropped out and disappeared.

His teacher wondered what went wrong;
It worried her, but not for long.

She'd seen this kind of thing before
And frankly she expected more.
Eddie's not the first or last
Forgotten as the years go past.

Part II

Down in a bar on Highway 3,
Today some guy sits next to me
And the bartender brings him a short draft beer,
Smiles and says, Hey, Eddie's here!
Then this beautiful girl runs across the floor
And gives him a look I've seen before.

She says, When you want to leave, I'm ready.
You're really something special, Eddie.
So he told his friends he would be back
And left in a dark blue Cadillac.
My drink went down like a glass of fire—
If it wasn't Eddie, I'm a liar.

I swallowed my drink, and swallowed my pride
And asked, Who's that who stepped outside?
Eddie, they laughed, Don't you know that face?
He's the guy who owns this place,
The laundromat and the bowling alley . . .
And half the land around the valley.

So he owned some little ginmill joint . . .
What's the moral and what's the point?
I sat awhile and kept on drinking,
Thought and thought and kept on thinking . . .
Does it take brains to make a buck?
Poor folks say it's mostly luck;
But he looked happy too, I guess,
In any terms he's a success.

continued ➲

He's not the first and not the last one.

Seems that someone pulled a fast one.

Did we help him succeed

And fill some special learning need?

Or did we only make it tough

For him to show his native stuff?

District schools around the nation

Play the game, Evaluation

Share the credit, pass the blame,

The funding tells who wins the game.

Uncertainty must never show . . .

So, never say that you don't know.

Maybe we should take our turn

At saying, We've a lot to learn.

And when we get OUR homework done,

Someday, we might just help someone.

Here's to that day of self-reliance

WHEN MAGIC ACTS BECOME A SCIENCE.

(Used with permission by Dick Sobsey, University of Alberta, 1976.)

Helping All Learners to Succeed

As this book has outlined, inclusive engagements will vary—direct instruction, more guidance, enrichment, repetition, small-group instruction, one-on-one interventions, related services, and other behavioral, social, emotional, communicative, physical, and learning accommodations and support. While interventions are intended to help students with special needs, they can actually benefit all students in the class. Well-trained teachers can implement best practices to ensure that each student receives optimum learning experiences in the optimum environment.

Students on the autism spectrum often benefit from visual prompts that allow the students to see transitions and structures, making situations more predictable (Fittipaldi & Mowling, 2009). What is wonderful about inclusion is that strategies such as posting transitions, schedules, and other such visuals as constant reminders are advantageous to all students, not just those with autism or those who have IEPs or 504 plans.

Students with and without special needs often need help to generalize, apply, and connect to concepts and topics, and to see things from different perspectives. All students in all grades have experienced boredom in school. Often, the motivation to learn determines whether or not understanding is gained. Teachers who connect their lessons to their students' lives are able to effectively deliver concepts, motivating students to gain more understanding. This strategy is just as effective for students without special needs as it is for students with special needs.

Teaching all students within the inclusive classroom is sometimes a challenging task, but not an impossible one, if you believe that successful outcomes will be achieved. Inclusion often requires additional preparation and a great deal more collaboration, flexibility, and patience. However, these added efforts honor students as integral members of the classroom and as future productive adults within inclusive societies.

Inclusion as an Evolutionary Process

Inclusion is an evolutionary process, and well-planned lessons yield gradual successes. What works effectively for one student with a learning difference will not necessarily be the best practice for another student with a learning difference. All students are unique, and educators must recognize, honor, and capitalize on students' strengths while providing inclusion strategies that respect students' differences. Academic, emotional, behavioral, and social skills are nurtured and strengthened through time as students advance in the grades.

When inclusion interventions and connections are continually explored, expanded, and reflected upon, we obtain positive results. We honor students' abilities by connecting the learning to the students' emotions, goals, and interests, making education truly *special* for every student.

Question to Investigate

What's next on the inclusion horizon?

There is no clear-cut image projecting on that GE/SE crystal ball. Inclusion interventions are practiced with increased diversity across districts within the state or province, states or provinces across the country, and countries around the world. Roles and expectations of schools change as legislation changes, often with more demands put on staff and students. Higher test scores and increased accountability seem to be the destination, but how will this translate to instructing diverse students in inclusive classrooms? Only time will determine whether those outcomes are realistic and whether the statistics meaningfully translate to productive learning. If collaboration, professional training, continual learning, and increased preparation and acceptance are standard practices, the horizon will be bright. Early interventions within general education classrooms before labeling occurs and high expectations for all students are steps in the right direction. The bottom line is that inclusion interventions involve more than grade-level or school successes. Effective inclusion interventions connect to the individual students.

Sum It Up

Collect your thoughts about inclusion in the following chart. In the heart column, write what you love about inclusion; under the question mark, write any questions or concerns about inclusion; and write important inclusive points under the star. Sum It Up can also be used as a generic graphic organizer by students for any content area.

♥	?	★

APPENDIX A
Abbreviations

AA-AAS	alternate assessments on alternate achievement standards
AAC	augmentative and alternative communication
AA-GLAS	alternate assessments on grade-level achievement standards
AA-MAS	alternate assessments on modified achievement standards
ABA	applied behavior analysis
ADA	Americans with Disabilities Act
ADAAA	Americans with Disabilities Act Amendments Act
ADHD	attention-deficit/hyperactivity disorder
ASD	autism spectrum disorder
AT	assistive technology
ATAP	Assistive Technology Act Project
BICS	basic interpersonal communication skills
BIP	behavior improvement plan
CAI	computer-assisted instruction
CALLA	cognitive academic language learning approach
CALP	cognitive academic language proficiency
CAPD	central auditory processing disorder
CAST	Center for Applied Special Technology
CBA	curriculum-based assessment
CBM	curriculum-based measurement
CEC	Council for Exceptional Children
CSR	collaborative strategic reading
CST	child study team
DBQ	document-based question
DI	differentiated instruction
DRA	Developmental Reading Assessment
EBP	evidence-based practice
ED	emotional disturbance
EIS	early intervening services
EL	English learner

ESEA	Elementary and Secondary Education Act
ESY	extended school year
FAPE	free and appropriate public education
FBA	functional behavioral assessment
GE	general education
IAES	interim alternative educational setting
IDEA	Individuals with Disabilities Education Act
IDEIA	Individuals with Disabilities Education Improvement Act
IEP	individualized education program
INTASC	Interstate New Teacher Assessment and Support Consortium
IST	instructional support team
LEA	local education agency
LRE	least restrictive environment
MDT	multidisciplinary team
NCLB	No Child Left Behind
OCD	obsessive-compulsive disorder
OCR	optical character recognition
ODD	oppositional defiant disorder
OHI	other health impairment
OT	occupational therapy
PALS	peer-assisted learning strategies
PECS	picture exchange communication system
PDD	pervasive developmental disorder
PLAAFP	present level of academic achievement and functional performance
PLC	professional learning community
PT	physical therapy
RT	reciprocal teaching
RTI	response to intervention
SE	special education
SLD	specific learning disability
SOP	summary of performance
SRL	self-regulated learner
SST	student support team
STO	short-term objective
TBI	traumatic brain injury
UbD	understanding by design
UDL	universal design for learning
VAKT	visual, auditory, kinesthetic/tactile
WPM	words per minute
ZPD	zone of proximal development

APPENDIX B
Legal Aspects of Inclusion

Legislation influences the writing of individualized education programs (IEPs) and the monitoring of individual student progress within inclusive classrooms. Many students fall under diversified and often shared general and special education umbrellas. The text that follows elaborates more about how legislation enters inclusive classrooms.

The Individuals with Disabilities Education Act (IDEA) guarantees that all students will receive free and appropriate public education (FAPE); states receive funding as specified under part B of IDEA. IDEA applies to students who fall under the classifications of autism, multiple disabilities, traumatic brain injury, specific learning disability, visual impairment or blindness, deaf-blindness, hearing impairment, speech-language impairments, deafness, other health impairments, orthopedic impairments, emotional disturbance, and intellectual disabilities (still labeled mental retardation under IDEA). The general education classroom with or without support services is the first option of student placement if it will appropriately service a student's needs. Prior to IDEA, when students with special needs first entered school systems, they were often educated in separate classrooms. Today, many students with IDEA classifications are educated in the inclusive classroom environment, alongside their peers, in preparation for productive independent lives alongside adults with whom they have shared successful prior academic and social school experiences.

If a child is thought to have a disability, the IEP school support team meets with the family to obtain feedback. It then collects information from a variety of sources to determine eligibility. This evaluation collects both formal (for example, cognitive tests) and informal (for example, observations and interviews) data to determine if a disability is present. A team of professionals—such as a social worker, learning disabilities consultant, and school psychologist—then compares the child's progress and testing results to typical achievements and expectations of child development. Considerations are given to the child's performance in a variety of environments, such as the home, community, and school.

Parental consent is always required for initial evaluations and reevaluations concerning eligibility for special education services under IDEA. An initial evaluation is conducted within sixty calendar days of parental consent with families kept in the loop and informed of their rights. Reevaluations are conducted every three years, unless the parent and public agency agree that such an evaluation is unnecessary. If disputes regarding students' services and educational decisions between parents or families and the school occur, informal meetings are the first course of action before more formal due process hearings begin.

If a child is determined to be eligible for special education services, a local education agency (LEA) and a local team, such as a student support team (SST), write an individualized education program for the child. The IEP includes the child's present level of academic achievement and functional performance (PLAAFP) with specific details that outline how the child's disability impacts involvement in the general education setting with regards to the curriculum and related activities. If the student is educated in an inclusive classroom and eligible for other special education services and placements, the IEP contains specific information that lists the types, dates, and duration of services, accommodations, and modifications. Supplementary aids and services also refer to nonacademic and extracurricular activities. Assessment information and ways to monitor and communicate the student's progress to his or her family are also indicated.

Short-term objectives with specific benchmarks are not required for students who take district assessments (IDEIA, 2004). If a student has the classification of a specific learning disability, then that student may or may not have goals stated, depending on whether he or she is expected to achieve the same outcomes as the curriculum delineates. As an example, there may be study skill, communication, or occupational therapy goals if evaluations determine that the student requires those related objectives but no separate reading goals if the goal is for the student to succeed in the general education classroom. Some school districts translate this to mean that only students with more significant disabilities or only those receiving replacement instruction have short-term objectives, not students who are instructed in inclusive environments. The students who take alternate assessments have written goals that are aligned to achieve curriculum standards comparable to the grade-level standards of students within the general education population. Some students may also require extended school year (ESY) services if it is determined that the student would lose skills over a summer or vacation break.

Annual goals are set and monitored and include measurable academic and functional goals as appropriate to meet each child's needs as related to his or her disability. For example, in order to determine a student's reading fluency, he or she may take a test to determine the number of words accurately read per minute. After a set period of time, a posttest is given to measure the effectiveness of the reading interventions. Curriculum-based measurements (CBMs) may in this case be a graded word list or a reading passage to determine fluency and comprehension. Overall, CBMs are a practical way to ascertain how students are functioning in a classroom and are often more valuable than a standardized assessment that just gives a snapshot of a student's knowledge for that day or a few days of what is often viewed as a grueling testing period. Informal observations, ratings, and portfolios of both academic and behavioral competencies help document students' progress within inclusive classrooms. If changes are made to IEPs, parents are involved and informed through meetings or other contacts. Every person involved in the deliverance or implementation of an IEP reviews the document.

With regards to discipline, schools may review students' needs on a case-by-case basis. A manifestation determination is conducted to determine whether the student's behavior was related to his or her disability or if it was a failure of the school to properly implement that student's IEP. If a student with a disability breaks a school rule, then the parents and school must agree upon a change of placement. If no agreement is reached, and the child is facing more than ten consecutive days of suspension, then the parent, family member, or guardian may assert the "stay put rule," which allows the student to remain in his or her placement until revisions are made to the IEP. If the suspension is fewer than ten days, the school can offer the student ways to make up the missed work but does not have to provide alternate education for that time period. In the event of unacceptable behavior such as carrying weapons or illegal drugs, or causing serious bodily harm, a student may be removed for up to forty-five days and placed in an interim alternative educational setting (IAES) regardless of what the manifestation determination reveals.

If the behavior in question had a direct and substantial relationship to the student's disability or was the result of the LEA's failure to implement the IEP, then the student's program is reviewed and a functional behavioral assessment (FBA) and behavior improvement plan (BIP) are created. The FBAs with written BIPs of some students are frequently revisited to continually provide appropriate services that address each student's emotional difference. The staff within the inclusive classroom enlist the help of trained staff such as a behavior therapist who may set up a program to improve or extinguish the unwanted behaviors and replace them with acceptable behaviors. If a student has uncontrollable outbursts, requires more social skills, or is impulsive and needs to refine his or her behavior, a BIP is a necessary part of that student's IEP.

When the Individuals with Disabilities Education Improvement Act of 2004 (IDEIA) passed, RTI was implemented in school districts. RTI helps students with learning differences before more formal intensive evaluations and classifications are given. With RTI as an option, students receive interventions in the general education classroom with documented and monitored research-based programs that value evidence-based practices (EBP). It is no longer assumed that students with special needs will be automatically pulled out for separate instruction. RTI includes a combination of tiered instruction and core instruction, smaller groups receiving targeted programs, and more intensive programs for other groups of students with EBPs.

Another piece of legislation, commonly known as Section 504 or simply 504, specifies that when life activities such as speaking, walking, working, caring for oneself, eating, sleeping, standing, lifting, bending, learning, reading, concentrating, thinking, and communicating are limited, student eligibility for specialized services and classroom accommodations is considered. School personnel gather information from families and other sources (for example, medical experts, school performance records, and teacher observations).

Section 504 plans grew out of the Rehabilitation Act of 1973 and are monitored by the Office of Civil Rights. This act's purpose was to end discrimination against people with disabilities. The 504 plans are similar to IEPs in that these plans offer accommodations and related services with family input, but the funding that school districts receive differs.

Some students may receive preferential seating, testing accommodations, or modified schedules as stated in their 504 plans. These plans may provide trained staff equipped to give an EpiPen, monitor glucose levels, teach appropriate calming measures, or ensure that unsafe snacks are excluded from the classroom for students with health issues such as asthma, diabetes, epilepsy, or food allergies. These plans help many students with a range of needs, from a student with ADHD receiving extra time on a test to a student with short stature requiring a modified chair or desk height. Overall, 504 plans offer reasonable accommodations to students in inclusive classrooms who do not always fall under IDEA classifications.

When the Elementary and Secondary Education Act (ESEA) of 1965 was reauthorized and renamed by George W. Bush as No Child Left Behind (NCLB), schools were held accountable for producing students who could achieve academic proficiencies. Research-based programs and increased testing were emphasized along with more school scrutiny and parental options to ensure that students were receiving educational programs that matched their needs. As this book is going to press, ESEA 2001 is up for reauthorization again, with changes on the horizon that may lessen sanctions for nonperforming schools by reviewing a multitude of factors to somewhat level the playing field for student populations, such as alternative schools and differing requirements and accountability for students with more severe cognitive impairments. Reauthorization may involve more flexibility for different subgroups to acknowledge students' unique needs and assessments based on more than one standardized test, such as portfolios or observations (Hardy, 2009). There may also be changes that acknowledge growth, not just passing grades.

The Americans with Disabilities Act (ADA), a document that opened doors in the private sector for people with disabilities who in the past had been denied access, has also impacted inclusive environments. The ADA (1990) was a legislative milestone in that it changed the way the public accepted people with disabilities. It allowed the provision of reasonable accommodations in areas such as transportation, communication, and employment for people with mental or physical impairments who were limited in life activities. It was amended in 2008 as the Americans with Disabilities Act Amendments Act (ADAAA), which broadened the definition of a disability. This antidiscrimination law protects people with limitations in the activities of communicating, self-caring, walking, breathing, seeing, hearing, speaking, learning, working, eating, sleeping, standing, lifting, bending, reading, concentrating, and thinking. This legislation enters school systems, for example, if a student with ADHD has difficulty concentrating, if a parent who is deaf attends a school meeting and needs a sign language interpreter, or if someone in a wheelchair needs access to a school building. Although ADA usually comes into play in the private sector, communities and schools are also impacted by this legislation.

Inclusive classrooms are influenced by legislative mandates that require equal opportunities for all students regardless of evidenced differences. Education is not for some students, but for all students. This includes the students with above-average skills and those with different learning, physical, sensory, communicative, emotional, behavioral, social, and developmental needs. Legislation such as IDEA and ADA exist to guarantee that inclusion becomes a reality in all classrooms and all walks of life.

References and Resources

Abeel, S. (2007). *My thirteenth winter: A memoir*. New York: Scholastic.

Adams, G., & Carnine, D. (2003). Direct instruction. In H. L. Swanson, K. R. Harris, & S. Graham (Eds.), *Handbook of learning disabilities* (pp. 403–416). New York: Guilford Press. Accessed at www.nichcy.org /Research/Summaries/Pages/Abstract1.aspx on May 3, 2010.

Ahlfeld, K. (2010). Hands-on learning with a hands-off approach for professional development. *School Library Month*, *26*(6), 16–18.

Algozzine, B., Browder, D., Karvonen, M., Test, D. W., & Wood, W. M. (2001). Effects of interventions to promote self-determination for individuals with disabilities. *Review of Educational Research*, *71*, 219–277.

Allsopp, D., Kyger, M., Lovin, L., Gerretson, H., Carson, K., & Ray, S. (2008). Mathematics dynamic assessment: Informal assessment that responds to the needs of struggling learners in mathematics. *Teaching Exceptional Children*, *40*(3), 6–16.

American Educational Research Association (AERA). (2009). Ensuring early literacy success. *Research Points*, *6*(1), 1–4. Accessed at www.aera.net/uploadedFiles/Journals_and_Publications/Research_Points/RP_Winter09_PDF .pdf on February 16, 2010.

American Speech-Language-Hearing Association. (2002). *Augmentative and alternative communication: Knowledge and skills for service delivery*. Rockville, MD: Author. Accessed at www.asha.org/docs/html /KS2002–00067.html on May 5, 2009.

Angelle, P., & Bilton, L. (2009). Confronting the unknown: Principal preparation training in issues related to special education. *AASA Journal of Scholarship & Practice*, *5*(4), 5–9.

Arreaga-Mayer, C., Utley, C. A., Perdomo-Rivera, C., & Greenwood, C. R. (2003). Ecobehavioral assessment of instructional contexts in bilingual special education programs for English language learners at risk for developmental disabilities. *Focus on Autism and Other Developmental Disabilities*, *18*(1), 28–40.

Artiles, A., Trent, S., & Palmer, J. (2004). Culturally diverse students in special education: Legacies and prospects. In J. A. Banks & C. A. McGee Banks (Eds.), *Handbook of research on multicultural education* (2nd ed., pp. 716–735). San Francisco: Wiley.

Artiles, A. J., Rueda, R., Salazar, J. J., & Higareda, I. (2005). Within-group diversity in minority disproportionate representation: English language learners in urban school districts. *Exceptional Children*, *71*, 283–300.

Atherton, J. T. (2010). Learning and teaching: Assimilation and accommodation. Accessed at www.learning andteaching.info/learning/assimacc.htm on September 4, 2010.

Atwood, T. (2005). *What is Asperger syndrome?* Accessed at www.aspergersyndrome.org/Articles/What-is -Asperger-Syndrome-.aspx on February 15, 2010.

Baca, L., & Cervantes, H. (2004). *The bilingual special education interface* (4th ed.). Upper Saddle River, NJ: Pearson/Merrill/Prentice Hall.

Baker, J. (2003). *The social skills picture book.* Arlington, TX: Future Horizons.

Baker, J. (2008). *No more meltdowns.* Arlington, TX: Future Horizons.

Baker, S., Gersten, R., & Scanlon, D. (2002). Procedural facilitators and cognitive strategies: Tools for unraveling the mysteries of comprehension and the writing process, and for providing meaningful access to the general curriculum. *Learning Disabilities Research & Practice, 17*, 65–77.

Bandura, A. (1977). *Social learning theory.* New York: General Learning Press.

Barton, R., & Stepanek, J. (2009). Three tiers to success. *Principal Leadership, 9*(8), 16–20.

Barton-Arwood, S., Murrow, L., Lane, K., & Jolivette, K. (2005). Project IMPROVE: Improving teachers' ability to address students' social needs. *Education & Treatment of Children, 28*(4), 430–443.

Bausch, M., & Ault, M. (2008). Assistive technology implementation plan: A tool for improving outcomes. *Teaching Exceptional Children, 41*(1), 6–14.

Bausch, M. E., Quinn, B. S., Chung, Y., Ault, M. J., & Behrmann, M. M. (2009). Assistive technology in the individualized education plan: Analysis of policies across ten states. *Journal of Special Education Leadership, 22*(1), 9–23.

Baxter, J., Woodward, J., Voorhies, J., & Wong, J. (2002). We talk about it, but do they get it? *Learning Disabilities Research & Practice, 17*, 173–185.

Beattie, J., Jordan, L., & Algozzine, B. (2006). *Making inclusion work: Effective practices for ALL teachers.* Thousand Oaks, CA: Corwin Press.

Beck, I. L., McKeown, M. G., & Kucan, L. (2002). *Bringing words to life: Robust vocabulary instruction.* New York: Guilford Press.

Begeny, J., & Martens, B. (2007). Inclusionary education in Italy: A literature review and call for more empirical research. *Remedial and Special Education, 28*, 80–94.

Bellini, S. (2006). *Building social relationships: A systematic approach to teaching social interaction skills to children and adolescents with autism spectrum disorders and other social disorders.* Shawnee Mission, KS: Autism Asperger Publishing.

Bernstein, S. (2009). Phonology, decoding, and lexical compensation in vowel spelling errors made by children with dyslexia. *Reading and Writing: An Interdisciplinary Journal, 22*(3), 307–331.

Bhattacharya, A., & Ehri, L. (2004). Graphosyllabic analysis helps adolescent struggling readers read and spell words. *Journal of Learning Disabilities, 37*, 331–348.

Black, P., & Wiliam, D. (1998). Assessment and classroom learning. *Educational Assessment: Principles, Policy, and Practice, 5*(1), 7–74.

Blair, K. S. C., Umbreit, J., & Dunlap, G. (2007). Promoting inclusion and peer participation through assessment-based intervention. *Topics in Early Childhood Education, 27*(3), 134–147.

Blom-Hoffman, J., Wilcox, K., Dunn, L., Leff, S., & Power, T. (2008). Family involvement in school-based health promotion: Bringing nutrition information home. *School Psychology Review, 37*(4), 567–577.

Bock, M. A. (2001). SODA strategy: Enhancing the social interaction skills of youngsters with Asperger's syndrome. *Intervention in School and Clinic, 36*, 272–278.

Bond, M., & Wasik, B. (2009). Conversation stations: Promoting language development in young children. *Early Childhood Education Journal, 36*(6), 467–473.

Boon, R., Fore, C., Ayres, K., & Spencer, V. (2005). The effects of cognitive organizers to facilitate content-area learning for students with mild disabilities: A pilot study. *Journal of Instructional Psychology, 32*(2), 101–117.

Boscardin, M. L. (2005). The administrative role in transforming secondary schools to support inclusive evidence-based practices. *American Secondary Education, 33*(3), 21–32.

Brennan, H. R. (2005). *Behavioral and social effects of inclusion at the preschool level: Exploring an integrated early childhood classroom.* Unpublished master's thesis, Keuka College. Accessed at www.eric.ed.gov on May 6, 2010.

British Columbia Ministry of Children and Family Development. (2001). *Transition planning for youth with special needs.* Victoria, British Columbia, Canada: Author. Accessed at www.mcf.gov.bc.ca/spec_needs/pdf/support_guide.pdf on April 17, 2009.

Broer, S., Doyle, M., & Giangreco, M. (2005). Perspectives of students with intellectual disabilities about their experiences with paraprofessional support. *Exceptional Children, 71,* 415–430.

Browder, D., Ahlgrim-Delzell, L., Courtade-Little, G., & Snell, E. (2006). General curriculum access. In M. Snell & F. Brown (Eds.), *Instruction of students with severe disabilities* (6th ed., pp. 489–525). Upper Saddle River, NJ: Pearson/Merrill/Prentice Hall.

Browder, D., Flowers, C., Ahlgrim-Delzell, L., Karvonen, M., Spooner, F., & Algozzine, R. (2004). The alignment of alternate assessment content with academic and functional curricula. *Journal of Special Education, 37*(4), 211–223.

Browder, D., Spooner, F., Ahlgrim-Delzell, L., Harris, A., & Wakeman, S. (2008). A meta-analysis on teaching mathematics to students with significant cognitive disabilities. *Exceptional Children, 74*(4), 407–432.

Browder, D. M., Spooner, F., Algozzine, R., Ahlgrim-Delzell, L., Flowers, C., & Karvonen, M. (2003). What we know and need to know about alternate assessment. *Exceptional Children, 70,* 45–61.

Browder, D., Wakeman, S., Spooner, F., Ahlgrim-Delzell, L., & Algozzine, B. (2006). Research on reading instruction for individuals with significant cognitive disabilities. *Exceptional Children, 72,* 392–408.

Brownell, M., Adams, A., Sindelar, P., Waldron, N., & Vanhover, S. (2006). The role of teacher qualities in collaboration. *Exceptional Children, 72,* 169–185.

Brownell, M., Sindelar, P., Kiely, M., & Danielson, L. (2010). Special education teacher quality and preparation: Exposing foundations, constructing a new model. *Exceptional Children, 76,* 357–377.

Bryant, D. P., Vaughn, S., Linan-Thompson, S., Ugel, N., Hamff, A., & Hougen, M. (2000). Reading outcomes for students with and without reading disabilities in general education middle-school content area classes. *Learning Disability Quarterly, 23,* 238–252.

Buckley, S., Bird, G., & Sacks, B. (2006). Evidence that we can change the profile from a study of inclusive education. *Down Syndrome Research and Practice, 9*(3), 51–53.

Burdette, P. (2007). *Response to intervention as it relates to early intervening services.* Alexandria, VA: National Association of State Directors of Special Education. Accessed at www.projectforum.org on January 30, 2010.

Burke, K., & Sutherland, C. (2004). Attitudes toward inclusion: Knowledge vs. experience. *Education, 125*(2), 163–172.

Burns, M. (1994). *I hate mathematics! book.* New York: Scholastic Books.

Campbell, P., Milbourne, S., & Silverman, C. (2001). Strengths-based child portfolios: A professional development activity to alter perspectives of children with special needs. *Topics in Early Childhood Special Education, 21*(3), 152–162.

Capizzi, A. (2008). From assessment to annual goal: Engaging a decision-making process in writing measurable IEPs. *Teaching Exceptional Children, 41*(1), 18–25.

Carnahan, C., Williamson, P., Clarke, L., & Sorensen, R. (2009). A systematic approach for supporting para-educators in educational settings: A guide for teachers. *Teaching Exceptional Children, 41*(5), 34–43.

Cascella, P., & McNamara, K. (2005). Empowering students with severe disabilities to actualize communication skills. *Teaching Exceptional Children, 37*(3), 38–43.

Causton-Theoharis, J. (2009). The golden rule of providing support in inclusive classrooms: Support others as you wish to be supported. *Teaching Exceptional Children, 42*(2), 36–43.

Causton-Theoharis, J. N., & Malmgren, K. W. (2005). Increasing peer interaction for students with severe disabilities via paraprofessional training. *Exceptional Children, 71*, 431–444.

Chamberlain, S. (2005). Kathleen McConnell Fad and James R. Patton: A practical perspective on functional assessments and behavior intervention plans. *Intervention in School & Clinic, 40*(3), 161–170.

Chandler-Olcott, K., & Kluth, P. (2009). Why everyone benefits from including students with autism in literacy classrooms. *The Reading Teacher, 62*(7), 548–557.

Childre, A., Sands, J., & Pope, S. (2009). Backward design: Targeting depth of understanding for all learners. *Educational Leadership, 41*(5), 6–14.

Chitiyo, M., & Wheeler, J. (2009). Challenges faced by school teachers in implementing positive behavior support in their school systems. *Remedial and Special Education, 30*(1), 58–63.

Chmelynski, C. (2006). ADHD play teaches what testing can't touch: Humanity. *Education Digest: Essential Readings Condensed for Quick Review, 72*(3), 10–13.

Chorzempa, B., & Lapidua, L. (2009). To find yourself, think for yourself: Using Socratic discussions in inclusive classrooms. *Teaching Exceptional Children, 41*(3), 54–59.

Cloud, J. (2009, April 13). Better learning through fidgeting. *TIME, 173*(14), 61.

Cochran-Smith, M. (2004). *Walking the road: Race, diversity, and social justice in teacher education.* New York: Teachers College Press.

Cole, J., & Wasburn-Moses, L. (2010). Going beyond "the math wars." *Teaching Exceptional Children, 42*(4), 14–20.

Conderman, G. (2003). Using portfolios in undergraduate special education teacher programs. *Preventing School Failure, 47*(3), 106–112.

Conroy, M. A., Dunlap, G., Clarke, S., & Alter, P. J. (2005). A descriptive analysis of positive behavioral intervention research with younger children with challenging behavior. *Topics in Early Childhood Special Education, 25*, 157–166.

Cook, R. (2004). *Adapting early childhood curricula in inclusive settings.* Upper Saddle River, NJ: Pearson/Merrill/Prentice Hall.

Cortiella, C. (2005). *NCLB: Determining appropriate assessment accommodations for students with disabilities.* New York: National Center for Learning Disabilities. Accessed at www.ncld.org/publications-a-more/parent-advocacy-guides/no-child-left-behind-determining-appropriate-assessment-accommodations-for-students-with-disabilities on March 1, 2010.

Council for Exceptional Children. (2007). *CEC performance-based standards.* Accessed at www.cec.sped.org/ps/perf_based_stds/standards.html on February 23, 2010.

Courtade, G., Spooner, F., & Browder, D. (2007). A review of studies with students with significant cognitive disabilities that link to science standards. *Research and Practice in Severe Disabilities, 32*, 45–49.

Crain, W. (1985). *Theories of development.* Upper Saddle River, NJ: Prentice-Hall.

Crisman, B. (2008). Inclusive programming for students with autism. *Principal, 88*(2), 28–32.

D'Allura, T. (2002). Enhancing the social interaction skills of preschoolers with visual impairments. *Journal of Visual Impairment & Blindness, 96*(8), 576.

Damasio, A. (2003). *Looking for Spinoza: Joy, sorrow, and the feeling brain.* New York: Houghton Mifflin Harcourt.

Darling-Hammond, L., & Richardson, N. (2009). Teaching learning: What matters? *Educational Leadership, 66*(5), 46–53.

Deshler, D., Ellis, E., & Lenz, B. K. (1996). *Teaching adolescents with learning disabilities: Strategies and methods.* Denver, CO: Love.

Diamond, K., Hong, S., & Tu, H. (2009). Physical disability preschool children's inclusion decisions. *Journal of Applied Developmental Psychology, 30*(2), 75–81.

Dillon, N. (2006). Multiple choice. *American School Board Journal, 193*(1), 22–25.

Doing What Works. *School principal/reflective leadership strategies.* Accessed at http://dww.ed.gov/ on September 7, 2009.

Dollaghan, C. A. (2007). *The handbook of evidence-based practice in communication disorders.* Baltimore: Brookes.

Dong, Y. (2009). Linking to prior learning. *Educational Leadership, 66*(7), 26–31.

DuFour, R. (2004). Schools are learning communities. *Educational Leadership, 61*(8), 6–11.

Dukes, C., & Lamar-Dukes, P. (2009). Inclusion by design: Engineering inclusive practices in secondary schools. *Teaching Exceptional Children, 41*(3), 16–23.

Dull, L., & van Garderen, D. (2005). Bringing the story back into history: Teaching social studies to children with learning disabilities. *Preventing School Failure, 49*(3), 27–31.

Hawkins, J. D., Kosterman, R., Catalano, R. F., Hill, K. G., & Abbott, R. D. (2008). Effects of social development intervention in childhood 15 years later. *Archives of Pediatrics & Adolescent Medicine, 162*(12), 1133–1141.

Dunst, C. J., Trivette, C. M., & Cutspec, P. A. (2002). Toward an operational definition of evidence-based practices. *Centerscope: Evidence-Based Approaches to Early Childhood Development, 1*, 1–10.

DuPaul, G., & Eckert, T. (1997).The effects of school-based interventions for attention deficit hyperactivity disorder: A meta-analysis. *School Psychology Review, 26*, 5–27.

Edgemon, E., Jablonski, B., & Lloyd, J. (2006). Large-scale assessments: A teacher's guide to making decisions about accommodations. *Teaching Exceptional Children, 38*(3), 6–11.

Edward, B. (1999). *The new drawing on the right side of the brain.* New York: Tarcher/Penguin Books.

Egilson, S., & Traustadottir, R. (2009). Assistance to pupils with physical disabilities in regular schools: Promoting inclusion or creating dependency? *European Journal of Special Needs Education, 24*(1), 21–36.

Epstein, M., Atkins, M., Cullinan, D., Kutash, K., & Weaver, R. (2008). *Reducing behavior problems in the elementary school classroom: A practice guide* (NCEE No. 2008–012). Washington, DC: National Center for Education Evaluation and Regional Assistance, Institute of Education Sciences, U.S. Department of Education. Accessed at http://ies.ed.gov/ncee/wwc/publications/practiceguides on February 3, 2010.

Ervin, R. A. (2008). *Considering tier 3 within a response-to-intervention model.* Accessed at www.rtinetwork.org on February 1, 2010.

Espin, C., Shin, J., & Busch, T. (2005). Curriculum-based measurement in the content areas: Vocabulary matching as an indicator of progress in social studies learning. *Journal of Learning Disabilities, 38*(4), 353–363.

Ferguson, D. (2008). International trends in inclusive education: The continuing challenge to teach each one and everyone. *European Journal of Special Needs, 23*(2), 109–120.

Ferri, B. A., & Connor, D. J. (2005). In the shadow of Brown: Special education and overrepresentation of students of color. *Remedial and Special Education, 26*, 93–100.

Ferriter, B. (2009). Learning with blogs and wikis. *Educational Leadership, 66*(5), 34–38.

Field, S. (1996). Self-determination instructional strategies for youth with learning disabilities. *Journal of Learning Disabilities, 29*, 40–52.

Field, S., & Hoffman, A. (1996). *Steps to self-determination*. Austin, TX: Pro-Ed.

Fittipaldi, J., & Mowling, C. (2009). Using visual supports for students with autism in physical education. *The Journal of Physical Education & Dance, 80*(2), 39–43.

Fletcher, J., Lyon, G., Fuchs, L., & Barnes, M. (2007). *Learning disabilities: From identification to intervention*. New York: Guilford Press.

Foorman, B. R., & Al Otaiba, S. (2009). Reading remediation: State of the art. In K. Pugh & P. McCardle (Eds.), *How children learn to read: Current issues and new directions in the integration of cognition, neurobiology and genetics of reading and dyslexia research and practice* (pp. 257–275). New York: Psychology Press.

Foran, L. (2009). Listening to music: Helping children regulate their emotions and improve learning in the classroom. *Educational Horizons, 88*(1), 51–58.

Frankel, H. (2007, October 12). Another way of working. *Times Educational Supplement, 4758*, 44–45.

Fredembach, B., de Boisferon, A. H., & Gentaz, E. (2009). Learning of arbitrary association between visual and auditory novel stimuli in adults: The "bond effect" of haptic exploration. *PLoS ONE, 4*(3), e4844. Accessed at www.plosone.org on May 6, 2010.

Frederickson, N., Simmonds, E., Evans, L., & Soulsby, C. (2007). Assessing the social and affective outcomes of inclusion. *British Journal of Special Education, 34*(2), 105–115.

Friend, M., & Cook, L. (2009). *Interactions: Collaborative skills for school professionals* (6th ed.). Boston: Allyn & Bacon.

Fuchs, D., Fuchs, L., & Stecker, P. (2010). The blurring of special education in a new continuum of general education placements and services. *Exceptional Children, 76*(3), 301–323.

Fuchs, D., Mathes, P. G., & Fuchs, L. S. (1995). *Peabody peer-assisted learning strategies (PALS): Math methods*. Nashville, TN: Peabody College, Vanderbilt University.

Galef Institute. (2004). *The Different Ways of Knowing Arts Integration Framework™: Accelerates achievement for all students and student groups*. Accessed at www.differentways.org/services/integrating.html on May 6, 2010.

Galley, M. (2004). Not separate, but equal. *Teacher Magazine, 15*(5), 47.

Garcia, S. B., & Ortiz, A. A. (2006). Preventing disproportionate representation: Culturally and linguistically responsive pre-referral interventions. *Teaching Exceptional Children, 38*(4), 64–68.

Gardner, J., Wissick, C., Schweder, W., & Canter, L. (2003). Enhancing interdisciplinary instruction in general and special education. *Remedial and Special Education, 24*(3), 161–172.

Garner, J. (2009). Conceptualizing the relations between executive functions and self-regulated learning. *The Journal of Psychology, 143*(4), 405–426.

Gavish, B. (2009). Book review. *Journal of International Special Needs Education, 12*, 25–28.

Gersten, R., Beckmann, S., Clarke, B., Foegen, A., Marsh, L., Star, J. R., et al. (2009). *Assisting students struggling with mathematics: Response to intervention (RtI) for elementary and middle schools* (NCEE No. 2009-4060). Washington, DC: National Center for Education Evaluation and Regional Assistance, Institute of Education Sciences, U.S. Department of Education. Accessed at http://ies.ed.gov/ncee/wwc/publications /practiceguides/ on February 6, 2010.

Goldstein, A. P. (1999). *The PREPARE curriculum.* Champaign, IL: Research Press.

Gresham, F. M., Cook, C. R., Crews, S. D., & Kern, L. (2004). Social skills training for children and youth with emotional and behavioral disorders: Validity considerations and future directions. *Behavior Disorders, 30*, 32–46.

Grigal, M., & Hart, D. (2010). *Think college! Postsecondary education options for students with intellectual disabilities.* Baltimore: Brookes.

Grisham-Brown, J., Pretti-Frontczak, K., Hawkins, S., & Winchell, B. (2009). Addressing early learning standards for all children within blended preschool classrooms. *Topics in Early Childhood Special Education, 29*(3), 131–142.

Guiberson, M. (2009). Hispanic representation in special education: Patterns and implications. *Preventing School Failure, 53*(3), 167–176.

Gurgur, H., & Uzuner, Y. (2010). A phenomenological analysis of the views of co-teaching applications in the inclusion classroom. *Educational Sciences: Theory and Practice, 10*(1), 311–331.

Guthrie, P., & Su, C. M. (1992, September 17–19). *The significance of young children's visual skills in graphic depiction of spatial representation: The testimony from two drawing researchers.* Paper presented at the Making Meaning Through Art: Art in Early Childhood Education Conference, Urbana, IL.

Haager, D., Klinger, J., & Vaughn, S. (Eds.). *Evidence-based reading practices for response to intervention.* Baltimore: Paul H. Brookes.

Haager, D., & Mahdavi, J. (2007). Teacher roles in implementing interventions. In D. Haager, J. Klingner, & S. Vaughn (Eds.), *Evidence-based reading practices for response to intervention* (pp. 245–264). Baltimore: Paul H. Brookes.

Hall, T., Strangman, N., & Meyer, A. *Differentiated instruction and implications for UDL implementation.* Wakefield, MA: Center for Applied Special Technology. Accessed at www.cast.org/publications/ncac /ncac_diffinstruc.html on July 22, 2010.

Halvorsen, A., & Neary, T. (2001). *Building inclusive schools: Tools and strategies for success.* Needham Heights, MA: Allyn & Bacon.

Hamilton, L., Halverson, R., Jackson, S., Mandinach, E., Supovitz, J., & Wayman, J. (2009). *Using student achievement data to support instructional decision making* (NCEE No. 2009-4067). Washington, DC: National Center for Education Evaluation and Regional Assistance, Institute of Education Sciences, U.S. Department of Education. Accessed at http://ies.ed.gov/ncee/wwc/publications/practiceguides/ on January 30, 2010.

Hardy, L. (2009). *Looking ahead to ESEA reauthorization: What will happen to NCLB?* Alexandria, VA: National School Boards Association. Accessed at www.nsba.org/HPC/Features/AboutSBN/Embrace-change.aspx on September 22, 2009.

Harmon, J. M., Katims, D. S., & Whittington, D. (1999). Helping middle school students learn with social studies texts. *Teaching Exceptional Children, 32*, 70–75.

Hart, J. (2009). Strategies for culturally and linguistically diverse students with special needs. *Preventing School Failure*, *53*(3), 197–208.

Hartman, M. (2009). Step by step: Creating a community-based transition program for students with intellectual disabilities. *Teaching Exceptional Children*, *41*(6), 6–11.

Hasbrouck, J. (2006). For students who are not yet fluent, silent reading is not the best use of classroom time. *American Educator*, *30*, 2. Accessed at www.readingrockets.org/article/27202 on April 27, 2009.

Hess, F. (2009). The new stupid. *Educational Leadership*, *66*(4), 12–17.

Hessler, T., & Konrad, M. (2008). Using curriculum-based measurement to drive IEPs and instruction in written expression. *Teaching Exceptional Children*, *41*(2), 28–37.

Heward, W. L. (2006). *Exceptional children: An introduction to special education* (8th ed.). Upper Saddle River, NJ: Pearson/Prentice Hall.

Hilte, M., & Reitsma, P. (2008). What type of computer-assisted exercise supports young less skilled spellers in resolving problems in open and closed syllable words? *Annals of Dyslexia*, *58*(2), 97–114.

Hines, J. (2008). Making collaboration work in inclusive high school classrooms: Recommendations for principals. *Intervention in School & Clinic*, *43*(5), 277–282.

Hinshaw, C. (2006). Connecting to Curious George. *School Arts*, *105*(7), 37.

Hoerr, T. (2009). Data that count. *Educational Leadership*, *66*(4), 93–94.

Hollingsworth, H., Boone, H., & Crais, E. (2009). Individualized inclusion plans at work in early childhood classrooms. *Young Exceptional Children*, *13*(1), 19–35.

Horvath, L., Kampfer-Bobach, S., & Kearns, J. (2005). The use of accommodations among students with deaf-blindness in large-scale assessment systems. *Journal of Disability Policy Studies*, *16*(3), 177–187.

Hourigan, R., & Hourigan, A. (2009). Teaching music to children with autism: Understandings and perspectives. *Music Educators Journal*, *96*(1), 40–45.

Hughes, C., & Rollins, K. (2009). RtI for nurturing giftedness: Implications for the RtI school-based team. *Gifted Child Today*, *32*(3), 31–39.

Huitt, W., & Hummel, J. (2003). *Piaget's theory of cognitive development*. Valdosta, GA: Valdosta State University. Accessed at http://chiron.valdosta.edu/whuitt/col/cogsys/piaget.html on May 1, 2009.

Hyde, A. (2007). Mathematics and cognition. *Educational Leadership*, *65*(3), 43–47.

Idol, L. (2006). Toward inclusion of special education students in general education. *Remedial and Special Education*, *27*(2), 77–94.

Individuals with Disabilities Education Act of 1990 (IDEA), Pub. L. No. 101–476.

Individuals with Disabilities Education Improvement Act of 2004 (IDEIA), Pub. L. No. 108–466.

Interstate New Teacher Assessment and Support Consortium. (2001). *Model standards for licensing general and special education teachers of students with disabilities: A resource for state dialogue*. Washington, DC: Author. Accessed at www.ccsso.org/content/ pdfs/SPEDStds.pdf on February 22, 2010.

Irving, M., Nti, M., & Johnson, W. (2007). Meeting the needs of the special learner in science. *International Journal of Special Education*, *22*(3), 109–118.

Isbell, C., & Isbell, R. (2005). *The inclusive learning center for preschool children with special needs*. Beltsville, MD: Gryphon House.

Iseminger, S. (2009). Keys to success with autistic children: Structure, predictability, and consistency are essential for students on the autism spectrum. *Teaching Music*, *16*(6), 28.

Jacobs, H. (2006). *Active literacy across the curriculum: Strategies for teaching reading, writing, speaking and listening.* Larchmont, NY: Eye on Education.

James, P. (1983). *Teaching art to special students.* Portland, ME: J. Weston Walch.

Jenkins, A., & Ornelles, C. (2009). Determining professional development needs of general education educators in teaching students with disabilities in Hawaii. *Professional Development in Education, 35*(4), 635–654.

Jenkins, R. (2005). Building strong school communities: Interdisciplinary instruction in the inclusion classroom. *Teaching Exceptional Children, 37*(5), 42–48.

Johns, B., Crowley, E., & Guetzloe, E. (2005). The central role of teaching social skills. *Focus on Exceptional Children, 37*(8), 1–8.

Johnson, C., Brown, P., & Edgar, G. (2000). *Transition guide for Washington State.* Seattle: The C Services, University of Washington.

Johnson, E., Mellard, D. F., Fuchs, D., & McKnight, M. A. (2006). *Responsiveness to intervention (RTI): How to do it.* Lawrence, KS: National Research Center on Learning Disabilities.

Johnson, G., & Bonaiuto, S. (2009). Accountability with roots. *Educational Leadership, 66*(4), 26–29.

Joseph, N. (2010). Metacognition needed: Teaching middle and high school students to develop strategic learning skills. *Preventing School Failure, 54*(2), 99–103.

Just Read, Florida!. (2005). *An example of the 90 minute reading block.* Tallahassee, FL: Author. Accessed at www.justreadflorida.com on May 4, 2010.

Kamens, M. W., Loprete, S. J., & Slostad, F. A. (2003). Inclusive classrooms: What practicing teachers want to know. *Action Teacher Education, 25*(1), 20–26.

Karten, T. (2007a). *Inclusion activities that work! Grades K–2.* Thousand Oaks, CA: Corwin Press Classroom.

Karten, T. (2007b). *Inclusion activities that work! Grades 3–5.* Thousand Oaks, CA: Corwin Press Classroom.

Karten, T. (2007c). *Inclusion activities that work! Grades 6–8.* Thousand Oaks, CA: Corwin Press Classroom.

Karten, T. (2007d). *More inclusion strategies that work! Aligning student strengths with standards.* Thousand Oaks, CA: Corwin Press.

Karten, T. (2008a). *Embracing disABILITIES in the classroom: Strategies to maximize students' assets.* Thousand Oaks, CA: Corwin Press.

Karten, T. (2008b). *Facilitator's guide to* More inclusion strategies that work!. Thousand Oaks, CA: Corwin Press.

Karten, T. (2008c). *Inclusion succeeds with effective strategies: Grades K–5* [Laminated guide]. Port Chester, NY: National Professional Resources.

Karten, T. (2008d). *Inclusion succeeds with effective strategies: Grades 6–12* [Laminated guide]. Port Chester, NY: National Professional Resources.

Karten, T. (2010a). *Inclusion strategies that work! Research-based methods for the classroom* (2nd ed.). Thousand Oaks, CA: Corwin Press.

Karten, T. (2010b). *Inclusion lesson plan book for the 21st century.* Port Chester, NY: Dude Publishing.

Kauffman, J. (1999). Today's special education and its messages for tomorrow. *Journal of Special Education, 32*(4) 244–254.

Kearsley, G. (2009). Social development theory Vygotsky. Accessed at http://tip.psychology.org/vygotsky.html on September 13, 2010.

Keefe, E., Moore, V., & Duff, F. (2004). The four "knows" of collaborative teaching. *Teaching Exceptional Children, 36,* 36–42.

Kilpatrick, J., Swafford, J., & Findell, B. (Eds.). (2001). *Adding it up: Helping children learn mathematics.* Washington, DC: National Academies Press. Accessed at www.nap.edu/catalog.php?record_id = 9822 on March 20, 2008.

King-Sears, M. (2005). Scheduling for reading and writing small-group instruction using learning center designs. *Reading and Writing Quarterly, 21,* 401–405.

King-Sears, M. (2007). Designing and delivering learning center instruction. *Intervention in School and Clinic, 42,* 137–147.

King-Sears, M. (2008). Facts and fallacies: Differentiation and the general education curriculum for students with special education needs. *Support for Learning, 23*(2), 55–62.

King-Sears, M., Maccini, P., McNaughton, D., & Ruhl, K. (1999). Algebra instruction for students with learning disabilities: Implications from a research review. *Learning Disability Quarterly, 22,* 113–126.

Kirch, S., Bargerhuff, M., Turner, H., & Wheatly, M. (2005). Inclusive science education: Classroom teacher and science educator experiences in CLASS workshops. *School Science & Mathematics, 105*(4), 175–196.

Klein, S. D., & Schive, K. (Eds.). (2001). *You will dream new dreams: Inspiring personal stories by parents of children with disabilities.* New York: Kensington Books.

Kliewer, C. (2008). *Seeing all kids as readers: A new vision for literacy in the inclusive early childhood classroom.* Baltimore: Brookes.

Klingner, J. K., & Harry, B. (2006). The special education referral and decision-making process for English language learners: Child study team meetings and placement conferences. *Teachers College Record, 108,* 2247–2281.

Klingner, J. K., Vaughn, S., & Schumm, J. S. (1998). Collaborative strategic reading during social studies in heterogeneous fourth-grade classrooms. *Elementary School Journal, 99,* 3–22.

Knight-McKenna, M. (2008). Syllable types: A strategy for reading multisyllabic words. *Teaching Exceptional Children, 40*(3), 18–24.

Konrad, M., & Test, D. (2007). Effects of GO 4 IT . . . NOW! Strategy instruction on the written IEP goal articulation and paragraph-writing skills of middle school students with disabilities. *Remedial and Special Education, 28*(5), 277–291.

Konrad, M., Walker, A., Fowler, C., Test, D., & Wood, W. (2008). A model for aligning self-determination and general curriculum standards. *Teaching Exceptional Children, 40*(3), 53–64.

Kroesbergen, E. H., & Van Luit, J. E. H. (2003). Mathematics interventions for children with special educational needs. *Remedial and Special Education, 24*(2), 97–114.

Kunsch, C., Jitendra, A., & Sood, S. (2007). The effects of peer-mediated instruction in mathematics for students with learning problems: A research synthesis. *Learning Disabilities Research & Practice, 22*(1), 1–12.

Lachat, M., & Smith, S. (2004). *Data use in urban high schools.* Providence, RI: Education Alliance at Brown University.

Lahm, E. (2003). Assistive technology specialists: Bringing knowledge of assistive technology to school districts. *Remedial and Special Education, 24*(3), 141–153.

Lamar-Dukes, P., & Dukes, C. (2005). Consider the roles and responsibilities of the inclusion support teacher. *Intervention in School & Clinic, 4*(1), 55–61.

Lane, K. L., Gresham, F. M., & O'Shaughnessy, T. E. (Eds.). (2002). *Interventions for children with or at-risk for emotional and behavioral disorders*. Boston: Allyn & Bacon.

Lane, K. L., & Wehby, J. (2002). Addressing antisocial behavior in the schools: A call for action. *Academic Exchange Quarterly, 6*, 4–9.

Learning Disabilities Association of Minnesota. (2005). Dysgraphia defined. *NetNews, 5*(3), 1–4. Accessed at www.eric.ed.gov:80/ERICDocs/data/ericdocs2sql/content_storage_01/0000019b/80/1b/ed/7e.pdf on May 6, 2010.

Learning-Theories.com. (2010). Learning theories knowledgebase. Accessed at www.learning-theories.com on September 12, 2010.

LeDoux, J. (2002). *Synaptic self: How our brains become who we are*. New York: Viking.

Lee, J., Grigg, W., & Dion, G. (2007). *The nation's report card: Mathematics 2007* (NCES No. 2007–494). Washington, DC: National Center for Education Statistics. Accessed at http://nces.ed.gov/pubsearch/pubsinfo.asp?pubid=2007494 on March 20, 2009.

Lee, J., Grigg, W., & Donahue, P. (2007). *The nation's report card: Reading 2007* (NCES No. 2007–496). Washington, DC: National Center for Education Statistics.

Lee, M. (2007). Spark up the American Revolution with math, science and more: An example of an integrative curriculum unit. *Social Studies, 98*(4), 159–164.

Light, J. C., Roberts, B., DiMarco, R., & Greiner, N. (1998). Augmentative and alternative communication to support receptive and expressive communication for people with autism. *Journal of Communication Disorders, 31*, 153–180.

Littky, D. (2004). *The big picture: Education is everyone's business*. Alexandria, VA: Association for Supervision and Curriculum Development.

Luke, S. (2006). The power of strategy instruction evidence for education. Washington, DC: National Dissemination Center for Children with Disabilities. Accessed at http://research.nichcy.org/NICHCY_EE_Strategy.pdf on May 1, 2009.

Luiselli, J., McCarty, J., Coniglio, J., Zorilla-Ramirez, C., & Putnam, R. (2005). Social skills assessment and intervention review and recommendations for school practitioners. *Journal of Applied School Psychology, 21*(1), 21–38.

Lynch, S., & Adams, P. (2008). Developing standards-based individualized education program objectives for students with significant needs. *Teaching Exceptional Children, 40*(3), 36–39.

Maccini, P., McNaughton, D., & Ruhl, K. (1999). Algebra instruction for students with learning disabilities: Implications from a research review. *Learning Disabilities Quarterly, 22*(2), 113–126.

Macswan, J., & Rolstad, K. (2006). How language proficiency tests mislead us about ability: Implications for English language learner placement in special education. *Teachers College Record, 108*, 2304–2328.

Marchant, M., & Womack, S. (2010). Book in a bag: Blending social skills and academics. *Teaching Exceptional Children, 42*(4), 6–12.

Marzano, R. (Ed.). (2010). *On excellence in teaching*. Bloomington, IN: Solution Tree Press.

Mastropieri, M. A., Scruggs, T. E., & Graetz, J. E. (2003). Reading comprehension instruction for secondary students: Challenges for struggling students and teachers. *Learning Disability Quarterly, 26*, 103–116.

Mastropieri, M., Scruggs, T., Graetz, J., Norland, J., Gardizi, W., & McDuffie, K. (2005). Case studies in co-teaching in the content areas: Successes, failures, and challenges. *Intervention in School & Clinic, 40*(5), 260–270.

Mathur, S., Quinn, M., Forness, S., & Rutherford, R. (1998). Social skills interventions with students with emotional and behavioral problems: A quantitative synthesis of single-subject research. *Behavioral Disorders, 23*(3), 193–201.

McCrimmon, D. (2003). Nothing wrong with being wrong! *Independent School, 62*(3), 12.

McGarrell, M., Healy, O., Leader, G., O'Connor, J., & Kenny, L. (2009). Six reports of children with autism spectrum disorder following intensive behavioral intervention using the preschool inventory of repertoires for kindergarten. *Research in Autism Spectrum Disorders, 3*(3), 767–782.

McIntosh, A. S., Graves, A., & Gersten, R. (2007). The effects of response to intervention on literacy development in multiple-language settings. *Learning Disability Quarterly, 30*(3), 197–212.

McKinley, L., & Stormont, M. (2008). The school supports checklist: Identifying support needs and barriers for children with ADHD. *Teaching Exceptional Children, 41*(2), 14–19.

McLanahan, B. (2009). Help! I have kids who can't read in my world history class! *Preventing School Failure, 53*(2), 105–112.

McLeskey, J., & Waldron, N. L. (2002). Inclusion and school change: Teacher perceptions regarding curricular and instructional adaptations. *Teacher Education and Special Education, 25*(1), 41–54.

McNamee, G., & Chen, J. (2005). Dissolving the line between assessment and teaching. *Educational Leadership, 63*(3), 72–76.

McNary, S., Glasgow, N., & Hicks, C. (2005). *What successful teachers do in inclusive classrooms: 60 research-based strategies that help special learners succeed.* Thousand Oaks, CA: Corwin Press.

Meadan, H., & Halle, J. W. (2004). Social perceptions of students with learning disabilities who differ in social status. *Learning Disabilities Research and Practice, 19,* 71–83.

Meadan, H., & Monda-Amaya, L. (2008). Collaboration to promote social competence for students with mild disabilities in the general classroom: A structure for providing social support. *Intervention in School & Clinic, 43*(3), 158–167.

Miami Museum of Science. (2001). Constructivism and the five E's. Accessed at www.miamisci.org/ph/lpintro5e.html on April 5, 2009.

Miller, M. (2008). What do students think about inclusion? *Phi Delta Kappan, 89*(5), 389–391.

Miller, T. W., Kraus, R. F., & Veltkamp, L. J. (2005). Character education as a prevention strategy in school-related violence. *The Journal of Primary Prevention, 26*(5), 455–466.

Mintz, J. (2007). Attitudes of primary initial teacher training students to special educational needs and inclusion. *Support for Learning, 22,* 3–8.

Moats, L., & Tolman, C. (2008). *Types of reading disability.* Accessed at www.readingrockets.org/article/28749 on May 6, 2010.

Montague, M., & Applegate, B. (2000). Middle school students' perceptions, persistence, and performance in mathematical problem solving. *Learning Disability Quarterly, 23,* 215–226.

Montgomery County Public Schools. (2009). *Montgomery schools preschool education.* Rockville, MD: Author. Accessed at www.montgomeryschoolsmd.org/curriculum/pep/description.shtm on May 2, 2009.

Moran, S., Kornhaber, M., & Gardner, H. (2006). Orchestrating multiple intelligences. *Educational Leadership, 64*(1), 22–27.

Munro, J. (2003). The influence of student learning characteristics on progress through the extended essay. *Journal of Research in International Education, 2*(1), 5–24.

Murawski, W., & Dieker, L. (2004). Tips and strategies for co-teaching at the secondary level. *Teaching Exceptional Children, 36*, 52–58.

Murawski, W., & Dieker, L. (2008). 50 ways to keep your co-teachers: Strategies for before, during, and after co-teaching. *Teaching Exceptional Children, 40*(4), 40–48.

Murawski, W., & Hughes, C. (2009). Response to intervention, collaboration, and co-teaching: A recipe for successful systematic change. *Preventing School Failure, 53*, 267–275.

Myers, C. (2007). "Please listen, it's my turn": Instructional approaches, curricula and contexts for supporting communication and increasing access to inclusion. *Journal of Intellectual & Developmental Disability, 32*(4), 263–278.

Nasir, N. (2008). Everyday pedagogy: Lessons from basketball, track, and dominoes. *Phi Delta Kappan, 89*(7), 529–532.

National Association of Secondary School Principals. (2009). *Recommendations for the reauthorization of IDEA.* Accessed at www.principals.org/portals/0/content/60910.pdf on February 28, 2010.

National Association of State Directors of Special Education. (2010). *Project Forum: Principal preparedness to support students with disabilities and other diverse learners—A Project Forum proceedings document.* Accessed at www.projectforum.org on February 26, 2010.

National Council for the Social Studies. (2002). *National standards for social studies teachers.* Accessed at http://mmf.cu.edu.tr/dokuman/NCSS.pdf on September 10, 2010.

National Council of Teachers of Mathematics. (n.d.). Curriculum focal points for prekindergarten through grade 8. Accessed at www.nctm.org/standards/content.aspx?id = 270 on September 5, 2009.

National Early Literacy Panel. (2008). *Developing early literacy: Report of the National Early Literacy Panel—A scientific synthesis of early literacy development and implications for interventions.* Louisville, KY: National Center for Family Literacy.

National Institute of Child Health and Human Development. (2000). *Report of the National Reading Panel: Teaching children to read—An evidence-based assessment of the scientific research literature on reading and its implications for reading instruction* (NIH Publication No. 00–4769). Washington, DC: U.S. Government Printing Office.

National Research Council. (2001). *Educating children with autism.* Washington, DC: National Academies Press.

Nelson, J., Caldarella, P., Young, K., & Webb, N. (2008). Using peer praise notes to increase the social involvement of withdrawn adolescents. *Teaching Exceptional Children, 41*(2), 6–13.

Neubert, D., & Moon, M. (2006). Postsecondary settings and transition services for students. *Focus on Exceptional Children, 39*(4), 1–8.

Neuschwander, C. (2001). *Sir circumference and the great knight of Angleland.* Watertown, MA: Charlesbridge.

Nevin, A., Cramer, E., Voigt, J., & Salazar, L. (2008). Instructional modifications, adaptations, and accommodations of coteachers who loop. *Teacher Education and Special Education, 31*(4), 283–297.

Northwest Regional Educational Laboratory. (2001). *Thematic or integrated instruction.* Accessed at www.ncrel.org/sdrs/areas/issues/students/atrisk/at7lk12.htm on May 1, 2009.

Obi, S. O., Obiakor, F. E., & Algozzine, B. (1999). *Empowering culturally diverse exceptional learners in the 21st century: Imperatives for U.S. educators* (Tech. Rep. No. 307730). Frankfort, KY: Kentucky State University, Division of Educational and Human Services. (ERIC Document Reproduction Service No. ED439551)

Odom, S. (2000). Preschool inclusion: What we know and where we go from here. *Topics in Early Childhood Special Education, 20*(1), 20–27.

Ollerton, M. (2009). Inclusive mathematics classrooms. *Mathematics Teaching, 216,* 5–7.

Olson, J., & Mokhtari, K. (2010). Making science real. *Educational Leadership, 67*(6), 56–62.

OSEP Technical Assistance Center on Positive Behavioral Interventions and Supports. (2006). *PBIS goals.* Accessed at www.pbis.org/main.htm on September 9, 2009.

OurChildrenLeftBehind.org. (2006). *Position paper on the reauthorization of the Individuals with Disabilities Education Act.* Accessed at www.ednews.org/articles/position-paper-on-the-reauthorization-of-the -individuals-with-disabilities-education-act-(idea)-.html on February 12, 2010.

PACER Center. (2007). Your 3-step plan to stopping childhood bullying. *Exceptional Parent, 37*(2), 64–66.

Paine, S. (2008). Supporting a school-wide reading initiative with curriculum, instruction and assessment. Accessed at www.readingrockets.org/article/25035 on July 21, 2010.

Palincsar, A. S., & Brown, A. L. (1984). Reciprocal teaching of comprehension-fostering and comprehension-monitoring activities. *Cognition and Instruction, 1*(2), 117–175.

Palincsar, A. S., Magnusson, S. J., Collins, K. M., & Cutter, J. (2001). Making science accessible to all: Results of a design experiment in inclusive classrooms. *Learning Disability Quarterly, 24,* 15–32.

Paris, C., & Combs, B. (2006). Lived meanings: What teachers mean when they say they are learner-centered. *Teachers and Teaching: Theory and Practice, 12*(5), 571–592.

Pashler, H., Bain, P., Bottge, B., Graesser, A., Koedinger, K., McDaniel, M., et al. (2007). *Organizing instruction and study to improve student learning* (NCER No. 2007–2004). Washington, DC: National Center for Education Research. Accessed at http://ncer.ed.gov on February 15, 2010.

Paterson, D. (2007). Teachers' in-flight thinking in inclusive classrooms. *Journal of Learning Disabilities, 40*(5), 427–435.

Patterson, K., Webb, K., & Krudwig, K. (2009). Families as faculty parents: Influence on teachers' beliefs about family partnerships. *Preventing School Failure, 54*(1), 41–50.

Paulson, F., Paulson, P., & Meyer, C. (1991). What makes a portfolio? *Educational Leadership, 48*(5), 60–63.

Pereles, D., Omal, S., & Baldwin, L. (2009). Response to intervention and twice-exceptional learners: A promising fit. *Gifted Child Today, 32*(3), 40–51.

Porter, G. (2008). Making Canadian schools inclusive: A call to action. *Canadian Education Research, 48*(2), 62–66.

Pransky, K. (2009). There's more to see. *Educational Leadership, 66*(7), 74–78.

Pressley, M. (2006, April 29). *What the future of reading research could be.* Paper presented at the International Reading Association's Reading Research 2006, Chicago, IL.

Qirmbach, L., Lincoln, A., Feinberg-Gizzo, M., Ingersoll, B., & Andrews, S. (2009). Social stories: Mechanisms of effectiveness in increasing game play skills in children diagnosed with autism spectrum disorder using a pretest posttest repeated measures randomized control group design. *Journal of Autism and Developmental Disorders, 39*(2), 299–321.

Quenemoen, R., Rigney, S., & Thurlow, M. (2002). *Use of alternate assessment results in reporting and account-ability systems: Conditions for use based on research and practice* (Synthesis Report 43). Minneapolis, MN: National Center on Educational Outcomes. Accessed at http://education.umn.edu/NCEO/OnlinePubs /Synthesis43.html on April 16, 2009.

Rasinski, T., Padak, N., McKeon, C., Krug-Wilfong, L., Friedauer, J., & Heim, P. (2005). Is reading fluency a key for successful high school reading? *Journal of Adolescent and Adult Literacy, 49,* 22–27.

reachAbility. (n.d.). The rights of special needs children. Accessed at http://reachability.org/news/articles /the-rights-of-special-needs-children/ on September 8, 2010.

Reeves, D. (2009). Looking deeper into the data. *Educational Leadership, 66*(4), 89–90.

Regan, K., & Page, P. (2008). "Character" building: Using literature to connect with youth. *Reclaiming Children and Youth: The Journal of Strength-Based Interventions, 16*(4), 37–43.

Rice, D., & Zigmond, N. (2000). Co-teaching in secondary schools: Teachers' reports of developments in Australian and American classrooms. *Learning Disabilities Research and Practice, 15*(4), 13–25.

Richburg, R. (2000). Learning from mistakes in history: A thematic instructional unit. *Social Studies, 91*(6), 279–285.

Ringelblum, E. (1999). Life in the Warsaw Ghetto. Accessed at www.jewishvirtuallibrary.org/jsource /Holocaust/life_in_warsaw.html on September 8, 2010.

Roach, A., & Elliott, S. (2008). Best practices in facilitating and evaluating intervention integrity. In A. Thomas & J. Grimes (Eds.), *Best practices in school psychology V*. Bethesda, MD: National Association of School Psychologists.

Roberts, J., Keane, E., & Clark, T. (2008). Making inclusion work: Autism Spectrum Australia's satellite class project. *Teaching Exceptional Children, 41*(2), 22–27.

Roberts, G., Torgesen, J., Boardman, A., & Scammacca, N. (2008). Evidence-based strategies for reading instruction of older students with learning disabilities. *Learning Disabilities Research & Practice, 23*(2), 63–69.

Roeber, E. (2002). *Setting standards on alternate assessments* (Synthesis Report No. 42). Minneapolis, MN: National Center on Educational Outcomes. Accessed at http://cehd.umn.edu/NCEO/OnlinePubs/ Synthesis42.html on November 28, 2005.

Rogers, G. (2004). Interdisciplinary lessons in musical acoustics. *Music Educators Journal, 91*(1), 25–30.

Rogers, J. (1993). The inclusion revolution. *Phi Delta Kappa Research Bulletin, 11*, 2–7.

Rossow, A., & Hess, C. (2001). Engaging students in meaningful reading: A professional development journey. *Teaching Exceptional Children, 33*(6), 15–20.

Sackett, D., Rosenberg, W., Muir Gray, J., Haynes, R., & Richardson, W. (1996). Evidence based medicine: What it is and what it isn't. *British Medical Journal, 312*, 71–72.

Salend, S. (2005). *Creating inclusive classrooms: Effective and reflective practices for ALL students* (5th ed.). Upper Saddle River, NJ: Pearson Education.

Salisbury, J., Jephcote, M., Rees, G., & Roberts, J. (2007). *The learning journey: Young people's experiences of further education*. Cardiff, United Kingdom: Cardiff School of Social Sciences, Cardiff University.

Samuels, C. (2010, September 2). New common core tests to shelve "Modified Achievement Standards." Accessed at http://blogs.edweek.org/edweek/speced/2010/09/duncan_common_core_tests_to_be.html on September 13, 2010.

Sangster, M. (2007). Reflecting on pace. *Mathematics Teaching, 204*, 34–36.

Sasso, G., Conroy, M., & Stichter, J. (2001). Slowing down the bandwagon: The misapplication of functional assessment for students with emotional or behavioral disorders. *Behavioral Disorders, 26*(4), 282–296.

Scherer, M. (2009). Driven dumb by data? *Educational Leadership, 66*(4), 5.

Scruggs, T., Mastropieri, M., & McDuffie, K. (2007). Co-teaching in inclusive classrooms: A metasynthesis of qualitative research. *Exceptional Children, 73*(4), 392–416.

Shapiro, L., Hurry, J., Masterson, J., Wydell, T., Taeko, N., & Doctor, E. (2009). Classroom implications of recent research into literacy development: From predictors to assessment. *Dyslexia, 15*(1), 1–22.

Sharkey, W. (1997). *Erik Erikson.* Accessed at http://fates.cns.muskingum.edu/%7Epsych/psycweb/history /erikson.htm on May 6, 2010.

Shaw, E., Baggett, P., Daughenbaugh, R., Santoli, S., & Daughenbaugh, L. (2005). From boxed lunch to learning boxes. *Science Activities, 42*(3), 16–25.

Sheridan, S. (1995). *The tough kid social skills book.* Frederick, CO: Sopris West.

Shure, M. B. (2001). *I can problem solve: Interpersonal cognitive problem solving (ICPS).* Champaign, IL: Research Press.

Silva, J. (2004). *Teaching inclusive mathematics to special learners, K–6.* Thousand Oaks, CA: Corwin Press.

Siperstein, G., Parer, R., Bardon, J., & Widaman, K. (2007). A national study of youth attitudes toward the inclusion of students with intellectual disabilities. *Exceptional Children, 73*(4), 435–455.

Smith, M. K. (2002). *Jerome Bruner and the process of education.* Accessed at www.infed.org/thinkers/bruner .htm on July 22, 2010.

Snowman, J., & Biehler, R. (2009). *Psychology applied to teaching.* Boston: Houghton Mifflin.

Sousa, D. (2007). *How the special needs brain learns.* Thousand Oaks, CA: Corwin Press.

Spear-Swerling, L. (2005). *Components of effective mathematics instruction.* Accessed at www.ldonline.org /article/5588 on February 10, 2009.

Spellings, M. (2008). *U.S. Secretary of Education Margaret Spellings announces proposed regulations to strengthen No Child Left Behind.* Accessed at www.ed.gov/news/pressreleases/2008/04/04222008.html on April 26, 2009.

Spence, D. (2007). A roadmap to college and career readiness. *Education Week, 26*(11), 93–96.

Spencer, T., Petersen, D., & Gillam, S. (2008). Picture exchange communication system (PECS) or sign language. *Teaching Exceptional Children, 41*(2), 40–47.

Spinney, L. (2009). How dyscalculia adds up. *New Scientist, 201*(2692), 40–43.

Spooner, F., Ahlgrim-Delzell, L., Kohprasert, K., Baker, J., & Courtade, G. (2008). Content analysis of science performance indicators in alternate assessment. *Remedial and Special Education, 29*(6), 343–351.

Spooner, F., Baker, J., Harris, A., Ahlgrim-Delzell, L., & Browder, D. (2007). Effects of training in universal design for learning on lesson plan development. *Remedial and Special Education, 28*, 108–116.

Stage, S., Jackson, H., Jensen, M., Moscovitz, K., Bush, J., Violette, H., Thurman, S., et al. (2008). A validity study of functionally-based behavioral consultation with students with emotional/behavioral disabilities. *School Psychology Quarterly, 23*(3), 327–353.

Stage, S., Jackson, H., Moscovitz, K., Erickson, M., Thurman, S., Jessee, W., et al. (2006). Using multimethod-multisource functional behavioral assessment for students with behavioral disabilities. *School Psychology Review, 35*(3), 451–471.

Steedly, K., Dragoo, K., Arafeh, S., & Luke, S. D. (2008). *Effective mathematics instruction.* Washington, DC: National Dissemination Center for Children With Disabilities. Accessed at www.nichcy.org/Research /EvidenceForEducation/Documents/NICHCY_EE_Math.pdf on May 6, 2010.

Steedly, K. M., Schwartz, A., Levin, M., & Luke, S. D. (2008). *Social skills and academic achievement.* Washington, DC: National Dissemination Center for Children With Disabilities. Accessed at www.nichcy .org/Research/EvidenceForEducation/Pages/SocialSkillsIntro.aspx on May 6, 2010.

Steen, L. (2007). How mathematics counts. *Educational Leadership, 65*(3), 8–14.

Stiggins, R. (2007). Assessment through the student's eyes. *Educational Leadership, 64*(8), 22–26.

Stuart, S., & Rinaldi, C. (2009). A collaborative planning framework for teachers implementing tiered instruction. *Teaching Exceptional Children, 42*(2), 52–57.

Swanson, H. L. (2001). Searching for the best model for instructing students with learning disabilities. *Focus on Exceptional Children, 34*(2), 1–15.

Swanson, H. L., & Hoskyn, M. (2001). Instructing adolescents with learning disabilities: A component and composite analysis. *Learning Disabilities Research & Practice, 16*(2), 109–119.

Taylor, A., & Kuo, F. (2009). Children with attention deficits concentrate better after walk in the park. *Journal of Attention Disorders, 12*(5), 402–409.

Teaching history's big picture. (2005). Accessed at www.fossils-facts-and-finds.com/history.html on May 6, 2010.

Thangham, C. V. (2008, December 7). *No two snowflakes are alike.* Accessed at www.digitaljournal.com /article/263168 on May 6, 2010.

Thousand, J. S., Villa, R. A., & Nevin, A. I. (Eds.). (2002). *Creativity and collaborative learning: The practical guide to empowering students, teachers, and families* (2nd ed.). Baltimore: Paul H. Brookes.

Thurlow, M. (2002). Positive educational results for all students. *Remedial and Special Education, 23*(4), 195.

Thurlow, M., Elliott, J., & Ysseldyke, J. (1998). *Testing students with disabilities: Practical strategies for complying with district and state requirements.* Thousand Oaks, CA: Corwin Press.

Tincani, M. (2004a). Improving outcomes for college students with disabilities. *College Teaching, 52*(4), 128–132.

Tincani, M. (2004b). Comparing the picture exchange communication system and sign language training for children with autism. *Focus on Autism and Other Developmental Disabilities, 19*, 152–163.

Tomlinson, C. (2003). *Fulfilling the promise of the differentiated classroom: Strategies and tools for responsive teaching.* Alexandria, VA: Association for Supervision and Curriculum Development.

Tomlinson, C. (2008). The goals of differentiation. *Educational Leadership, 66*(3), 26–30.

Tomlinson, C. (2010). One kid at a time. *Educational Leadership, 67*(5), 12–16.

Tomlinson, C., & McTighe, J. (2006). *Implementing differentiation of instruction with understanding by design: Connecting content and kids.* Alexandria, VA: Association for Supervision and Curriculum Development.

Tomsho, R. (2007, November 27). Parents of disabled students push for separate classes. *Wall Street Journal,* pp. A1–A17.

Towles-Reeves, E., Kleinert, H., & Muhomba, M. (2009). Alternate assessment: Have we learned anything new? *Exceptional Children, 75*(2), 233–252.

University of Florida Department of Special Education. (2003). *Study of personnel needs in special education (SPeNSE).* Accessed at http://ferdig.coe.ufl.edu/spense/ on May 6, 2010.

U.S. Department of Education. (2005). *Alternate achievement standards for students with the most significant cognitive disabilities: Non-regulatory guidance.* Washington, DC: Office of Elementary and Secondary Education.

U.S. Department of Education. (2007). *Modified academic achievement standards: Non-regulatory guidance.* Washington, DC: Author. Accessed at http://vvTvw.ed.gov/policy/speced/guid/modachieve-summary.html on July 30, 2007.

U.S. Department of Education. (2008). *Foundations for success: The final report of the National Mathematics Advisory Panel.* Washington, DC: Author. Accessed at www.ed.gov/about/bdscomm/list/mathpanel/report /final-report.pdf on July 21, 2010.

U.S. Department of Education, Office for Civil Rights. (2007). *Students with disabilities preparing for postsecondary education: Know your rights and responsibilities.* Washington, DC: Author. Accessed at www.ed.gov /about/offices/list/ocr/transition.html on July 15, 2009.

U.S. Government Accountability Office. (2005). *Federal science, technology, engineering, and mathematics programs and related trends* (GAO-06–114). Washington, DC: Author. Accessed at www.gao.gov/new.items /d06114.pdf on April 10, 2009.

Vaughn, S., & Ortiz, A. (n.d.). *Response to intervention in reading for English language learners.* Accessed at www.RTInetwork.org/Learn/Diversity/ar/EnglishLanguage on May 6, 2010.

Vincent, C. G., Horner, R. H., & Sugai, G. (2002). *Developing social competence for all students: ERIC/OSEP digest.* Arlington, VA: ERIC Clearinghouse on Disabilities and Gifted Education. Accessed at www.eric .ed.gov:80/ERICDocs/data/ericdocs2sql/content_storage_01/0000019b/80/1a/63/b4.pdf on May 6, 2010. (ERIC Document Reproduction Service No. ED468580)

Voltz, D., Sims, M., Nelson, B., & Bivens, C. (2008). Engineering successful inclusion in standards-based urban classrooms. *Middle School Journal, 39*(5), 24–30.

Vygotsky, L. (1962). *Thought and language.* Cambridge, MA: MIT Press.

Waddington, E., & Reed, P. (2009). The impact of using the "Preschool Inventory of Repertoires for Kindergarten" (PIRK[R]) on school outcomes of children with autism spectrum disorders. *Research in Autism Spectrum Disorders, 3*(3), 809–827.

Wagner, K. (n.d.). *Kohlberg's theory of moral development.* Accessed at http://psychology.about.com/od /developmentalpsychology/a/kohlberg.htm on September 22, 2009.

Wagner, M., Newman, L., Cameto, R., & Levine, P. (2005). *Changes over time in the early postschool outcomes of youth with disabilities: A report of findings from the National Longitudinal Transition Study (NLTS) and the National Longitudinal Transition Study-2 (NLTS2).* Menlo Park, CA: SRI International. Accessed at www.nlts2.org/pdfs/str6_completereport.pdf on April 10, 2009.

Walker-Dalhouse, D., Risko, V. J., Esworthy, C., Grasley, E., Kaisler, G., McIlvain, M., et al. (2009). Crossing boundaries and initiating conversations about RTI: Understanding and applying differentiated classroom instruction. *Reading Teacher, 63*(1), 84–87.

Wang, M., & Brown, R. (2009). Family quality of life: A framework for policy and social service provisions to support families of children with disabilities. *Journal of Family Social Work, 12*(2), 144–167.

Wanzek, J., & Haager, D. (2003). Teaching word recognition with blending and analogizing: Two strategies are better than one. *Teaching Exceptional Children, 36*(1), 32–38.

Watson, S., & Johnston, L. (2004). Teaching science to the visually impaired. *Science Teacher, 71*(6), 30–35.

Wehmeyer, M. L., & Palmer, S. B. (2003). Adult outcomes for students with cognitive disabilities three years after high school: The impact of self-determination. *Education and Training in Developmental Disabilities, 38,* 131–144.

Wei, R., Andree, A., & Darling-Hammond, L. (2009). How new nations invest in teachers. *Educational Leadership, 66*(5), 28–33.

Wiener, J., & Mak, M. (2009). Peer victimization in children with attention deficit/hyperactivity disorder. *Psychology in the Schools, 46*(2), 116–131.

Wiggins, G., & McTighe, J. (2006). *Understanding by design* (2nd ed.). Upper Saddle River, NJ: Prentice Hall.

Williams, J. (2008). Lev Semenovich Vygotsky, 1896–1934. *Times Educational Supplement, 4816*(3), 25.

Willis, C. (2009). *Creating inclusive learning environments for young children: What to do on Monday morning.* Thousand Oaks, CA: Corwin Press.

Winebrenner, S. (2003). *Teaching gifted kids in the regular classroom: Strategies and techniques every teacher can use to meet the academic needs of the gifted and talented.* Minneapolis, MN: Free Spirit.

Winter, E. C. (2006). Preparing new teachers for inclusive schools and classrooms. *Support for Learning, 21,* 85–91.

Winzer, M., & Mazurek, K. (2009). Inclusive schooling: Global ideals and national realities. *Journal of International Special Needs Education, 12,* 1–9.

Witzel, B., Mercer, C., & Miller, M. (2003). Teaching algebra to students with learning difficulties: An investigation of an explicit instruction model. *Learning Disabilities Research & Practice, 18,* 121–131.

Wolfe, P. (2002). *Brain matters: Translating research into classroom practice.* Alexandria, VA: Association for Supervision and Curriculum Development.

Wolfe, P. (2008). *Brain compatible practices for the classroom: Grades K–6* [DVD]. Port Chester, NY: National Professional Resources.

Woodward, J., Monroe, K., & Baxter, J. (2001). Enhancing student achievement on performance assessments in mathematics. *Learning Disability Quarterly, 24,* 33–46.

Worell, J. (2008). How secondary schools can avoid the seven deadly school "sins" of inclusion. *American Secondary Education, 36*(2), 43–56.

Wormeli, R. (2006). *Fair isn't always equal: Assessing and grading in the differentiated classroom.* Portland, ME: Stenhouse.

Wright, J. (2007). *RTI toolkit: A practical guide for schools.* Port Chester, NY: National Professional Resources.

Wright, P., & Wright, P. (2006). *Wrightslaw: From emotions to advocacy—The special education survival guide* (2nd ed.). Hartfield, VA: Harbor House Law Press.

Young, S., & Amarasinghe, J. M. (2010). Practitioner review: Non-pharmacological treatments for ADHD—A lifespan approach. *Journal of Child Psychology and Psychiatry, 51*(2), 116–133.

Zins, J., Weissbert, R., Wang, M., & Walberg, H. (2004). *Building academic success on social and emotional learning: What does the research say?* New York: Teachers College Press.

Index

A

abbreviations, 165–166

About.com: Special Education, 55

above-average skills, interventions for students with, 50

accommodations

difference between modifications and, 64

examples of, 65–68, 69

need for meaningful and realistic, 68, 70

sample curriculum lessons, 70–71

accountability, data and, 63–64

administrators, 151

alternate assessments on alternate achievement standards (AA-AAS), 72

alternate assessments on grade-level achievement standards (AA-GLAS), 72

alternate assessments on modified achievement standards (AA-MAS), 72–73

American Association of Intellectual and Developmental Disabilities, 55

American Foundation for the Blind, 57

American Society for Deaf Children, 53

American Speech-Language-Hearing Association, 51, 52

Americans with Disabilities Act (ADA), 3, 170

Americans with Disabilities Act Amendments Act (ADAAA), 170

Anxiety Disorders Association of America, 54

applied behavior analysis (ABA), 35

apraxia of speech, interventions for, 52

Arc of the United States, 55

art, accommodations, 130–131

ASLPro.com, 53

Asperger's syndrome

interventions for, 50–51

resources on, 14

assessments

accommodations, 64–71

alternative, 71–73

data used, 63–64

formative, 73

functional behavioral, 54, 75–76

modifications, 64, 68–71

portfolios, 73–74

sample curriculum lessons, 70–71

self-, 73

summative, 73

tips, 58, 77

assistive technology, 34

Assistive Technology Act (2004), 34

Association for the Gifted, 50

attention, 46–47

attention-deficit/hyperactivity disorder (ADHD), interventions, 51

auditory processing difficulties, interventions for, 51

augmentative and alternative communication (AAC), 35, 92

autism

communication issues, 17

interventions for, 51–52

resources on, 14, 16

technology for, 35

Autism Society of America, 52

Autism Speaks, 52

awareness, raising, 13–14, 159–162

B

Baker, J., 16

Ballad of Special EDDIE, The (Sobsey), 159–162

Bandura, A., 47

behavioral disabilities, resources on, 14

behavioral problems
   impact of, 14–15
   interventions for, 15
behavior improvement plan (BIP), 75–76
belonging, 12–13
bibliotherapy, 13–14
blindness, 57
Brain Injury Association of America, 56
Bright Solutions for Dyslexia, 54

C

Center for Applied Special Technology, 35
Child Find, 150
Children and Adults with Attention Deficit/
   Hyperactivity Disorder, 51
collaboration
   administrators, 151
   checklist, 158
   families, 150
   interventions, 154
   local education agencies, 150
   reading and, 86
   related staff and services, 150–151
   RTI and, 24–25
   teaching practices and, 49–50
   team/inclusion players, types of, 149–150
   tips, 155
communication
   augmentative and alternative, 35, 92
   differences, accommodating, 91–92
   disorders, interventions for, 52
   issues, 17–18, 151–153
   profile, creating, 92–93
   promoting, 91
   strategies, 90–93
   technology and, 35
content and meaning, reading and, 83
contingency management, 51
cooperative learning, 26
Co-Teaching Planner, 152, 157
co-teaching practices, 49–50
Council for Exceptional Children, 16–17
curriculum-based measurements (CBM), 25

D

data, accountability and, 63–64
deafness, interventions for, 52–53
developmental delay, 10
differentiated instruction (DI), 27

disabilities
   classifications of, 9–10
   raising awareness, 13–14, 159–162
Doing What Works, 37
Don Johnston, 53
Down syndrome
   communication issues, 17
   resources on, 14
Dragon Naturally Speaking, 53
Dull, L., 118
dyscalculia, interventions for, 53
dysgraphia, 35
   interventions for, 53
dyslexia, 81–82
   interventions for, 53–54

E

Early Literacy Skills, 82, 95
Ed's Car mnemonic, 88–89
Education of All Handicapped Children Act (1975), 3
educators, role of, 18
Elementary and Secondary Education Act (ESEA)
   (1965), 3, 170
Elliott, S., 37
emotional differences, interventions for, 54
emotional well-being, promoting, 20
engaged learning, 119–120
English learners (ELs), 10
   strategies for, 93–94
Enlightening Details, 125–126, 128
epilepsy, interventions for, 54
Epilepsy Foundation, 54
executive dysfunction, interventions for, 54–55
expressive language, 17

F

families, involvement of, 150
feedback, 47
Field, S., 144
504 plans, 169–170
FOIL mnemonic, 109
formative assessments, 73
Franklin Electronic Publishers, 53
full inclusion, defined, 2
functional behavioral assessments (FBAs), 54, 75–76

G

Gardner, H., 12, 32–33

Geometer's Sketchpad, 106
GO 4 IT NOW strategy, 89
Goleman, D., 12
graphic organizers, 120–126
Gray, C., 16
Guthrie, P., 130

H

Handwriting without Tears, 53
hearing impaired, interventions for, 52–53
Hearing Loss Association of America, 53
Hoffman, A., 144
Hundreds Chart, 110, 116
hyperlexia, 82

I

Ideal versus Pseudo Inclusion, 62
Illuminations, 109
inclusion
    concept of, 1–2
    defined, 13
    full, 2
    future for, 163
    goals of, 2
    ideal versus pseudo, 62
    laws regarding, 3–4, 167–170
Inclusive Classroom Checklist, 61
inclusive classrooms
    behavioral issues, 14–15
    belonging, 12–13
    communication issues, 17–18
    diversity in, 9–10
    educators, role of, 18
    importance of knowing students, 10–11
    raising awareness, 13–14
    self-knowledge, importance of, 11
    social issues, 15–17
    stereotypes, exercise on, 18–20
Inclusive Educator Checklist, 60
individualized education programs (IEPs), 3–4, 89
individualized program plans (IPPs), 3
Individuals with Disabilities Education Act (IDEA), 3, 22, 167–169
    classifications of disabilities, 9–10
    technology defined by, 34
Individuals with Disabilities Education Improvement Act (IDEIA), 169
instructional pacing, 47–49

instructional strategies and organization for diverse groups, 35–37
intellectual disabilities, interventions for, 55
interdisciplinary approach
    benefits of, 139
    examples of lesson strategies, 136–139
    setting up, 135
    thematic planning, 139
Interdisciplinary Thematic Planner, 139, 140
interdisciplinary writing, 90
Interests and Strengths Questionnaire, 141–142, 146
International Dyslexia Association, 54, 81
Interstate New Teacher Assessment and Support Consortium (INTASC), 16–17
interventions
    for above-average skills, 50
    for apraxia of speech, 52
    for Asperger's syndrome, 50–51
    for attention-deficit/hyperactivity disorder, 51
    for auditory processing difficulties, 51
    for autism, 51–52
    collaborative, 154
    for communication disorders, 52
    for deafness and hearing impaired, 52–53
    for dyscalculia, 53
    for dysgraphia, 53
    for dyslexia, 53–54
    for emotional differences, 54
    for epilepsy, 54
    for executive dysfunction, 54–55
    for intellectual disabilities, 55
    for physical disabilities, 55
    for specific learning disabilities, 55–56
    for Tourette's syndrome, 56
    for traumatic brain injury, 56
    for twice-exceptional learners, 56–57
    for visual impairment, 57

J

Jung, C., 76

K

KidsHealth, 51
KWL charts, 45–46

L

laws/legal issues, 3–4, 167–170
ldinfo.com, 53, 56

learning disabilities, resources on, 14
Learning Disabilities Association of America, 56
least restrictive environments (LREs), 3
lesson plans
    My Lesson Plan, 78
    sample, 70–71
Lesson Review, 156
Letters Mastery, 82, 96
life skills, 133–134
literacy. *See* communication; reading; writing
Living the Math, 107, 112–115
local education agencies (LEAs), 150

M

MAD mnemonic, 109
mathematics
    computational fluency, 109–110
    Hundreds Chart, 110, 116
    Living the Math, 107, 112–115
    relevancy and, 106–107
    representations, 105–106
    RTI recommendations, 107–108
    strategies, 108–109
    tips, 110
Math Interview Assignment, 107, 111
Mental Health America, 54
mental retardation. *See* intellectual disabilities
mind maps, 120–121
mistakes, learning from, 76
mnemonics
    for math, 109
    for writing, 88–89
modifications
    difference between accommodations and, 64
    examples of, 68, 69
    sample curriculum lessons, 70–71
Montessori, M., 118
motivation, 46–47
movement. *See* physical education
multiple intelligences theory, 32–33
multisensory approaches, reading and, 85
music, benefits of teaching, 131–132
My Lesson Plan, 78

N

Nasir, N. S., 76
National Association for Gifted Children, 50
National Center for Learning Disabilities, 56

National Council for the Social Studies (NCSS), 118
National Council of Teachers of Mathematics (NCTM), 105
National Dissemination Center for Children with Disabilities, 54, 55
National Early Literacy Panel (NELP), 82
National Institute of Mental Health, 51, 54
National Institute of Neurological Disorders and Stroke (NINDS), 50–51
National Science Education Standards, 118
No Child Left Behind (NCLB) Act (2001), 3, 118, 170
No More Meltdowns (Baker), 16
nutrition, teaching, 133

O

OCD Foundation, 54
Online Asperger Syndrome Information and Support (OASIS), 50
organizers, graphic, 120–126
Orton-Gillingham Institute for Multi-Sensory Education, 54
outlines, 121–123

P

pacing, instructional, 47–49
partner reading, 86
peer tutoring, 86
People Finder, 134
PEPs, 123, 127
physical disabilities
    interventions for, 55
    resources on, 14
physical education
    accommodations, 133
    nutrition, 133
    People Finder, 134
    teaching strategies, 132–133
picture exchange communication system (PECS), 35
portfolios, 73–74
Posit Science, 51
pragmatic language, 17
professional development, 153–154
professional learning communities (PLCs), 153
progress monitoring, RTI and, 25, 40–41

Q

QIAT, 35

R

reading
    collaborative, 86
    content and meaning, 83
    deficits, types of, 81
    differences, 81–82
    Early Literacy Skills, 82, 95
    Letters Mastery, 82, 96
    multisensory approaches, 85
    sounds and syllables, 84–85
    strategies, 82–86
    strategy books, 45–46
    structural analysis, 83–84
receptive language, 17
Recording for the Blind and Dyslexic, 54, 57
Rehabilitation Act (1973), 3, 169
reinforcements, types of, 16
response to intervention (RTI), 4
    collaboration and, 24–25
    curriculum examples, 22–24
    description of, 22–25
    intervention plan, 38–39
    progress monitoring, 25, 40–41
    recommendations for math, 107–108
    tiers of, 22
revisions, writing, 88–89
Roach, A., 37
RubiStar, 73
rubrics, 73, 74

S

Schwab Foundation, 56
science
    curriculum, 118–119
    graphic organizers, 120–126
    strategies, 119–126
    tips, 126
self-assessments, 73
self-efficacy, improving, 94
self-image and performance, 12–13
self-knowledge, importance of, 11
sensory disabilities, resources on, 14
sensory modalities, 33–34
Sensory Word Lists, 88, 101–102
Show What You Know List, 33, 42
Sobsey, D., 159–162
social issues, 15–17
Social Skills Picture Book (Baker), 16
social stories, 16

social studies
    curriculum, 117–118
    graphic organizers, 120–126
    strategies, 119–126
    tips, 126
sounds and syllables, 84–85
specific learning disabilities (SLDs), interventions
        for, 55–56
Speechville Express, 52
sponge activities, 48, 49, 59
stereotypes, exercise on, 18–20
Story Element Planner, 88, 97
Story Frame, 88, 98
strategic learners
    KWL charts and reading strategy books, 45–46
    strategies for creating, 45
structural analysis, reading and, 83–84
Su, C-M, 130
success, fourteen points for, 43–44
Sum It Up, 164
summary of performance (SOP), 142
summative assessments, 73
Support Groups for Children with Autism, Aspergers,
        PDD, 52
syllables, 84–85

T

Teaching History's Big Picture, 118
technology
    assistive, 34
    defined, 34
    use of, 34–35
thinkcollege.net, 55
timelines, boxed, 123–124
Tomlinson, C., 10
Tourette's syndrome, interventions for, 56
transitional plans
    Interests and Strengths Questionnaire, 141–142,
        146
    role of, 141
    setting goals, 141–142
    strategies, 142–144
    tips, 144–145
Transitional Word Lists, 88, 99–100
traumatic brain injury (TBI), interventions for, 56
twice-exceptional learners, interventions for, 56–57

U

understanding by design (UbD), 28–30

Uniquely Gifted, 57
United Cerebral Palsy, 55
U.S. Department of Education, Doing What Works, 36–37
universal design for learning (UDL), 30–32

V

Van Garderen, D., 118
visual, auditory, kinesthetic/tactile (VAKT) elements, 32, 33–34
visual impairment, interventions for, 57
Vygotsky, L., 12, 26, 108

W

Wilson Reading Program, 85

writing
    accommodations, 87–88
    exercise, 89, 103
    formal, outline for, 89–90
    IEP narratives, 89
    interdisciplinary, 90
    revisions, 88–89
    Sensory Word Lists, 88, 101–102
    Story Element Planner, 88, 97
    Story Frame, 88, 98
    strategies, 86–90
    Transitional Word Lists, 88, 99–100

Z

zones of proximal development (ZPD), 108

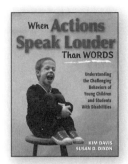

When Actions Speak Louder Than Words
Understanding the Challenging Behaviors of Young Children and Students With Disabilities
Kim Davis and Susan D. Dixon
Build your understanding of behavior as communication and learn to interpret the messages behind the actions. This book provides information and tools to support all children whose primary way to communicate is through challenging behaviors. **BKF274**

Making Math Accessible to English Language Learners
r4 Educated Solutions
Help English language learners build academic vocabulary and proficiency in meaningful mathematics while keeping the entire class engaged. A great tool for strengthening classroom instruction, this manual offers research-based strategies that address the affective, linguistic, and cognitive needs of ELLs.
K–2 **BKF284**, 3–5 **BKF285**, 6–8 **BKF286**, 9–12 **BKF287**

Making Math Accessible to Students With Special Needs Series
Practical Tips and Suggestions
r4 Educated Solutions
These manuals offer grade-appropriate research-based strategies for increasing confidence and capability among students with special needs. Reflective questions and tasks make this a perfect book for self-guided or group study. Appendices offer sample answers and additional supports.
K–2 **BKF288**, 3–5 **BKF289**, 6–8 **BKF290**, 9–12 **BKF291**

40 Reading Intervention Strategies for K–6 Students
Research-Based Support for RTI
Elaine K. McEwan-Adkins
This well-rounded collection of reading intervention strategies, teacher-friendly lesson plans, and adaptable miniroutines will support and inform your RTI efforts. Many of the strategies motivate all students as well as scaffold struggling readers. Increase effectiveness by using the interventions across grade-level teams or schoolwide. **BKF270**

Beyond the RTI Pyramid
Solutions for the First Years of Implementation
William N. Bender
This book helps schools deepen the RTI experience by extending the processes beyond initial implementation. Examples from real schools show how to apply RTI in reading, math, and behavior at elementary and secondary schools.
BKF323